MODERN CAMBRIDGE ECONOMICS

THE EVOLUTION OF ECONOMIC IDEAS

MODERN CAMBRIDGE ECONOMICS

Editors   Phyllis Deane
          Joan Robinson

THE EVOLUTION OF ECONOMIC IDEAS

Phyllis Deane

Reader in Economic History in the University of Cambridge and Fellow of Newnham College

CAMBRIDGE UNIVERSITY PRESS

CAMBRIDGE

LONDON   NEW YORK   NEW ROCHELLE

MELBOURNE   SYDNEY

Published by the Press Syndicate of the University of Cambridge
The Pitt Building, Trumpington Street, Cambridge CB2 1RP
32 East 57th Street, New York, NY 10022, USA
296 Beaconsfield Parade, Middle Park, Melbourne 3206, Australia

First published 1978
Reprinted 1979

Printed in Great Britain at the
University Press, Cambridge

Library of Congress Cataloguing in Publication Data
Deane, Phyllis.
    The evolution of economic ideas.
    (Modern Cambridge economics series)
    Includes index.
    1. Economics – History. I. Title.
HB75.D29   330'.09   77-88674
ISBN 0 521 21928 0 hard covers
ISBN 0 521 29315 4 paperback

SERIES PREFACE

The modern Cambridge Economics series, of which this book is one, is designed in the same spirit as and with similar objectives to the series of Cambridge Economic Handbooks launched by Maynard Keynes soon after the First World War. Keynes' series, as he explained in his introduction, was intended 'to convey to the ordinary reader and to the uninitiated student some conception of the general principles of thought which economists now apply to economic problems'. He went on to describe its authors as, generally speaking, 'orthodox members of the Cambridge School of Economics' drawing most of their ideas and prejudices from 'the two economists who have chiefly influenced Cambridge thought for the past fifty years, Dr Marshall and Professor Pigou' and as being 'more anxious to avoid obscure forms of expression than difficult ideas'.

This series of short monographs is also aimed at the intelligent undergraduate and interested general reader, but it differs from Keynes' series in three main ways: first in that it focuses on aspects of economics which have attracted the particular interest of economists in the post Second World War era; second in that its authors, though still sharing a Cambridge tradition of ideas, would regard themselves as deriving their main inspiration from Keynes himself and his immediate successors, rather than from the neoclassical generation of the Cambridge school; and third in that it envisages a wider audience than readers in mature capitalist economies, for it is equally aimed at students in developing countries whose problems and whose interactions with the rest of the world have helped to shape the economic issues which have dominated economic thinking in recent decades.

Finally, it should be said that the editors and authors of this Modern Cambridge Economics series represent a wider spectrum of economic doctrine than the Cambridge School of Economics to which Keynes referred in the 1920s. However, the object of the series is not to propagate particular doctrines. It is to stimulate students to escape from conventional theoretical ruts and to think for themselves on live and controversial issues.

JOAN ROBINSON
PHYLLIS DEANE

CONTENTS

INTRODUCTION

There are basically two approaches to a study of the development of ideas in a discipline. The first concentrates on the dialectical sequence of change in the theories, concepts and analytical techniques which constitute the substance of the discipline; the second traces the historical process of change in the way successive generations of scientists have adapted their explanatory techniques to a solution of the problems they regarded as important and soluble. The two approaches are not mutually exclusive, they overlap, and most historians of economic thought have taken both into account. But they raise different sets of questions. The approach from the first aspect is primarily concerned with a rational justification and critique of the theoretical basis of economic analysis in successive epochs; the second with explaining the historical process of innovation and adaptation in the analytical framework which economists have typically accepted as appropriate to the pursuit of their enquiries. The predominant trend in recent histories of economic thought has been towards increasing the emphasis on the first approach. Schumpeter's *History of Economic Analysis* and Blaug's *Economic Theory in Retrospect* are among the more widely known examples of the genre. This book, mainly intended for students committed to a systematic study of economic theory, shifts the weight of its emphasis in the direction of the second approach and seeks to interpret the history of economic thought as a process of change in the ideas of successive generations of economists.

A prime difficulty in pursuing this kind of socio-historical approach in a study of the evolution of economic ideas lies in specifying the relevant economic consensus, the analytical framework which a given generation of economists accepts as authoritative. It would appear that it is easier to do this for one of the natural sciences. According to Sir Karl Popper, for example, 'A scientist engaged on a piece of research in, say, physics, can attack his problems straight away. He can go at once to the heart of the matter; that is to the heart of an organized structure. For a structure of scientific doctrines is already in existence; and with it the generally accepted problems situation.'[1] Philosophers of science concerned with how and why successive generations of practising scientists cling to, or rearrange, or alter the explanatory techniques in which they have been trained, have used the word 'paradigm' to denote the doctrinal core that the majority of practising scientists are prepared to take for granted. Thomas Kuhn, for example, has defined a paradigm in its generally accepted connotation as a disciplinary matrix '"disciplinary" because it refers to the common possession of the practitioners of a particular discipline; "matrix" because it is composed of ordered elements of various sorts each requiring further specification',[2] though he also identifies a broader, sociological, use for the term in which 'it stands for the entire constellation of beliefs, values, techniques and so on shared by the members of a given community'.[3]

Since Kuhn popularised the term by elevating the concept of a paradigm to a key role in a theory of scientific progress, in which 'normal' cumulative advance is punctuated by revolutionary episodes defined as paradigm-switches, it has become a somewhat sensitive category. In the intense controversy sparked off by Kuhn's theory of scientific revolution his concept of a paradigm has been attacked as ill-defined,[4] as being inapplicable to most scientific disciplines, and as implying that the theories embraced by different generations of scientists were so heavily rooted in dogmatism as to be outside the range of rational confrontation.[5] Those who prefer to stress the continuities rather than the

[1] K. Popper, *The Logic of Scientific Discovery* (1959), Preface.
[2] T. S. Kuhn, *The Structure of Scientific Revolutions* (1969), p. 182.
[3] *Ibid*, p. 175. Both references are to the postscript added to the second (1969) edition.
[4] A sympathetic critic has distinguished 21 different senses in which Kuhn used the term in the first edition of his *Structure of Scientific Revolutions* (1962): see Margaret Masterman, 'The Nature of a Paradigm', in I. Lakatos and A. Musgrave (eds.), *Criticism and the Growth of Knowledge* (1970). Less sympathetic critics have felt it sufficient evidence of Kuhn's confusion to point to this fact or to select the senses which they choose to attack.
[5] E.g. K. Popper, 'Normal Science and its Dangers', in Lakatos and Musgrave (eds.), *op. cit.*, p. 54 'His schema of normal periods dominated by *one* ruling theory (a "paradigm" in Kuhn's terminology) and followed by exceptional revolutions seems to fit astronomy fairly well. But it does not fit, for example, the evolution of the theory of matter; or of the biological sciences since, say, Darwin and Pasteur.'

discontinuities in scientific progress (a preference which tends to be associated with an interest in the logic of discovery as opposed to the sociology of knowledge) react particularly strongly against the notion of a total paradigm-switch, and/or deny that it is ever possible to express the full range of explanatory techniques available to a discipline at any one time in a systematic network of ideas. Both objections have considerable force in the context of economics. Among the philosophers of science the sharpest reaction to Kuhn's use of the paradigm concept has been associated with its irrational or sociological content. Those whose interest in the history of intellectual development is focused on a critical appraisal of past theories in terms of their approximation to absolute or objective truth have little use for a theory which postulates a significant irrational element in the common framework of ideas accepted by scientists at a given point of time.[6] To the extent that economic theory is regarded as 'value-free' this objection also has force for economics.

More recently, economists unwilling either to take a dogmatic view of what constitutes progress in economic theory, or to abandon the search for the holy grail of objective internalist (i.e. rationalist) criteria of progressive change, have been attracted by the 'methodology of scientific research programmes' suggested by Imre Lakatos. This approach, which brings normative methodological criteria to the fore, interprets the history of science in terms of a continuous competition between alternative research programmes, rather than as a succession of conjectures and refutations on the one hand, or of total paradigm-switches on the other.[7] As was demonstrated by the papers presented to the economics sessions of a colloquium inspired by Lakatos, attempts to interpret the evolution of particular sub-sets of economic ideas as sequences of competing research programmes can yield new insights and unusual perspectives on the way certain theories have developed.[8] One of the contributors, Mark Blaug, went so far as to conclude that 'if we have regard to professional rather than popular opinion' the 'externalist' (i.e. socio-psychological)

[6] E.g. K. Popper again: 'The Myth of the Framework is, in our time, the central bulwark of irrationalism', Lakatos and Musgrave (eds.). *op. cit.*, p. 56.

[7] See Imre Lakatos and Alan Musgrave (eds.), *Criticism and the Growth of Knowledge* (1970), p. 177: 'Kuhn's conceptual framework for dealing with continuity in science is socio-psychological: mine is normative...Where Kuhn sees "paradigms", I *also* see rational "research programmes".'

[8] Spiro Latsis (ed.), *Method and Appraisal in Economics* (1976).

factors are redundant to the history of scientific progress in economics and 'a Lakatosian "rational reconstruction" would suffice to explain virtually all past successes and failures of economic research programmes'.[9] Such a judgment, however, seems to rest on a rather narrower definition of a professional economist than I would wish to adopt, and to beg the question of how one defines success or failure.

The upshot of the debate on Kuhn's theory of scientific revolutions seems to be that there is a strong element of 'rhetorical exaggeration'[10] in his concept of a paradigm which fully determines both the world-view of practising scientists and the research agenda of 'normal' scientific activity and also in the associated notion of a scientific revolution involving a total paradigm-switch. What the Kuhnian interpretation did bring out, however, more effectively than any other, is the connection between the socio-historical development of professional schools of thought and the intellectual development in the theoretical content of a discipline. Nor is it necessary to embrace Kuhn's theory of scientific revolutions to find the concepts of a 'paradigm' and of an intellectual 'revolution' convenient description categories to apply in a review of the evolution of economic ideas which seeks to take into account the socio-historical context of their development. No doubt there are dangers in using a term such as paradigm which may imply that the average economist's repertoire of theories and concepts is a more fully articulated system than it in practice is: just as there are dangers in applying the term revolution to highlight the discontinuities in a process of continuous conceptual change. But it is scarcely in dispute that there have been ruling paradigms in economics in that the textbooks describe a related set of theories, concepts and analytical techniques accepted as authoritative (though not necessarily as beyond criticism) by a majority of economists; and that there have been radical changes in the structure of economic

[9] *Ibid*, p. 177.
[10] The term is Toulmin's. See Stephen Toulmin, *Human Understanding*, Vol. I (1972), pp. 105–6: 'If we are to make the theory of paradigms and revolutions fit the historical evidence...we can do so only on one condition. We must face the fact that paradigm-switches are never as complete as the fully-fledged definition implies: that rival paradigms never really amount to entire alternative world views; and that intellectual discontinuities on the theoretical level of science conceal underlying continuities at a deeper methodological level. This done, we must ask ourselves whether the use of the term "revolution" for such conceptual changes is not itself a rhetorical exaggeration.'

doctrines which determine the generally accepted problem situation. The questions which arise when one approaches the history of economic thought from this angle are, for example: when did economics acquire a sufficiently coherent and well-attested paradigm to rank as a distinct discipline? What were the distinguishing characteristics of successive paradigms? How revolutionary were the changes attributable to periods of significant conceptual innovation? How do we explain the success or failure of alternative paradigms in gaining a hold over the minds of a majority of economists? These are the kind of questions that will be raised in this book.

Moreover, whatever may be the case for the natural sciences, there is no doubt that in the social sciences the attraction of a paradigm, and the factors in its displacement, depend to a considerable extent on forces beyond the range of logical evaluation of its explanatory power. Political economy, born out of philosophy and ethics, has always been a discipline with strong normative implications in spite of a persistent effort on the part of its practitioners to develop its scientific and objective aspects. The philosophical and ideological premises of an economic theory thus play an important role both in its initial acceptance and in its tenacity. More important still perhaps in dislodging a ruling orthodoxy is the fact that both the empirical content of the economic problem and the boundaries of the discipline are changeable. Economic processes, for example, change through time with economic, social and political institutions. Theories and concepts may drift away from objective truth because the nature of economic reality is changing; and critical appraisal of the relative superiority of economic theories (whether competing at particular points of time or ruling in different epochs) must be conditioned by the knowledge that economists' views on the scope of the discipline, as well as on its problem priorities, shift inevitably with changes in the character of the political, social and economic context. It may be that changes in the doctrines which practising economists regard as orthodox are more often the result of an autonomous change in the problem-situation, leading to changes in the form of explanation, than of objective research designed to test the logical or empirical validity of existing theory.

The current paradigm for economics – the set of micro and macro theories, concepts, techniques and problems purveyed in the orthodox textbooks[11] – has come under increasing attack in recent years for reasons that will be considered later in this book. The result is that the discipline is in the throes of what Kuhn's model would categorise as a 'methodological crisis' such as typically precedes a complete paradigm-switch. Even a non-Kuhnian interpretation would indicate that some kind of paradigm change was in the air because both the textbook doctrines and their practical applications are being increasingly subjected to fundamental criticism. Students in faculties where orthodox theory is being actively questioned by individuals of acknowledged stature in the profession[12] are finding it particularly hard to digest a textbook-authenticated paradigm which appears to be already disintegrating.

The object of this book is neither to paper over the cracks nor to suggest ways of identifying a new paradigm awaiting its cue in the wings, but, by tracing some of the historical antecedents and parallels to contemporary theoretical controversies, to put them into perspective and to interpret some of the major issues at stake. The political quality of much of the contemporary methodological debate springs from profound disagreements about what economics is, and about what problems the economist should be concerned to solve – disagreements that will confirm some observers in their belief that economics is not a science at all, possibly not even a definable discipline. However, starting from the position that economics is a discipline whose terms of reference, theories and analytical techniques are defined by an invisible college of authoritative practitioners (i.e. economics is what economists do), I postulate that shifts in economists' views about what problems they ought to be solving, as well as how they ought to be solving them, are the key to understanding the historical changes that have taken place in the ruling paradigm for economics. From this angle of vision I have looked at the way leading theorists have adapted their theories and concepts – and with them the research orientation of the discipline – to major changes in the problem-situation confronting them. I have not

---

[11] There are of course plenty of unorthodox textbooks on the market, some of which are finding their way into the undergraduate reading lists in some strength (e.g. Joan Robinson and John Eatwell, *An Introduction to Modern Economics,* 1973), but they have not yet succeeded in displacing the conventional texts which most examiners can confidently be expected to accept, if not enthusiastically to approve.

[12] By the leaders of the institutional establishment as well as its self-styled heretics. See below pp. 222–3.

tried to be in any sense exhaustive, either in the range of theories or in the leading theorists discussed, for two reasons – first because the book was designed as one of a series of deliberately short student texts, and limitations of space thus made it necessary to select both the theories and the theorists considered. The second reason was that certain schools of thought, or theories, or writers, seemed to illustrate more effectively than others the main themes implicit in my starting point.

In consequence this book focuses particularly on the evolution of economic ideas in three distinctive branches of economic theory – value, growth and money. And because it was usually easier to trace that evolution from teacher to pupil I have more often focused on English (even Cambridge) theorists and their problem situations than on continental or American examples. I am conscious of the fact that the story could have been told with a different cast of characters and a different batch of intellectual problems. But on the assumption that critical students will have other, more comprehensive, sources to draw upon they should benefit by testing the arguments in alternative contexts. The object is not to provide readers with a complete account of the evolution of any one branch of theory, nor to identify all who have made a major contribution to its progress, but to illustrate the way economists' views on the scope and methodology of their discipline – and hence the assumptions and questions underlying their theories – have been subject to a variety of intellectual, historical and ideological influences.

A number of people have read one of the many drafts of this book, have rescued me from some shocking errors of logic or misconception or have helped to clarify some of its more opaque passages or to put the argument into better order. I am particularly grateful to Joan Robinson (who has combed patiently through several drafts), Geoff Harcourt, Don Moggridge, Sue Howson, Donald Winch, Colin Day and Mark Blaug. They are of course in no way responsible for the new confusions which have emerged in the process of redrafting or for my obstinate errors of omission. The quotations from Lionel Robbins, *The Nature and Significance of Economic Science*, and *The Collected Writings of John Maynard Keynes* are by permission of Macmillan, London and Basingstoke.

1

ORIGINS OF MODERN ECONOMICS

Ideas have been developed about economics – economic concepts and theories that might seem familiar to the students of twentieth-century textbooks – longer probably than written records survive to attest. Schumpeter, for example, refers to Kung Fu Tse (i.e. Confucius 551–478 B.C.) and Meng Tzu (372–288 B.C.) 'from whose works it is possible to compile a comprehensive system of economic policy' and who used 'methods of monetary management and of exchange control that seem to presuppose a certain amount of analysis'.[1] The standard histories of economic thought generally begin with references to Plato and Aristotle (sometimes also to the Old Testament) before launching into a discussion of theories of the just price: and it has become conventional to divide the history of western economic thought into four distinctive epochs:

(1) Classical Greek; the ideas of this period have come down to us embedded in political philosophy focused on the ethical problems of the aristocratic slave-based city-state.

(2) Mediaeval scholastic; in this period scholarship was a clerical monopoly and medieval economic ideas are to be found in essentially theological treatises where the focus of interest was moral rather than political and acquisitive motives were regarded as inherently disreputable. The scholastic discussions of the practice of usury, for example, or of a just price, were often concerned with deriving moral precepts of individual economic behaviour relevant to the context of a market economy, rather than with explaining the way the exchange economy actually worked, or ought to work.

(3) Mercantilist; this was the period when the economic problems of warring nationalist–monarchical states and the growth of capitalist commerce stimulated a stream of political pamph-

[1] J. Schumpeter, *History of Economic Analysis* (1954), p. 53.

lets focused on ways of increasing national wealth and power through regulation of trade.

(4) Modern; in the eighteenth century, beginning with the French physiocrats (who called themselves *économistes*) and with Adam Smith, we find the origins of a systematic study of economics as a distinctive discipline, a specialised technique of analysis, a science or a quasi-science.

The economic ideas which emerged in the first two of these epochs are mainly of historical or antiquarian interest. For the Greek philosophers and the medieval scholastics the study of economics was peripheral to their political or theological interests and their approach had little in common with modern economic thinking. It is difficult to imagine a modern economic theorist gaining any direct stimulus or inspiration from their techniques of analysis or policy conclusions. With the mercantilists, however, and particularly with the later generations of mercantilists it was different. Twentieth-century economists do not hesitate to acknowledge an intellectual debt to them. It may be that today's theorists distort the thought processes of their predecessors by reformulating yesterday's problems, concepts and analyses in modern terms; but they may still clarify their own ideas and sharpen their message by so doing. When looking back in this way, it is not hard to accept Sir William Petty, say, as an economist in the modern idiom or to link some of today's textbook theories and concepts directly to mercantilist writings of the late seventeenth and eighteenth centuries.

There were two main factors impelling educated men to take a lively interest in macroeconomic policy problems in the late sixteenth and seventeenth centuries. On the one hand, there were the needs of national governments to raise revenue on the scale required to finance mercenary armies and standing navies (or to subsidise allies) in the balance of power manoeuvres which dominated international politics after the end of the religious wars. On the other hand there was the growing realisation by merchants and bankers, operating on widening domestic and international markets, of their dependence on the specifically economic policies of governments. It became increasingly obvious that governments, producers and consumers were operating in an economic *system* of complex mutual interdependence and correspondingly important to explain the nature of the system.

It was the seventeenth-century Political Arithmeticians (e.g. Graunt, Petty and King) who began the modern tradition of empirical economic enquiry, consciously modelled on the natural sciences, deliberately objective in approach. Over the next half century or so a swelling stream of pamphlets and books (not always as objective) bearing on economic questions were published: Joseph Massie, for example, is reported to have amassed a library of 2,500 tracts and manuscripts on 'trade' by the mid eighteenth century.[2] Strictly speaking, however, the mercantilist economists were writing not about economic science as it came to be called later but about political economy. So although one can find mercantilists such as Barbon (*Discourse on Trade*) or Cantillon (*Essay on the Nature of Trade in General*) or Gervaise (*System of the Theory of the Trade of the World*) who offered explicit, theoretical explanations of the operations and logical interrelations of some aspect of the macroeconomic system, the avowed motive behind most mercantilist writings was to justify specific policy prescriptions of one kind or another. For the most part, the mercantilists were pamphleteers whose writings were designed as propaganda instruments focused on definite policy issues. In so far as they had begun to adopt common theories of the way the economy operated these were usually implicit in their writings rather than explicit – a by-product of their efforts to influence the politicians.

True, the seventeenth-century mercantilists had inherited or developed a basis of economic theory in the modern sense, even if this was often sketchy. For example, they had long ago abandoned the scholastic notion that the 'value' of a commodity was the price at which it *ought* to sell on the market (the Medieval Just Price) in favour of the idea that it was the price at which it actually *did* sell.[3] They thought of economics as the art of managing a household and, by natural extension, political economy as the art of managing a State. They had worked out the elements of a clear, if rudimentary, theory of supply and demand. They developed theories of the interest rate which took into account such factors as the yield of investment in capital stock and the supply of loanable funds.[4] Most of them focused

[2] W. Letwin, *Origins of Scientific Economics*.

[3] But see Raymond de Roover, 'The Concept of the Just Price: Theory and Economic Policy', *Journal of Economic History* (1958), who concludes that the just price was often equated by the scholastics to the competitive market price.

[4] Samuel Hollander, *The Economics of Adam Smith, op. cit.*, p. 70, finds evidence for the late seventeenth century of a breakthrough in mercantilist understanding of the process of saving and of the role of the rate of interest.

primarily on the external trading relationships of the nation, though this did not prevent them from discussing at length a wide range of economic variables and problems such as production, prices, money, interest, tariff policy, the relief of the poor, etc. The later mercantilists became increasingly concerned with problems of growth and development. In the debates on the East India trade, for example, it was apparently accepted that the desirability of any branch of trade depended more on its contribution to the national aggregate of production or employment than to the balance of overseas trade.[5]

Nevertheless it must be admitted that mercantilist economics does not amount to either a systematic discipline or a coherent doctrine, even if we confine our attention to the late seventeenth and eighteenth centuries when it can be said to have acquired its distinctive methodological and doctrinal characteristics.[6] The most famous, and the most systematic exposition of the economic doctrine of mercantilism at its eighteenth-century maturity is to be found in Book IV of Adam Smith's *Wealth of Nations*. But it was set up there by Smith only to be shot down; and his account needs to be taken with some reserve. It was a reflection of those aspects of mercantilism against which he was reacting, rather than an accurate synthesis of the doctrine as seen by its most sophisticated exponents. Subsequent rehabilitations of the doctrine whether by Schmoller or Cunningham in the later nineteenth century, or by Keynes in the twentieth, are also suspect as being highly selective accounts. It is only relatively recently that historians of economic thought have begun to examine the mercantilist pamphlets on their own terms in order to build up an objective picture of the mercantilist assumptions and analytical apparatus.

The results of these researches suggest that although it is possible to identify certain characteristics of mercantilist thought which effectively distinguish it from classical political economy – e.g. its bias towards state intervention in the economy, its stress on overseas trade as the prime mover in economic development and its tendency to assume underemployment of labour – it does not seem to have developed either a solid tradition of systematic economic inquiry and explanation, or a coherent set of generally-accepted principles of economic theory. It was not until the

---

[5] A. Coats, 'In Defence of Heckscher and the Idea of Mercantilism', *Scandinavian Economic History Review* (1957), p. 187.

[6] I.e. its generally accepted techniques of analysis and *a priori* principles.

eighteenth-century philosophers – primarily the physiocrats and Adam Smith – began systematically, and not merely incidentally, to apply to economic phenomena their theories of the natural order underlying the real world that economic theory began to develop into a unified system of explanation, a definitive technique of analysis.

In effect, Adam Smith and the physiocrats were contemporaneous and cross-fertilising. Both saw economic society as an organic unity. Both were philosophic system-builders concerned to establish the nature of the laws underlying the total socio-economic order – as it was and especially as it ought to be. Both classified the primary agents in the economic process on the same lines – viz as labourers, landlords and capitalists. Both operated with essentially pre-industrial analytical concepts, e.g. their concept of capital was of 'a stockpile of food and implements accumulated *before* the process of production began and subsequently *advanced* to labourers in anticipation of the returns from the final output'.[7] Both saw growth as the main economic problem and both emphasised the importance of the domestic market in economic development in contradistinction to the mercantilist pre-occupation with overseas trade. Both reacted against the mercantilist obsession with a favourable balance of trade and emphasised real capital accumulation as the key to faster growth that did not have to depend on 'beggar-your-neighbour' policies.

However, they emerged with different systems of explanation and a different bias in their policy prescriptions. Whereas the physiocrats analysed the economic system in terms of a circular flow best illustrated by Quesnay's *Tableau Economique*, Adam Smith analysed it less schematically in terms of a natural complex of harmony-promoting forces. Whereas the physiocrats assigned primacy to agriculture in generating economic development,[8] Adam Smith rested it on the division of labour.

The case for beginning a study of the evolution of economic ideas with Adam Smith rather than with the physiocrats does not rest, however, either on the innate superiority of his analytical

[7] A. W. Coats, 'Adam Smith: The Modern Re-Appraisal', *Renaissance and Modern Studies*, Vol. VI (1962), p. 38.

[8] See R. L. Meek, 'Ideas, Events and Environment: the Case of the French Physiocrats', in R. V. Eagly (ed.), *Events, Ideology and Economic Theory* (1968), for an analysis of the way the distinctive quality of physiocratic theory stemmed from the structure and organisation of the contemporary French economy and the problems involved in its development.

framework, or on his claims to chronological priority in the unified methodological approach which both shared. No doubt François Quesnay has as much right as Adam Smith to be regarded as a founder of modern political economy. Indeed his concept of a circular flow of incomes and his *Tableau Economique*, which can be interpreted as a kind of input–output table, will strike economists used to operating with social accounting tools of analysis as more relevant to modern macro-economics than any part of mainstream classical political economy from Smith onwards.

However, although few of the contributions which Adam Smith made were original in the sense that they cannot also be found in the published text of some eminent predecessor, he is the author to whom all orthodox nineteenth-century classical economists (on the continent of Europe as well as in Britain) consciously traced back the science they professed. The *Wealth of Nations* was an immediate best-seller. By 1800 the book had gone through nine English editions and had been published in the USA, Ireland and Switzerland. By the end of the first decade of the nineteenth century it had been published in the Danish, Dutch, French, German, Italian, Spanish and Russian languages. It was the undisputed, internationally accepted, bible of the new science of political economy not only for orthodox economists but also for theoretical revolutionaries who broke out of the orthodox stream. J. S. Mill's *Principles* published in 1848 was explicitly patterned on the *Wealth of Nations*. 'It appears to the present writer' Mill explained in his Preface 'that a work similar in its object and general conception to that of Adam Smith, but adapted to the more extended knowledge and improved ideas of the present age, is the kind of contribution which Political Economy at present requires.' Karl Marx too had no doubt where modern economics effectively began. Adam Smith 'must be given credit' he wrote 'for having more closely determined the abstract categories and for having securely labelled the differences analysed by the physiocrats'.[9] In effect, Adam Smith provided the infant science of political economy with its first generally accepted system of theories, concepts and analytical techniques, its first paradigm or disciplinary matrix.[10] He gave it a methodology, a conceptual system and an ideological slant which determined the

[9] K. Marx, *Theories of Surplus Value*, Part I.
[10] See the quotations from T. S. Kuhn, above p. vii.

main problems which economists studied, the analytical framework within which they normally discussed these problems and the policy bias implicit in their solutions for nearly half a century: and his model attracted lip-service if not close conformity for a good deal longer still.

Adam Smith, however, was far from being a specialist economist. He was an academic philosopher for whom political economy was a branch of moral philosophy. For him, as also for some of his eminent successors it was merely one section of a general theory of society involving philosophy, psychology, ethics, law and politics. Like other eighteenth-century philosophers, he had a strong propensity to generalise – in his own words 'to account for all appearances from as few principles as possible'.[11] The method to which all his contemporaries committed to a scientific approach consciously aspired was that of Isaac Newton, whose system Smith described as 'the greatest discovery that ever was made by man, the discovery of an immense chain of the most important and sublime truths, all closely connected together, by one capital fact, [gravity] of the reality of which we have daily experience'.[12] It was by the same kind of ordered thought-system based on a few plausible, because self-evident, assumptions that Adam Smith set out to explain the everyday phenomena of economic behaviour. 'Systems' he wrote 'in many respects resemble machines. A machine is a little system, created to perform, as well as to connect together, in reality, those different movements and effects which the artist has occasion for. A system is an imaginary machine, invented to connect together in the fancy those different movements and effects which are in reality performed.'[13] In effect, then, Adam Smith was fully committed to the rational[14] theistic mechanistic views of his time, to the view of society as a sublime machine which left to itself will tend to maximise social welfare. 'Human society, when we contemplate it in a certain abstract and philosophical light appears like a great, an immense machine, whose regular and harmo-

---

[11] A. Smith, *Theory of Moral Sentiments*, ed. D. D. Raphael and A. L. Macfie, Glasgow (1976).
[12] A. Smith, *Essays on Philosophical Subjects* (1795) p. 93.
[13] *Ibid.* p. 44.
[14] See, however, T. D. Campbell, *Adam Smith's Science of Morals* (1971), for a discussion of the difference between Smith's 'rationalism' and that of contemporary moral theorists with whom he took issue.

nious movements produce a thousand agreeable effects.'[15] The
'great architect' of this agreeable machine was a benevolent
deity variously called by him the great director of the universe,
the final cause, the divine being, the great judge of hearts, provi-
dence, an invisible hand, and very occasionally quite baldly God.

Smith's first major work *The Theory of Moral Sentiments* was
written when he was Professor of Moral Philosophy at the University of Glasgow and was first published in 1759. The *Wealth of
Nations* originated in a set of lectures written after he had
resigned his professorship, i.e. during the period 1767–76, when
he was a gentleman of independent means;[16] and he planned,
but never found the time, to write a book on jurisprudence,
possibly because he took the appointment of Commissioner of
Customs in 1778.

His fundamental theory of society is set out at length in the
Theory of Moral Sentiments. Basically the argument is that society
is designed to a Divine Plan, which operates so as to maximise
human happiness by means of the interplay of certain moral
sentiments which are among the 'original passions of human
nature'. Social and unsocial, selfish and altruistic motives all play
their 'necessary part of the plan of the universe' for social
harmony. 'The happiness of mankind as well as of all other
rational creatures, seems to have been the original purpose
intended by the Author of nature when he brought them into
existence...But by acting according to the dictates of our
moral faculties, we necessarily pursue the most effectual means
for promoting the happiness of mankind.'[17] The moral sentiments which ensure that men by responding to their natural
feelings and personal ambitions will fulfil the divine plan are
beneficence – including sympathy, generosity, kindness, friend-
ship – which 'cannot be extorted by force'; justice, the enforce-
ment of which is often necessary and always socially approved;
and prudence – including industry and frugality – 'that great
purpose of human life we call bettering our condition'.[18] These
virtues 'have no tendency to produce any but the most agreeable
effects'.[19] The essential cement for the system is the individual's

[15] A. Smith, *Theory of Moral Sentiments, op. cit.*, p. 316.
[16] He resigned his professorship in 1764 to take up a post as tutor to the Duke
of Buccleuch with whom he travelled in France in the mid 1760s and from whom
he got a pension of £300 a year which enabled him to be independent over this
period.
[17] *Moral Sentiments, op. cit.*, p. 166.   [18] *Ibid*, p. 50.
[19] *Ibid*, p. 264.

active concern for the social esteem of his contemporaries. For 'Nature, when she formed man for society, endowed him with an original desire to please, and an original aversion to offend his brethren.'[20]

As a basis for an abstract theory of society these assumptions about the strategic factors in human behaviour are debatable but not implausible. The need for social approval has been recognised by sociologists and psychologists as a powerful human incentive. The moral virtues of beneficence, justice and prudence might not be equally high in the social scale of virtues for all communities, but there is no obvious reason to reject the assumption that they were important in eighteenth-century Britain. For Smith the essential justification for their universality was their success.

In the middling and inferior stations of life, the road to virtue and that to fortune, to such fortune, at least, as men in such stations can reasonably hope to acquire, are, happily in most cases very nearly the same. In all the middling and inferior professions, real and solid professional abilities joined to prudent, just, firm and temperate conduct, can very seldom fail of success.[21]

Armed with their instinctive moral virtues or ideals, individuals are thus impelled to amass their own fortunes in ways that tend to maximise the total income of the community as well as their own.

In the *Wealth of Nations* the basic framework of this theory of society is taken for granted and Adam Smith goes on to work out a special case of its application – the economic case. A great deal has been written on the relationship between these two books and in particular about certain inconsistencies which appear when one sets them side by side. The debate may seem a little pedantic for it would not be altogether surprising if Smith had shifted his ground in certain respects in the period of a decade and a half that elapsed between the writing of the two books. On the other hand, the fact that he brought out a new edition of the first, long after the publication of the second, without disposing of the apparent inconsistencies, would seem to suggest that he did not himself attach any importance to these issues. In many ways, however, the *Wealth of Nations* is a more substantial, more mature,

---

[20] *Ibid*, p. 116.
[21] *Ibid*, p. 63. However, he goes on to note that 'In the superior stations of life the case is unhappily not always the same' and that 'flattery and falsehood too often prevail over merit and abilities'.

and more original book than the *Theory of Moral Sentiments*, for he worked into the former a great deal of illustrative material about the real world and a certain healthy scepticism about the 'agreeable effects' produced by that 'immense machine'. So that although the *Theory of Moral Sentiments* is essentially a set of armchair speculations derived from conventional philosophical abstractions, the *Wealth of Nations* is focused on the behaviour-patterns of real people within the constraints of existing institutions.

Thus by the time he came to write the *Wealth of Nations*, Adam Smith still had a clear view of the 'natural order' to which the economic system *ought* to approximate but was prepared to admit to certain flaws in its operation in the real world. The 'great architect' needed some cooperation from the economic policy makers to allow his machine to work in the most effective way. Hence Smith advocated an extensive programme of reforms designed to bring the economic system closer to the system of natural order which would maximise the social product. Governments in practice were inefficient and incompetent. Masters and workers were in constant conflict. Merchants and manufacturers found their interests opposed to farmers and landlords. To quote: 'rent and profits eat up wages, and the two superior orders of people oppress the inferior one.'[22] And again in a very famous passage: 'People of the same trade seldom meet together, even for merriment and diversion, but the conversation ends in a conspiracy against the public, or in some contrivance to raise prices. It is impossible indeed to prevent such meetings, by any law which either could be executed, or would be consistent with liberty and justice.'[23] As for those prudent moral sentiments that were assumed in the *Theory of Moral Sentiments* to be so widespread, by the time he had taken a hard look at the facts of economic life Smith was prepared to concede that: 'Men commonly over-estimate their chances of success in risky ventures with the consequence that too great a share of the nation's capital goes into such ventures.'[24]

In effect, the *Wealth of Nations* was the result of subjecting to empirical test in one sphere of human activity the theory of society that had been developed in the *Theory of Moral Sentiments*: and it was in applying this kind of essentially scientific analytical technique to the study of economics that Adam Smith achieved

[22] A. Smith, *Wealth of Nations*, Vol. II, p. 67.
[23] *Ibid*, Vol. I, p. 130.   [24] *Ibid*, p. 110.

a revolutionary impact on the discipline he helped to found. If we were to define a theoretical science as a set of 'general laws which can serve as instruments for systematic explanation and dependable prediction '[25] and a scientific methodology as a technical apparatus for logically or empirically verifying these laws it would be too much to say that Adam Smith had founded a science of economics. But it is reasonable to claim that he had at any rate made the first steps in this direction by devising a system and testing it. By postulating a logical system of economic relationships based on an underlying law of human nature (analogous to Newton's law of gravity), he set the course of theoretical political economy towards a system-building discipline. Schumpeter criticised him for too hastily dropping the mercantilist propositions and hence failing to develop an adequate theory of international economic relations.[26] However, what accounted for the tremendous impact that this book had on economic thought was not its components which, taken out of context, are easily criticised, but the way it built up into a logically interdependent whole, the first unified socio-economic model.

Also important no doubt in explaining the book's powerful impact on contemporary and nineteenth-century thought was the fact that its policy bias was peculiarly attractive to the entrepreneurs of an expanding industrialising economy. Paradoxically, although Smith thought of himself as a critic of the mercantile and manufacturing classes – and he certainly had some fierce criticisms to make – it was those classes which produced his most enthusiastic supporters. The book was actually written in the context of an essentially preindustrial economy and showed little sign of anticipating the revolutionary changes that were beginning to take place in the organisation, technology and structure of the British economy. There is no reference to any of the new textile inventions or to the coke-fired iron industry, though the *Wealth of Nations* was still being substantially revised and added to up to 1783 or 1784. The only reference to the cotton industry as such is a curious glancing allusion to its underdevelopment at the time of Christopher Columbus.[27] Smith knew presumably about the Carron iron works which set up a coke-fired blast-furnace near Falkirk in 1769 – for the company maintained a warehouse in his home town of Kirkcaldy. He was probably

[25] Ernest Nagel, *The Structure of Science* (1961), p. 450.
[26] Schumpeter, *op. cit.*, p. 376.
[27] *Wealth of Nations*, Vol. II, Bk. iv, p. 63.

familiar with an essay by his friend Edmund Burke praising 'the spirited, inventive and enterprising traders of Manchester' and drawing attention to the 'iron works of such magnitude even in their cradle which are set up on the Carron'.[28] Yet when he selected an industry to illustrate his observations on technical progress he chose what one writer has called his 'silly little pin factory'. and a nailery. On the other hand, as we shall see in Chapter 4, he had identified a crucial link between industrialisation and sustained economic growth, viz the continuous scope for increasing returns in manufacturing industry as a result of increasing specialisation of labour.

It is not surprising that Adam Smith's vision of the economic system was of an essentially pre-industrial economy, for it took a generation and more for the industrial revolution to produce generally the distinctive organisational, structural and technological changes that were its most significant consequences. In particular, for example, in Smith's theory technical progress was associated not primarily with new machinery, or new processes, or new products, but with improvements in the organisation and equipment of the labour force due to specialisation. In so far as he would have visualised *embodied* technical progress he would have seen it as embodied in the labour force rather than in machinery or plant.[29] By capital he generally meant circulating capital, i.e. capital invested in stocks of goods or work in progress, the most important capital of his day, rather than fixed capital. The strategic variable in the whole Smithian system is the division of labour, the extension of which he saw as dependent on the opening up of new sources of demand. He devoted a whole chapter to the proposition 'that the division of labour is limited by the extent of the market'.

In these respects, i.e. in emphasising the primary importance of the labour force in economic development and in treating the size of the market as a more important constraint on growth than the supply of natural resources, he followed in the main stream of mercantilist tradition. But in focusing on the primary impor-

[28] Quoted R. Koebner, 'Adam Smith and the Industrial Revolution', *Economic History Review* (1959), p. 386.
[29] For a modern definition of 'embodied technical progress' see e.g. R. Solow, 'Investment and Technical Progress', in K. J. Arrow, S. Karlin and P. Suppes (eds.), *Mathematical Methods in the Social Sciences*, e.g. p. 60: 'Investments in technology affect output only to the extent that they are carried into practice either by net capital formation or by the replacement of old-fashioned equipment by the latest models.'

tance of the domestic market (rather than the overseas market) he was closer to the French physiocrats than to the English mercantilists, for in a pre-industrial economy emphasis on the domestic market means an emphasis on agriculture as a major source of, though not necessarily the motive power for, economic growth. 'The different progress of opulence in different ages and nations' he wrote in the introduction to Book IV 'has given occasion to two different systems of political œconomy, with regard to enriching the people. The one may be called the system of commerce, the other that of agriculture.'[30] The one that is to say was the mercantilist system, the other the physiocratic system. But the physiocrats had seen agriculture as the *only* source of an economic surplus large enough to lift the circular flow to a higher level of national output: for them the manufacturing sector was 'sterile' in the sense that it yielded no surplus. Smith went beyond this essentially pre-industrial viewpoint to argue in favour of what might be called a strategy of free 'balanced' growth, in which 'the obvious and simple system of natural liberty' would maximise growth so long as the Divine Plan was allowed to operate without hindrance; e.g.

every system which endeavours, either, by extraordinary encouragements, to draw towards a particular species of industry a greater share of the capital of the society than what would naturally go to it; or, by extraordinary restraints, to force from a particular species of industry some share of the capital which would otherwise be employed in it; is in reality subversive of the great purpose which it means to promote. It retards instead of accelerating, the progress of the society towards real wealth and greatness; and diminishes, instead of increasing, the real value of the annual produce of its land and labour.[31]

In essence then Adam Smith provided political economy with an organised structure of assumptions, a problem orientation and a value system. What was the substance – the long-term significance – of this paradigm and what accounted for its powerful and tenacious impact?

First of all, Smith articulated political economy firmly within the ambit of moral philosophy as a normative study of society. As a moral rather than a natural, a philosophical rather than a logical or mathematical discipline it moved away from the empirical–quantitative bias of the political arithmeticians. As a normative study it gave intellectual backing to the political–propagandist predilections of eighteenth-century pamphleteers.

[30] *Wealth of Nations*, Vol. I, p. 395.   [31] *Wealth of Nations*, Vol. II, p. 184.

In effect he set the pattern for an abstract deductive science proceeding from a few general principles, ultimately of an introspective or philosophical, rather than of an empirically verifiable nature. True there is a continual appeal to history in the *Wealth of Nations* but it is what Dugald Stewart (his pupil, disciple and first biographer) called 'conjectural history' rather than recorded history. Its role, like that of the references to economic and social conditions of other countries at earlier stages of development, was to illustrate rather than to verify the philosophical arguments.

Smith's basic philosophical premises were materialistic and mechanistic, as evidenced by his assumption of an 'agreeable machine' designed by a 'divine architect' and powered by the natural and universal human instinct for self-preservation and self-advancement. His problem was to explain economic development, to elucidate 'the nature and causes of the wealth of nations'. His analytical method was to describe the 'natural' economic order by abstracting from the conflicts and imperfections which hindered its beneficent operations in the real world and by deducing logically its propensity to maximise economic welfare. The ideological bias implicit in his choice of assumptions and methodology was towards policies designed to minimise interference by authority (church or state) with individual freedom: it led unequivocally towards individualism and laissez-faire and away from collectivism and state intervention.

It is not hard to explain why Adam Smith's paradigm for political economy had such an instant success. For one thing, it gave intellectual status and appeal to the subject by unifying its basic theories and by systematically relating it to academic philosophy in a way that no other writer had succeeded or even attempted to do before. The task of exploring and extending this essentially simple and relatively comprehensive system of analysis became a challenge to educated minds, irrespective of their political predilection or affiliations.

In addition, it formulated the primary economic problem in terms that seemed appropriate to a society that was beginning to expand in population and wealth and to industrialise. Economic growth and change were the topical questions of the day. Smith's system of classification of the basic economic relationships of society, his emphasis on the pivotal significance of the characteristic social pattern of capitalism – landlords, labourers and capitalists, with their characteristic forms of income – rents, wages and profits – had special relevance for the emergent capitalist societies of Western Europe. His anatomy of the exchange economy illuminated the interdependence of incomes and prices with an unprecedented cogency and realism. E.g.:

As the price or exchangeable value of every particular commodity, taken separately, resolves itself into some one or other, or all of these three parts; so that of all the commodities which compose the whole annual produce of the labour of every country, taken complexly, must resolve itself into the same three parts, and be parcelled out among different inhabitants of the country, either as the wages of their labour, the profits or their stock, or the rent of their land. The whole of what is annually either collected or produced by the labour of every society, or what comes to be the same thing, the whole price of it, is in this manner originally distributed among some of its different members. Wages, profit, and rent, are the three original sources of all revenue as well as of all exchangeable value. All other revenue is ultimately derived from one or other of these.[32]

Thus, having formulated the economic problem in terms that his contemporaries regarded as relevant, having analysed the factors of production into categories they recognised as realistic, Adam Smith produced a reasoned solution to the fundamental problem of capitalist society; i.e. how order rather than chaos can emerge from the uncoordinated activities of a myriad of individuals each pursuing his own self-interest. To quote again:

As every individual, therefore, endeavours as much as he can both to employ his capital in the support of domestic industry, and so to direct that industry that its produce may be of the greatest value; every individual necessarily labours to render the annual revenue of society as great as he can. He generally, indeed, neither intends to promote the public interest, nor knows how much he is promoting it. By preferring the support of domestic to that of foreign industry, he intends only his own security; and by directing that industry in such a manner as its produce may be of the greatest value, he intends only his own gain, and he is in this, as in so many other cases, led by an invisible hand to promote an end which was no part of his intention... By pursuing his own interest he frequently promotes that of the society more effectually than when he really intends to promote it.[33]

Finally, of course, a part of the success of the Smithian paradigm – possibly the larger part of its tenacity – can be attributed to the nature of the implicit policy prescriptions. Sir Karl Popper,

---

[32] *Wealth of Nations*, Vol. I, p. 54.
[33] *Wealth of Nations*, Vol. I, p. 421.

in an essay on the testing of theories[34] distinguishes three types of theory: (1) logical and mathematical theories which can be refuted by logical testing; (2) empirical and scientific theories which can be tested by experimental methods; and (3) philosophical or metaphysical theories which are irrefutable by definition and not open to empirical experiment. In the main, Adam Smith's theory of the economic order falls into the third category and Popper proposes a series of critical questions in relation to this type of theory, e.g. 'Does it solve the problem? Does it solve it better than other theories? Has it perhaps merely shifted the problem? Is the solution simple? Is it fruitful? Does it perhaps contradict other philosophical theories needed for solving other problems?'[35] The Smithian paradigm would have stood up quite well to a barrage of questions of this kind in the late eighteenth and early nineteenth centuries. But for a theory of the economic system, which inevitably implies a set of economic policy prescriptions, the users of the paradigm may reasonably be expected to apply another critical question, viz 'Does the policy work?'

There seems little doubt that in the capitalist societies of the eighteenth and early nineteenth centuries, and *a fortiori* for the first country to experience an industrial revolution, the policy appeared to work to the extent of maximising the output of material goods and services. The reduction of incompetent state intervention, of restrictions on internal and external trade and on the movement of capital and labour could be seen to have positively assisted the process of economic growth. Whether it achieved other policy desiderata, e.g. a just and/or politically stable distribution of wealth within economic society, was of course another matter. And it was no accident that the only totally different alternative paradigm offered during the nineteenth century, the Marxian system, was focused on the failure of orthodox political economy to prescribe for a desirable *distribution* of wealth.

As far as mainstream political economy was concerned however the Smithian paradigm was revised, amended and extended piecemeal during the nineteenth and twentieth centuries: but the ideological bias has lasted virtually intact in some schools of thought right down to the modern neo-classical orthodoxy. The following passage, for example, written in 1943 by an eminent

[34] K. Popper, 'On the Status of Science and Metaphysics', in *Conjectures and Refutations* (1963).
[35] *Ibid*, p. 199.

American theorist of the Chicago school is almost unadulterated Adam Smith:

The practical relevance of economic theory is chiefly to the problems of social action. But in a free society the objective of social control is not usually to make individuals behave in one particular way rather than in another; it is simply to create the conditions under which individuals will be able to realize their individual objectives to the maximum degree, i.e. to act harmoniously, with a minimum of conflict and mutual frustration.[36]

FURTHER READING

A short list of books and articles designed to refer the student to some of the most accessible primary sources and to a few of the secondary sources bearing on issues raised in the text is appended to each chapter. A more complete and usefully annotated bibliography will be found in Mark Blaug's book referred to below.

Primary literature

Adam Smith, *The Theory of Moral Sentiments*, Glasgow edition, ed. by A. L. Macfie and D. D. Raphael (1976).
Adam Smith, *An Inquiry into the Nature and Causes of the Wealth of Nations*, ed. Cannan, 2 vols. (1950). See also the Glasgow edition, edited with an introduction by R. H. Campbell and A. S. Skinner (1976).

Secondary literature

M. Blaug, *Economic Theory in Retrospect* (1964).
Marian Bowley, *Studies in the History of Economic Theory before 1870* (1973).
T. D. Campbell, *Adam Smith's Theory of Morals* (1971).
D. C. Coleman (ed.), *Revisions in Mercantilism* (1969).
Samuel Hollander, 'On the Interpretation of the Just Price', *Kyklos* (1965).
Samuel Hollander, *The Economics of Adam Smith* (1973).
J. Ralph Lindgren, *The Social Philosophy of Adam Smith* (1973).
R. L. Meek (ed.), *Precursors of Adam Smith 1750–1775* (1973).
R. L. Meek, *The Economics of Physiocracy* (1962).
Raymond de Roover, 'The Concept of the Just Price: Theory and Economic Policy', *Journal of Economic History* (1958).
J. Schumpeter, *History of Economic Analysis* (1954).

[36] F. H. Knight in a review of E. M. MacIver, *Social Causation*, reprinted in *On the History and Method of Economics*, p. 145.

Andrew S. Skinner and Thomas Wilson, *Essays on Adam Smith* (1975).
J. Viner, 'Adam Smith and Laissez-faire' in *idem, The Long View and the Short* (1950).
J. Viner, 'English Theories of Foreign Trade before Adam Smith' in *idem, Studies in the Theory of International Trade* (1937).

2

ADAM SMITH'S THEORY OF VALUE

Whatever the philosophical or methodological approach economists have taken to their discipline, whatever view they have
taken of its scope, objectives and analytical techniques, the theory
of value – with its associated theory of distribution – has been a
key feature of the disciplinary matrix or paradigm to which they
have chosen to conform.[1] The prevailing concept of value and
the use made of it has altered, chameleon-fashion, to match the
currently accepted economic doctrines. In pre-mercantilist
periods, when it would be an exaggeration to say that there was
an explicit *theory* of value, the concept of value reflected current
attitudes to economic questions. For example, in medieval-
scholastic doctrine the value of the commodity tended to be
identified with the morally right price. In a static, parochialised
economic and social order the just price would equal the customary price, reflecting a socially accepted scale of values, and the
whole community would know what the fair price *ought* to be.
However when the market became more dominant in economic
life, there was an increasing tendency for the concept of the just
price to coincide with the normal (competitive) market price,
including an element of normal profit. For this too became a
customary price which could be justified as being the proper one.
Realists such as Thomas Aquinas did not hesitate to identify the
actual market price, even when inflated by temporary scarcity,
with the just price.[2]

As the exchange economy extended its range, domestically and
internationally, the possibility of prices fluctuating and of

[1] Cf. L. Robbins, *The Nature and Significance of Economic Science*, p. 73: 'The
most fundamental propositions of economic analysis are the propositions of the
general theory of value. No matter what particular "school" is in question, no
matter what arrangement of subject-matter is adopted, the body of propositions
explaining the nature and the determination of the relation between given goods
of the first order will be found to have a pivotal position in the whole system.'

[2] Raymond de Roover, *Journal of Economic History* (1958), *op. cit.*, p. 420.

yielding variable profits to the lengthening line of merchants involved in the distribution process became more common and more socially acceptable. To equate value with actual price charged – whatever that was – was not to explain it, however, and some writers began to develop an explanation by taking into account factors on the side of demand and supply. Nicholas Barbon, for example, asserted in the seventeenth century that: 'the market is the best Judge of Value...Things are just worth so much as they can be sold for, according to the Old Rule, *Valet Quantum Vendi Potest*'; and 'The Value of all Wares, arriveth from their Use and the Dearness or Cheapness of them, from their Plenty and Scarcity.'[3] Even in the pre-classical, pre-paradigm, era of political economy, however, when theories of value were at best rudimentary, implicit rather than explicit, it was clear that the concept of value was inextricably involved with questions relating to the social distribution of income and in particular with the question of profit. Abnormal profits were often held to be morally disreputable in the pre-mercantilist era while in mercantilist and later periods they came to be justified by an appeal to a supposedly objective concept of value.

When Adam Smith came to embark on his systematic analysis of the nature and causes of the wealth of nations, the concept of value had already developed a long way from the moralistic–customary levels of discussion and the philosophers had already identified some of the building blocks relevant to a full theory of value. Francis Hutcheson, for example, Smith's teacher and predecessor in the Glasgow Chair of Moral Philosophy, brought out clearly the demand and supply aspects necessary to an explanation of value, e.g. 'we shall find that the prices of goods depend on these two jointly, the *demand* on account of some use or other which many desire and the *difficulty* of acquiring, or cultivating for human use'. He seemed to assign to use a primary role: 'The natural ground of all value or price is some sort of *use* which goods afford in life' and he defined use in terms which approximate to the modern economists' notion of utility, i.e. as 'not only a natural sub-serviency for our support, or to some natural pleasure, but any tendency to give any satisfaction, by prevailing custom or fancy, as a matter of ornament or distinc-

[3] Nicholas Barbon, *A Discourse of Trade* (1960), ed. J. L. Hollander (1938), pp. 20 and 100. See R. L. Meek, *Studies in the Labour Theory of Value*, for a discussion of value theory before Adam Smith; and Marian Bowley, *Studies in the History of Economic Theory before 1870*, for a detailed discussion of the development of value theory in the seventeenth century.

tion'. On the supply side he listed effort, skill and the producer's social status among the factors determining scarcity value (or value in exchange):

Not only a great labour, or toil, but all other circumstances which prevent a great plenty of the goods or performances demanded... Price is increased by the rarity or scarcity of the materials in nature, or such accidents as prevent plentiful crops of certain fruits of the earth; and the great ingenuity and nice taste requisite in the artists to finish well some works of art, as men of such genius are rare. The value is also raised, by the dignity of the station in which according to the custom of a country, the men must live who provide us with certain goods or works of art.[4]

Smith himself brought in income distribution on the demand side of the account in his 1762/3 lectures when he listed the following three determinants of market price:

First the demand, or need for the commodity. There is no demand for a thing of little use; it is not a rational object of desire. Secondly, the abundance or scarcity of the commodity in proportion to the need of it. If the commodity be scarce, the price is raised, but if the quantity be more than sufficient to supply the demand, the price falls. Thus it is that diamonds and other precious stones are dear, while iron, which is more useful, is so many times cheaper, though this depends principally on the last cause, viz: Thirdly, the riches or poverty of those who demand.[5]

It is, however, one thing to list the determinants of value (or price) and another to combine them in a theory of value, i.e. an explanation of the way value (or price) comes to be what it is. It is something else again to produce a theory of value which is consistent with an overall theory of economic behaviour, e.g. an explanation of the 'nature and causes of the wealth of nations'.

There has been a running debate, beginning with Ricardo's *Principles*, about the nature and internal consistency of Adam Smith's theory of value and although his exposition of it leaves much room for argument the differences often shed more light on the methodological commitments of the protagonists than on Adam Smith's own beliefs. Thus, for the neo-classical economists for whom the marginal revolution had brought the concept of utility firmly back into the theory of value, it was Smith who had

[4] F. Hutcheson, *System of Moral Philosophy* (1755), Vol. II, pp. 53–4. These passages are quoted and discussed by H. M. Robertson and W. L. Taylor in 'Adam Smith's approach to the theory of value', *Economic Journal* (June 1957).

[5] *Lectures on Justice, Police, Revenue and Arms by Adam Smith Reported by a Student in 1763*, ed. E. Cannan, p. 176.

led the classical economists away from the concern with utility
and scarcity which was already apparent in mercantilist thinking
and into an inadequate cost of production theory of value.
According to Schumpeter, for example, Smith 'was not primarily
interested in the problem of value' in the sense of a 'causal
explanation of the phenomenon of value... What he wanted was
a price theory by which to establish certain propositions that do
not require going into the background of the value phenomenon
at all.'[6] Indeed, some of Smith's statements lend themselves to
interpretation as a mere 'adding up' theorem whereby natural
price (i.e. value) is explained in terms of a summation of the
natural wages, profits and rents entering into the exchangeable
value of a commodity. In short, his theory of value and his theory
of distribution both stem from the doctrine of the invisible hand
which tends to bring about a naturally – and by definition
harmoniously – integrated set of exchange relationships in both
commodity and factor markets.[7]

Recently, however, there has been a tendency to see more
dimensions in Smith's analysis, partly perhaps because the mid
twentieth century methodological debate has encouraged researchers in economic thought to re-examine primary sources
from a more neutral stance. In a recent monograph on *The
Economics of Adam Smith*, Samuel Hollander, for example, concludes both that 'there was less emphasis on utility and scarcity
in mercantilist economic thought than has been read into it by
subsequent commentators',[8] and that Smith explained exchange
value in traditional terms taking full account of utility and
scarcity.[9] Marian Bowley has also re-examined Smith's theory of
value or natural price as set out in his *Lectures* and the *Wealth
of Nations* and sees a continuity between Adam Smith's explanation of the price mechanism and the scholastic school's analysis
of the just price. She argues that Smith demonstrated the resource allocation function of divergencies between market and
natural prices and so solved the difficulty, apparent in the school-
men's discussions, of finding a way to reconcile both market and
supply prices to the just price concept.[10] More recently still Dr

---

[6] J. Schumpeter, *History of Economic Analysis* (1954), p. 309.
[7] See the passage quoted on p. 15 above.
[8] Samuel Hollander, *The Economics of Adam Smith* (1973), p. 134.
[9] *Ibid*, p. 137.
[10] Marian Bowley, *Studies in the History of Economic Theory* (1973), *op. cit.*, pp.
126–7. For another recent rehabilitation of Smith's theory of value see S. Kaushil,
'The case of Adam Smith's value analysis', *Oxford Economic Papers* (March

O'Brien has argued that the apparent shift from a predominantly utility–scarcity explanation of value in the *Lectures* to an essentially cost-of-production explanation in the *Wealth of Nations*, reflected Adam Smith's need to accommodate a theory of distribution with his theory of value: 'Without the concept of marginal productivity there was no very obvious way of linking distribution to value except by a cost of production theory of value.'[11]

There are four prime inter-related difficulties involved in devising an acceptable theory of value. The first lies in explaining how and why a commodity acquires value. Another lies in disentangling the complex, shifting relationships between value considered as some intrinsic, lasting (though not necessarily constant attribute) of a commodity or service on the one hand, and its market price, whether expressed in money terms or in terms of some other commodities or services, on the other. Another lies in relating the theory of value to a theory of the distribution of incomes. The fourth lies in actually measuring value in operational terms – for if value is not measurable the theory is not testable.

Adam Smith faced all these problems in the following passage with which he opened his discussion of value in Book I of the *Wealth of Nations*.

The word VALUE, it is to be observed, has two different meanings, and sometimes expresses the utility of some particular object, and sometimes the power of purchasing other goods which the possession of that object conveys. The one may be called 'value in use'; the other, 'value in exchange'. The things which have the greatest value in use have frequently little or no value in exchange; and on the contrary, those which have the greatest value in exchange have frequently no value in use. Nothing is more useful than water, but it will purchase scarce anything: scarce anything can be had in exchange for it. A diamond, on the contrary, has scarcely any value in use; but a very great quantity of other goods may frequently be had in exchange for it.

In order to investigate the principles which regulate the exchangeable value of commodities, I shall endeavour to shew.

First, what is the real measure of this exchangeable value; or, wherein consists the real price of all commodities.

1973). Marxist writers have generally been more sympathetic in their critique than the orthodox neo-classicists. See e.g. R. L. Meek, *Studies in the Labour Theory of Value* (1956 and 1973), and M. Dobb, *Theories of Value and Distribution since Adam Smith* (1973). But it is noteworthy that Meek in the preface to his second edition considers that he may have over-estimated and over-simplified Smith's contribution (Meek, *op. cit.*, 1973 edn, p. iii).

[11] D. P. O'Brien, *The Classical Economists* (1975), p. 78.

Secondly, what are the different parts of which this real price is composed, or made up.

And, lastly, what are the different circumstances which sometimes raise some or all of these different parts of price above, and sometimes sink them below their natural or ordinary rate; or, what are the causes which sometimes hinder the market price, that is, the actual price of commodities from coinciding exactly with what may be called their natural price.[12]

There were thus two aspects of value or price to be explained and related – the actual market price and the natural price. Smith explained the first of these in terms of a simple supply and demand mechanism in a competitive market. He agreed that when demand exceeds supply it will be factors on the side of demand (competition between buyers) which effectively determine price – taking into account such influences as incomes ('the wealth and wanton luxury of competitors') and special market conditions such as war or harvest failure; and that when supply exceeds 'effectual demand' it will be competition among sellers that sets the price – taking into account such constraints as the possibility of adding to stocks (e.g. the perishability of commodities).[13]

To express the relationship between value, as a relatively long-lasting quality, and market price, as a relatively transient phenomenon dependent upon the conditions of a particular market, Smith invoked the concept of a 'natural' price defined in effect as price in long-run stable equilibrium, e.g.

The natural price, therefore, is, as it were, the central price, to which the prices of all commodities are continually gravitating. Different accidents may sometimes keep them suspended a good deal above it, and sometimes force them down even somewhat below it. But whatever may be the obstacles which hinder them from settling in this center of repose and continuance, they are constantly tending towards it.[14]

The concept of a natural price gives Smith's theory of value a pivotal position in his general theory of a harmonious economic order in which the self-interest of individuals operating in a freely competitive market economy tends naturally to produce an optimum allocation of resources and thus to maximise total output. At the same time it connects his theory of value with his theory of distribution by linking the commodity markets to the

[12] *Wealth of Nations*, Vol. 1, p. 30.
[13] *Ibid*, Vol. 1, pp. 58–9.   [14] *Ibid*, Vol. 1, p. 60.

factor markets, though in so far as he had a theory of distribution it was a mere byproduct of his theory of value.

> There is in every society or neighbourhood an ordinary or average rate both of wages or profit in every different employment of labour and stock. This rate is naturally regulated, as I shall show hereafter, partly by the general circumstances of the society, their riches or poverty, their advancing, stationary, or declining condition; and partly by the particular nature of each employment.
>
> There is likewise in every society or neighbourhood an ordinary or average rate of rent, which is regulated too, as I shall show hereafter, partly by the general circumstances of the society or neighbourhood in which the land is situated, and partly by the natural or improved fertility of the land.
>
> These ordinary or average rates may be called the natural rates of wages, profit, and rent at the time and place in which they commonly prevail.
>
> When the price of any commodity is neither more nor less than what is sufficient to pay the rent of the land, the wages of the labour, and the profits of the stock employed in raising, preparing, and bringing it to market, according to their natural rates, the commodity is then sold for what may be called its natural price.[15]

The natural price is in effect the crucial element in the allocative mechanism postulated by Smith for he went on to argue that whenever the market price of a commodity stood above the natural price, viewed as a sum of natural factor prices, it would tend to attract the factors of production into the industry concerned: and whenever it stood below, it would induce factors of production to withdraw. It thus tends to maximise output and to minimise long-run costs: 'The natural price, or the price of free competition...is the lowest which can be taken, not upon every occasion, indeed, but for any considerable time together.'[16] The natural price is then an abstraction which reflects real value in terms of a relationship between minimum costs and effective demand in a free market economy where the distribution of incomes is partly determined by the initial social and economic circumstances and partly by social and economic change.

Measuring value, however, so as to be able to make comparisons between countries or over time raises another set of problems. For prices are normally expressed in money terms and money itself is a variable yardstick. So Smith distinguished between a real price and a nominal price. 'The same real price is always of the same value; but on account of the variations in the

---

[15] *Ibid*, p. 57.   [16] *Ibid*, p. 63.

value of gold and silver, the same nominal price is sometimes of very different values.'[17] What is needed is a numeraire which is itself relatively stable over time and space. Smith discussed corn as a solution. 'The rents which have been reserved in corn have preserved their value much better than those which have been reserved in money, even where the denomination of the coin has not been altered.'[18] Similarly, in a poor, stagnant, economy the amount of corn required to provide for the subsistence of a labourer is relatively invariable: but in a growing economy 'a society advancing to opulence' this too will become a variable amount. In the end Smith came down to the view that: 'Labour...is the only universal, as well as the only accurate measure of value, or the only standard by which we can compare the values of different commodities at all times and at all places.'[19] There has been a good deal of argument as to what precisely Smith meant by his labour measure of value and since he never actually applied the measure empirically there is plenty of scope for debate.

On balance the discussion in the *Wealth of Nations* seems to suggest that it was not the labour *embodied* in a commodity that Smith regarded as 'the only accurate measure of value' in a capitalist economy but the labour *commanded* by a commodity. Were he to apply the measure, that is to say, he would presumably be looking not for data on the labour involved in producing the good in question, but on the amount of labour for which it could currently be exchanged on the market. Of course, as Smith points out, in 'the early and rude state of society which precedes both the accumulation of stock and the appropriation of land', the labour embodied in and the labour commanded by a commodity would come to the same thing. But in a capitalist economy, where 'the whole produce of labour does not always belong to the labourer' the two indices part company unless (as Ricardo later noted) wages move in step with the productivity of labour or, to put it another way, wages constitute a constant fraction of the total value of production.[20] To quote Smith again:

The value of any commodity, therefore, to the person who possesses it, and who means not to use or consume it himself, but to exchange

---

[17] *Ibid*, pp. 35–6.   [18] *Ibid*, p. 36.

[19] *Ibid*, p. 38.

[20] See below p. 61 for the relevant quotation from Ricardo. The point is also made by M. Dobb, *Theories of Value and Distribution since Adam Smith*. See his footnote on p. 49 making the point by numerical example.

it for other commodities, is equal to the quantity of labour which it enables him to purchase or command. Labour, therefore, is the real measure of the exchangeable value of all commodities.

The real price of everything, what everything costs to the man who wants to acquire it is the toil and trouble of acquiring it. What everything is really worth to the man who has acquired it, and who wants to dispose of it or exchange it for something else, is the toil and trouble which it can save to himself, and which it can impose upon other people.[21]

To sum up then: most of the confusion, the textual problems and the apparent inconsistencies raised by subsequent debate about what Adam Smith 'really' meant in this context hinge on questions which he did not set out to answer or on a reformulation of his questions in terms of a different disciplinary matrix. If we now go back to the questions which he posed at the outset of his investigation into 'the principles which regulate the exchangeable value of commodities' in a capitalist society[22] the answers are as follows:

(1) The real measure of the exchangeable value of commodities is the labour currently commanded by these goods in the market: for it is this which is the ultimate measure of real income, of poverty or wealth. E.g.

Every man is rich or poor according to the degree in which he can afford to enjoy the necessaries, conveniences, and amusements of human life. But after the division of labour has once thoroughly taken place, it is but a very small part of these with which a man's own labour can supply him. The far greater part of them he must derive from the labour of other people, and he must be rich or poor according to the quantity of that labour which he can command, or which he can afford to purchase.[23]

(2) This 'real price' of each commodity and of the national output as a whole can be resolved into components which reflect the rewards of the factors – land, labour and capital – involved in its production. Smith's formal definition of price as a sum of wages, profits and rent has already been quoted on p. 15 above.[24]

This and similar passages have often been adduced as evidence that Smith held a pure 'cost of production' theory of value.

[21] *Wealth of Nations*, Vol. 1, p. 32.
[22] Quoted above, pp. 23–4.
[23] *Wealth of Nations*, Vol. 1, p. 32.
[24] See the first quotation on p. 15.

However it can also be regarded as no more than a breakdown of the components of value, with taxonomic rather than explanatory significance.

(3) Finally, Smith found the reasons for the divergence between the market price of commodities and their natural prices or real value *either* in purely transitory conditions affecting particular markets where supply had not yet adjusted to 'effectual demand' *or* to imperfections in the market (monopoly, government intervention, etc.). In the long run and in a stable competitive exchange economy where individuals were free to pursue their own self-interest costs would be at a minimum, supply would be fully adjusted to 'effectual demand' and market prices would tend to coincide with real values in commodity and factor markets alike.

Running through the whole of Smith's analysis of value (as of other questions) was a strong normative content. Its main thrust, that is to say, was towards economic policies which militated against any kind of interference with the free market – whether in the form of private monopoly or combination or government intervention. It was also, and in this it was sharply distinguished from Ricardo's theory, primarily designed to serve the purposes of an inquiry into the conditions of economic progress.

FURTHER READING

(See also references at end of Chapter 1.)

Maurice Dobb, *Theories of Value and Distribution since Adam Smith* (1973).
Ronald L. Meek, *Studies in the Labour Theory of Value* (1973).
H. M. Robertson and W. L. Taylor, 'Adam Smith's Approach to the Theory of Value', *Economic Journal* (1957).

3

ORIGINS OF MODERN GROWTH THEORY

The leading writers on economic issues – theoretical, empirical or polemical – have always defined the subject of their investigations in the light of current economic problems. The central economic problem for Adam Smith, as for most other economists in the eighteenth and early nineteenth centuries was how to explain, and to prescribe policies for, economic growth. The mercantilists, for example, were keenly aware of inter-country differences in economic strength and of the fact that trade expansion or trade decline could alter, and indeed had altered, the balance of economic power and the relative ranking of countries. They were also prone to believe that economic expansion could be promoted by appropriate state intervention. The message of Mandeville's *Fable of the Bees* for example was that: 'Private Vices by the dextrous Management of a Skilful Politician may be turned into Public Benefits.'[1]

The mercantilists however were concerned not so much with a sustained process of economic growth resting on a growth in output per head, as with economic expansion in the limited aggregative sense of an increase in total output. In other words they were interested in GNP as an indicator of national opulence or national power. Accordingly they saw growth in the *total* labour force as the primary condition of economic progress. Relatively few of them discussed the possibility that an increase in population might be associated with a fall in output per head[2] and the majority of them favoured active pro-natalist policies. Perhaps if their man–land ratios had been less favourable and their mortality rates less crippling they would have seen some of the implications for productivity and hence long-term growth, of

---

[1] Concluding sentence of the essay on 'A Search into the Nature of Society' added to the 1723 edition of the *Fable*.

[2] B. F. Hoselitz (ed.), *Theories of Economic Growth*. Spengler (p. 28) quotes Cantillon as one of the few who did notice this.

these policies. The fact remains, however, that it is difficult to identify anything, however sketchy, corresponding to the basic elements of a mercantilist theory of economic growth as a continuous process. For the mercantilists, promoting the economic strength of the nation seemed to depend essentially on manipulating the international power structure and achieving a surplus on the balance of payments.

The physiocrats developed more fruitful ideas in this context. Like the mercantilists they saw the economy as a whole, an interdependent whole, and focused on aggregate output rather than average product but they developed a more systematic technique of analysing the mechanics of the interdependence of the individual sectors. Quesnay's *Tableau Economique* for example, was designed to illustrate diagrammatically the way expenditures in one sector generated incomes in other sectors. Although some later writers (e.g. Marx) appreciated the analytical insight involved in Quesnay's *Tableau* it was not until the macroeconomic model-builders of the mid twentieth century claimed him as their predecessor that it began to be seriously discussed by modern economists. When in 1955 Professor Phillips translated the data of the Quesnay *Tableau* into a modern input–output matrix it took on a new significance for many modern economists.[3] In this form it can be seen as a static closed Leontief system, a circular flow model in which the sectors were farmers, landlord and artisans.

Quesnay, however, had a continuous process in mind – for example he traced the expenditure of the landlord class back to the rents received in the previous period – and his *Tableau Economique* provided the analytical framework for a distinctive theory of growth. The physiocrats started from the pre-industrial assumption that the only productive class in the community was the agricultural sector. The artisan (manufacturing) class added nothing to the value of the social product beyond the value of its labour and so was deemed 'sterile': the landlords produced nothing: neither the 'sterile' nor the 'proprietary' classes added anything to the social surplus. However the productive class (the farmers) generated a surplus which gave rise to three sorts of capital outlays from which the next season's output stemmed viz (1) *avances annuelles* or working capital (i.e. outlays on preparing, planting, cultivating and harvesting the land, on maintaining

---

[3] A. Phillips, 'The Tableau Economique as a Simple Leontief Model', *Quarterly Journal of Economics* (1955).

farm workers and animals etc.); (2) *avances primitives* (i.e. replacement or maintenance of agricultural tools, implements, cattle etc.); (3) *avances foncières* (i.e. maintenance or supplementation of overhead capital of a semi-permanent character such as land improvement, drainage, hedges, buildings). Some physiocrats also distinguished a fourth kind of capital investment, *avances souveraines*, corresponding to what we might now call social overhead capital (e.g. highways, canals, rivers, ports etc.) generally provided out of the government's share in the gross national product.

Maintaining the level of agricultural output (and hence of GNP) depended under the physiocratic system on maintaining these '*avances*', and more especially on the *avances annuelles*. Should the amount available for *avances annuelles* in a given period diminish, either because the agricultural surplus held over from the previous period was lower, or because there was a redistribution of income in the direction of the 'consuming' classes rather than the 'investing' classes in the community, then GNP must fall. An expansion in output depends on raising the level of the agricultural surplus and making a larger sum available for capital formation than was necessary to maintain the current level of working capital (*avances annuelles*) or to replace fixed or overhead capital (*avances primitives* or *foncières*). The prime mover in this system, the factor generating economic growth, is thus the agricultural surplus and it is on capital accumulation in agriculture that economic development essentially depends. An increase in the surplus could take place either as a result of technical improvements in agriculture, or a reduction in agricultural taxation, or a fall in the rate of interest, or a freeing of the restrictions and tolls on domestic or international trade. So some physiocrats advocated putting a legal ceiling on the rate of interest in agriculture. Others advocated lightening the tax burden on the agricultural sector or spreading the tax burden so that it encouraged expenditure on primary products at the expense of processed products (manufactures) or services. Most were in favour of freeing trade from the numerous internal tolls that hindered the movement of agricultural produce in France, and also of institutional reforms (e.g. longer leases) and other measures which might encourage the adoption and diffusion of improved agricultural techniques. The key to *growth*, however, in the physiocratic system was the rate of capital accumulation.

In view of Adam Smith's interest in the physiocrats, whom he met on his visit to France, and with whose laissez-faire policy prescriptions he sympathised more than with the interventionist propensities of the English mercantilists, it is not surprising to find that the Smithian theory of growth has some affinities to this model. Professor Hicks has distilled what he calls Smith's 'pure economic model' in a form which brings out the similarity rather well. Although this distillation is clearly a greatly simplified interpretation of the Smithian message it also pinpoints some of the features that are of interest to modern growth theorists.[4]

Briefly, Hicks' version starts with an initial capital stock given by last year's harvest and expressed as a certain quantity of corn. This provides the resources which the labour force is to transform into more corn in the current period – the period being the agricultural year. The size of the initial capital stock (the amount of corn carried over from last year) determines the number of labourers that can be employed. Then the output of the current year X_t depends on last year's output X_{t-1}, the productivity of the average labourer (p) and the amount consumed (as food and as seed) by each labourer (w): so that $X_t = (p/w)X_{t-1}$. If the product of the average labourer (p) is larger than the corn he uses up (w) then X_t will be larger than X_{t-1} and the economy will be growing at the rate $(p/w) - 1$. Conversely, if the wage rate of (corn consumed by) the average labourer rises; or if any corn is taken out of this process to unproductive (non corn-producing) sectors then the agricultural surplus will be reduced i.e. $K_t = kX_{t-1}$ where k represents the fraction left after all non-productive 'leaks' are accounted for. Then the capital available to finance corn production next year K_t will be only part of this year's production and the wages fund, i.e. the stock of wage goods available to support next year's labour force, will be correspondingly reduced. The number of labourers employed will be K_t/w so that $X_t = (p/w)K_t = k(p/w)X_{t-1}$. The growth rate of the economy is now only $k(p/w) - 1$, so that a positive growth rate hinges on productivity rising faster than the wage rate and the level of unproductive consumption.

When the Smith model is put into this kind of form it resembles a highly simplified modern growth model but it is only a dynamic model under very special assumptions. If p and w and k were

[4] J. R. Hicks, *Capital and Growth*, pp. 36–8. See also W. T. Eltis 'Adam Smith's Theory of Economic Growth', in *Essays on Adam Smith*, ed. Andrew Skinner and Thomas Wilson (1975).

regarded as constants and $p > w$ it could constitute the model for a regularly progressive economy. Smith however gives no indication that he regards them as constants. 'It follows' says Hicks 'that Smith's model though it looks like a growth model is not a growth model in the modern sense. It does not exhibit a sequence.'[5]

Putting Smith's theory in this purely economic format, however, does not capture either the spirit or the novelty of his approach to an explanation of growth. For one thing he did not attempt to visualise the growth process in exclusively economic terms. For another he explicitly rejected the physiocratic view that the *only* productive sector in the economy, the only source of a social surplus, was the agricultural sector. Writing as he did on the threshold of the first industrial revolution, he perceived more clearly than any of his predecessors had done, the wide scope for increasing returns in industry. In commenting on the physiocratic model which he described as 'the nearest approximation to the truth that has yet been published upon the subject of political economy'[6] he wrote: 'The capital error of this system, however, seems to lie in its representing the class of artificers, manufacturers and merchants, as altogether barren and unproductive.'[7] He then went on to shift the emphasis from the landed classes to the manufacturing classes as the main source of economic growth, which he saw as depending on two main inter-related elements: (1) the productivity of labour arising out of specialisation; and (2) the accumulation of capital by saving out of profits. The crucial requirements for growth, that is to say, were that there should be increasing subdivision of labour, raising average productivity, and that savings out of profits should be more than enough to maintain existing capital.

In both respects he regarded the manufacturing classes as having an advantage over the landed classes. Thus he said of the first of his two sources of growth:

The improvement in the productive powers of useful labour depend, first, upon the improvement in the ability of the workman; and secondly upon that of the machinery with which he works. But the labour of artificers and manufacturers, as it is capable of being more subdivided, and the labour of each workman reduced to a greater simplicity of operation than that of farmers and country labourers, so it is like-

---

[5] *Op. cit.*, p. 39, n. 1.
[6] *Wealth of Nations*, Cannan edn, Vol. II, p. 176.
[7] *Ibid*, p. 172.

wise capable of both these sorts of improvement in a much higher degree.[8]

On his second source of growth, capital accumulation he wrote:

The increase in the quantity of useful labour actually employed within any society, must depend altogether upon the increase of the capital which employs it; and the increase of that capital again must be exactly equal to the amount of the savings from the revenue, either of the particular persons who manage and direct the employment of that capital, or of some other persons who lend it to them. If merchants, artificers and manufacturers are, as this system seems to suppose, naturally more inclined to parsimony and saving than proprietors and cultivators, they are, so far, more likely to augment the quantity of useful labour employed within their society and consequently to increase its real revenue, the annual produce of its land and labour.[9]

Finally he observed as a fact of life, confirming his assumptions, that incomes per head earned in trading and manufacturing activities are higher than average incomes in the agricultural sector and he used this fact as another reason for emphasising the crucial importance of the non-agricultural sectors in economic growth. Thus:

though the revenue of the inhabitants of every country was supposed to consist altogether, as this [physiocratic] system seems to suppose, in the quantity of subsistence which their industry could procure to them; yet even upon this supposition, the revenue of a trading and manufacturing country must, other things being equal, always be much greater than that of one without trade or manufactures...A small quantity of manufactured produce produces a great quantity of rude produce. A trading and manufacturing country therefore naturally purchases with a small part of its manufactured produce a great part of the rude produce of other countries; while on the contrary a country without trade and manufactures is generally obliged to purchase, at the expence of a great part of its rude produce, a very small part of the manufactured produce of other countries.[10]

The empirical evidence for this proposition was Holland, a trading and manufacturing country with relatively limited natural resources, then in Smith's estimation the most affluent country in the world. The explanation though not explicit in this context can be found in his argument connecting the division of labour and the size of the market opened up by international trade.[11]

[8] *Ibid*, pp. 174–5.   [9] *Ibid*, p. 175.
[10] *Ibid*, p. 175.
[11] See e.g. the chapter in Book I of the *Wealth of Nations* entitled 'That the Division of Labour is limited by the extent of the Market'.

The keystone of Adam Smith's theory of growth was capital accumulation associated with an increasingly specialised and hence productive labour force. On his account capital accumulation provided both the employment opportunities which determined the extent of the market for manufactured goods (and thereby the scope for specialisation of labour) and the machinery which was one element in the increasing productivity of the labour force.

This great increase of the quantity of work, which, in consequence of the division of labour, the same number of people are capable of performing, is owing to three different circumstances; first to the increase of dexterity in every particular workman; secondly to the saving of time which is commonly lost in passing from one species of work to another; and lastly, to the invention of a great number of machines which facilitate and abridge labour, and enable one man to do the work of many.[12]

The growth process generated by these twin elements – capital accumulation and division of labour – was likely to continue so long as product per head grew faster than consumption per head, for this would ensure a continuing surplus, a rising demand for labour and hence a growing population.[13]

It is worth noting in the light of later developments in economic theory two crucial links in this analysis. The first is that Smith did not entertain the possibility of savings lying unspent in normal conditions: 'In all countries where there is tolerable security, every man of common understanding will endeavour to employ whatever stock he can command, in procuring either present enjoyment or future profit.'[14] In going on to argue that 'a man must be perfectly crazy' who does not spend his surplus either on present consumption or on investment in fixed or circulating capital he laid the foundation for what later became known as Say's Law, viz that supply creates its own demand. The second crucial link in Smith's view of a continuous growth process was that connecting the demand for labour with the growth of population, because 'the demand for men, like that for any other commodity necessarily regulates the production of men; quickens it when it goes on too slowly, and stops it when it

[12] *Wealth of Nations*, Vol. I, p. 9.

[13] See *ibid*, pp. 81–2: 'If this demand [for labour] is continually increasing, the reward of labour must necessarily encourage in such a manner the marriage and multiplication of labourers, as may enable them to supply that continually increasing demand by a continually increasing population'.

[14] *Ibid*, p. 267.

advances too fast'.[15] Here of course he was anticipating in part
at any rate Malthus' theory of population.

Finally Smith did not expect growth to go on for ever. The
long-term limits to growth were apparently set by natural resources which would ultimately put limits on population growth.
'In a country fully peopled in proportion to what either its
territory could maintain or its stock employ, the competition for
employment would necessarily be so great as to reduce the wages
of labour to what was barely sufficient to keep up the number
of labourers, and, the country being fully peopled, that number
could never be augmented.'[16] There are various references in the
Wealth of Nations to what later came to be called the 'stationary
state' but they do not amount to a systematic explanation of the
transition from a growing to a non-growing economy. It seemed
to be self-evident to Smith that a country which 'had acquired
that full complement of riches which the nature of its soil and
climate, and its situation with respect to other countries, allowed
it to acquire'[17] would stop growing. His own focus of interest
however lay not on that distant horizon but on the more immediate problems raised by the short-term and surmountable limits
to growth set by political rather than economic factors.

This then was the nub of the eighteenth-century growth problem: how to identify the economic policies which would promote
rather than retard the growth of national output. Like the physiocrats Smith had seen beyond the limited mercantilist horizons
to a world in which economies could grow by generating an
annual surplus and using it to increase next year's output. Here
was the real breakthrough that permitted a theory of modern
economic growth. The peculiar virtue of Adam Smith's analysis,
for a historical period in which the first industrial revolution was
beginning spontaneously to take shape, was that it offered a
natural explanation for international income differentials and for
differing growth rates; natural in the sense that it was inherent
in the capitalist economic system he described. Thus:

The natural effort of every individual to better his own condition, when
suffered to exert itself with freedom and security, is so powerful a
principle, that it is alone, and without any assistance, not only capable
of carrying on the society to wealth and prosperity, but of surmounting
a hundred impertinent obstructions with which the folly of human laws
too often incumbers its operations; though the effect of these obstruc-

[15] *Ibid*, p. 82.   [16] *Ibid*, p. 96.
[17] *Ibid*.

tions is always more or less either to encroach upon its freedom, or to diminish its security.[18]

In sum, the distinctive features of Adam Smith's theory of economic growth were: (i) his emphasis on the role of labour specialisation and its relation to the size of the market; (ii) the importance he attached to the role of the manufacturing sector in accelerating the pace of productivity growth for three reasons – (a) because there was more scope for division of labour in manufacturing, (b) because the commercial and manufacturing sectors tended to save a relatively high proportion of income, and (c) because the demand for their products was less readily satiated than the demand for, e.g. foodstuffs; and (iii) the way he made the growth of population, output and productivity all hinge on the rate of growth of capital accumulation. No one before him had produced as complete and plausible an explanation of the process of economic development for a country in the early stages of unprecedentedly rapid industrialisation. In the event, however, it was the third of these characteristics – the pivotal importance of capital accumulation – which had the most power- ful impact on the subsequent evolution of growth theory.

The classical economists who followed Smith, for example, accepted as axiomatic his emphasis on capital accumulation but developed the argument along a narrower line to a more pessi- mistic conclusion. The most distinctive feature of classical growth theory was that it came to see the growth process as an inexorable movement in the direction of a stationary state. The argument rests essentially on the Malthusian population prin- ciple (already foreshadowed by Smith) and the law of historically diminishing returns. It is perhaps not surprising that it should have taken this form. In the first quarter of the nineteenth century the Census returns showed the British population to be growing at an accelerating rate. At the same time the enclosure movement was slowing down because the surplus of cultivable land in the form of wastes or commons was rapidly being ex- hausted. In this context growth theory tended to stress the tendency of diminishing returns (generated by the pressure of a rapidly rising population on a limited stock of natural re- sources) to outrun the pace of technical innovation. Agriculture was still the premier industry and even the remarkable burst of innovation in manufacturing and transport that characterised

[18] *Ibid*, Vol. II, p. 43.

the late eighteenth and nineteenth centuries affected a relatively small sector of national economic activity.

Briefly, then, the classical theory of the growth process ran as follows. An economy will tend to expand so long as natural resources are abundant in relation to the population dependent on them, for capital will be attracted by the profit opportunities of investing in resources not fully exploited and the labour force will grow in response to the demand associated with increasing capital accumulation. However, given land (hence natural resources) in fixed supply, and given population (hence labour force) tending to increase whenever average wages rise above the conventional subsistence minimum, the increase in total wages will tend to squeeze down total profits – the source of the nation's investible surplus. As profits (hence investment) fall and the demand for labour accordingly declines, average wages will sink back to subsistence level, but total wages will continue to press on total profits while population increases. When the working population reaches the point at which total wages equal total product minus rent, i.e. where profits drop to zero, new net investment will cease because there is no longer any incentive to invest. When average wages drop below the conventional subsistence level, poverty or moral restraint will curb the population increase. And with zero net investment and a static population the stationary state will have been reached. Of course, technical progress, making labour more productive, will set the growth process off again but as soon as wages rise above the conventional subsistence level the tendency for population to rise will recur and set in motion the retardative factors that lead back to a stationary state (probably at a higher real wage because the conventional subsistence minimum tends to shift upward).

Classical dynamics was thus essentially the theory of the progression towards the stationary state. Not all classical economists explained this progression in terms of the same mechanism but all saw it as an imminent historical necessity in the long run. The most rigorous and internally consistent version of the classical theory of growth was Ricardo's. Like Adam Smith, he saw capital accumulation (defined in terms of employment of productive labour) plus technical progress (defined as labour-saving or labour-improving innovation) as the two motive forces promoting growth. Like Adam Smith he saw the price of corn as ultimately determining the subsistence level in all industries[19] but he went further than Adam Smith in spelling out the mechanism of the interaction between agriculture and the rest of the economy. The heart of the Ricardian system was the theory that the yield of corn per acre of land (taken a proxy for a kind of composite agricultural productivity) was the ultimate determinant of the rate of return on capital invested in all sectors of the economy. Given free competition the rate of profit or the return on investment tends to be the same in all uses. Now in agriculture corn is both input and output, capital as well as product so that the money rate of return on agricultural investment cannot diverge from the corn rate of return: and since in long-run equilibrium the rate of return on investment in agriculture must equal that of all other industries the 'total profits of the farmer regulate the profits of all other trades'. However, with population tending to press on limited agricultural resources the long-term rate of return on investment in agriculture (and hence in other industries) must inevitably decline. To quote: 'With the progress of society the market price of labour has always a tendency to rise because one of the principal commodities by which its natural price is regulated [corn], has a tendency to become dearer from the greater difficulty of producing it'.[20] Ricardo was prepared to allow that in the short period the natural price might diverge from the market price of labour, e.g. because competition among capitalists for labour would drive market wages up, but held that in the long run any increase in market wages, above the 'natural' rate (determined by the conventional subsistence minimum) would raise the labour supply.

The virtue of this system was its extreme simplicity and – given acceptance of the necessary simplifying assumptions – its completeness and consistency. It was essentially a two-factor (almost a one-factor) model of growth. Land, being ultimately fixed in supply, could be left out of the growth equation. Capital, being defined in terms of the labour it gave employment to, would automatically grow at the same rate as the labour force, i.e. employment grows in step with the wages fund. Assuming equality of return to capital and labour in all industries made it

[19] See e.g. *Wealth of Nations*, Vol. II, p. 11: 'the money price of corn regulates that of all other home-made commodities'; and Vol. I, p. 187: 'Corn...or whatever else is the common and favourite vegetable food of the people, constitutes, in every civilized country, the principal part of the subsistence of the labourer.'

[20] Sraffa (ed.), *Works and Correspondence of David Ricardo*, Vol. I, p. 93.

possible to analyse the growth process essentially in terms of the growth of one industry – agriculture – and one product – corn. Assuming an elastic supply of labour meant that growth was generated by the rate of technical progress and the level of thrift and limited by the stock of natural resources. For if technical progress raised the productivity of labour or a change in savings habits increased the supply of capital, the resultant increase in the demand for labour would eventually increase the supply sufficiently to raise output to the full new potential – up to the point at which the increased labour demand for consumption goods outran the capacity of the agricultural industry to produce more corn. In the end, assuming savings habits constant (or all profits devoted to capital accumulation), the national growth rate depended essentially on the outcome of the conflict between technical progress in agriculture and diminishing returns in agriculture.

Actually in the third edition of his *Principles* published in 1821 Ricardo showed signs that he was beginning to move away from some of the artificial simplications of this model for he was beginning to develop a concept of capital as a factor of production substitutable for and not merely complementary to labour. In the chapter called 'On Machinery' he analysed the effects of substituting fixed capital for labour and recognised that this could in fact result in unemployment and 'a diminution of gross produce'. However, the significant conclusion he drew from it was more directly concerned with his theory of income distribution than with his theory of growth viz: 'that the substitution of machinery for human labour, is often very injurious to the interests of the class of labourers.'[21] He turned away from drawing the implications of this for fluctuations in growth. He suggested, for example, that for the economy as a whole the introduction of machinery is too gradual to be disruptive. He stressed its dependence on the price of labour: 'Machinery and labour are in constant competition, and the former can frequently not be employed until labour [i.e. the share of wages in national product] rises.'[22] And he stressed its long-run growth-promoting effects through increasing profits and hence capital accumulation.

These savings, it must be remembered are annual, and must soon create a fund, much greater than the gross revenue, originally lost by the

---

[21] *Ibid*, p. 388.   [22] *Ibid*, p. 395.

discovery of the machine, when the demand for labour will be as great as before, and the situation of the people will be still further improved by the increased savings which the increased net revenue will still enable them to make.[23]

In sum then, what did the classical economists provide in the way of building blocks relevant to growth theory? First, of course, they provided a check list of factors which can be expected to determine the pace of growth in income per head in any economy and which are therefore candidates for inclusion as the elements of any growth theory, viz: natural resources, population, capital, technology and the institutional setting of economic activity. Second, they developed certain propositions concerning the relationships between these elements. For example, since natural resources are assumed limited, their combination with other factors of production (capital and labour) can be expected to lead to historically diminishing returns. On the other hand technical progress, which raises output per unit of input and can be expected to continue indefinitely, can offset the effects of diminishing returns. So the pace of economic growth depends on the balance between these two underlying forces. Third, they suggested some ranking in the growth-promoting properties of the different elements, some crucial factors on which to focus. Without exception the classical economists (including their most unconventional follower, Marx) put capital accumulation as their crucial dynamic factor with labour following a close second.

Succeeding generations of growth theorists have suggested different kinds of relationships between the elements and defined the elements themselves differently. It is not surprising in retrospect to find that the classical economists who wrote when agriculture was still the premier industry expected the balance to be tipped by diminishing returns and saw the ultimate condition as being that of the stationary state: and that the neo-classical economists, writing when primary production had ceased to be the typical form of economic activity, were prepared to assume without argument that the balance would always be tipped in the long run by increasing returns.[24]

[23] *Ibid*, p. 396.
[24] J. S. Mill illustrates a kind of transitional stage in this context. E.g. in the 1848 *Principles*, p. 751, he wrote that 'hitherto it is questionable if all the mechanical improvements yet made have lightened the day's toil of any human being'; but he anticipated considerable improvements in political and social and institutional factors which would make the inevitable stationary state an agreeable way of life – one in 'which while no one is poor, no one desires to be richer or

Conventionally, moreover, classical growth theory assumed that natural resources and institutions could be regarded as constants (even over the long term) and that the crucial changes were those taking place in technology (treated by all except Marx as an exogenous variable) and in the inputs of capital and labour. Capital however was generally defined in such a way that it was a complement to labour (and not a substitute for it) so that the rates of growth of the inputs of capital and labour were always in step. These assumptions permitted the development of a fairly general and easily manipulable sort of theory with which the classical economist could be sure of never getting out of his analytical depth. Only Marx was bold enough to introduce technical and institutional change into his theory as variables, to define capital in a more disaggregated way, and to take explicit account of the influence of technological change on the way capital and labour were combined in the productive process. The effect was to make his theory more complicated, to reduce its generality and internal consistency by comparison for example with the Ricardian model but to give it a certain realism and an unquestioned dramatic power.[25]

FURTHER READING

Primary literature

Quesnay's *Tableau Economique*, ed. for the Royal Economic Society by Marguerite Kuczynski and Ronald L. Meek (1972).

T. R. Malthus, *First Essay on Population*, reprinted for the Royal Economic Society (1966).

David Ricardo, *On the Principles of Political Economy and Taxation*, Vol. 1 of *Works and Correspondence of David Ricardo*, ed. for the Royal Economic Society by Piero Sraffa with the collaboration of M. H. Dobb (1951).

Adam Smith, *Wealth of Nations, op. cit.*

Secondary literature

W. A. Eltis, 'Adam Smith's Theory of Economic Growth', in *Essays on Adam Smith*, ed. Skinner and Wilson, *op. cit.*

W. A. Eltis, 'François Quesnay: A reinterpretation', *Oxford Economic Papers* (1975).

has any reason to fear being thrust back by the efforts of others to push themselves forward' (*Principles*, pp. 748–9).

[25] See below, Chapter 9 for a discussion of the Marxian model.

B. F. Hoselitz (ed.), *Theories of Economic Growth* (1960).

A. Lowe, 'The Classical Theory of Economic Growth' *Social Research* (1957).

A. Phillips, 'The Tableau Economique as a Simple Leontief Model', *Quarterly Journal of Economics* (1955).

4

CLASSICAL MONETARY THEORY

The British classical economists who took up the torch which Adam Smith lit with the *Wealth of Nations* and who set out to perfect the 'science' of political economy won for their discipline a more significant prize than recognition as a minor academic subject. They turned it into a system of thought which commanded wide political respect: for the questions which gave direction and shape to their theoretical enquiries were questions of urgent practical concern to contemporary policy makers. When they found the analytical apparatus they had inherited from Smith lacking it was generally because it failed to provide them with the technique they needed to analyse current economic policy problems. The issues which dominated the first decade of the nineteenth century and which first drew Ricardo into active economic controversy were problems of monetary policy.

Monetary theory and monetary controversy have always evolved in intimate relation with real-world policy needs and economic debate on domestic, as distinct from international monetary issues, has generally been associated with a failure of the authorities responsible for regulating the money supply to steer a confident course between the Scylla of inflation and the Charybdis of deflation. So, although writers on economic questions have analysed the role of money in the economy for as long as they have been interested in the workings of an exchange economy, it is easy enough to decide where modern British monetary theory essentially begins, viz in the controversy set off by the problems involved in supplying the economy with the abnormal needs for money and credit facilities, necessitated by the prolonged French and Napoleonic wars of the late eighteenth and early nineteenth centuries. Additionally, moreover, this was a period in which the industrial revolution was gathering momentum, population growth and urbanisation were accelerating and when there occurred an abnormally high concentration of spectacularly poor harvests. There were thus three levels of monetary problem emerging at this period: first, the relationship between changes in the supply of money and the general level of economic activity or the rate of foreign exchange; second, the problem of the relation of the stock of an acceptable medium of exchange to the flow of payments to be made; and third, the problem of the availability of credit in relation to the possibilities of expanding business. Not surprisingly the problems of monetary policy loomed larger and demanded a more understanding helmsman than the existing monetary institutions were able to supply.

It was when paper notes, particularly small banknotes, began to rival coin as an everyday medium of exchange and thus to lift the ultimately technological constraints on the supply of money imposed by the accessible stock of monetary minerals that the problems of monetary policy began to assume their modern shape. Eighteenth-century writers became increasingly pre-occupied by the inflationary danger involved in the issue of paper money,[1] though all the while Bank of England notes were redeemable in gold (and other bank notes in either gold or Bank of England notes) the traditional assumption that 'real' money was metallic money could continue to support monetary analysis. The break came when the Bank of England snapped the automatic link between its notes and the precious metals for which they were in principle exchangeable, by suspending cash payments. From the Suspension of Cash Payments which began in 1797, and the essentially new problems of practical policy with which it presented the Bank, dates the emergence of a new branch of economic theory which developed largely independently of the mainstream economic doctrine stemming directly from Adam Smith's *Wealth of Nations*. The Suspension shattered the traditional mould of banking practice and called for a basic reappraisal of customary ideas on money and banking.

The challenge was met first by Henry Thornton, a practising City banker and MP, who had been giving thought to these questions even before he was called to give evidence to the 1797 parliamentary committee on the Suspension and who published in 1802 an *Enquiry into the Nature and Effects of the Paper Credit*

[1] E.g. David Hume's essays 'Of Money' and 'Of Balance of Trade', published in his *Political Discourses* (1752), were concerned with the balance of payments implications of an excess issue of paper currency.

of Great Britain.[2] Thornton's book was the first systematic exposition of a theory of money and credit on modern lines. It
embodies the development and first application of a number of
ideas which were eventually to fall into place as integral features
of monetary theory – though some of them were neglected by
mainstream nineteenth-century theorists and were brought into
play again only in the twentieth century. Thornton, for example,
presented the first complex analysis of the self-correcting balance
of payments mechanism, through which an increase in paper
currency circulating in a gold-standard country would, by raising
its price level relative to that of its trading partners, reduce exports and raise imports, and, via the resulting disequilibrium in
its balance of trade, lead to an export of bullion (and a tendency
to convert gold coin into bullion) and so to a fall in the domestic
circulation of gold-backed paper and coin. He recognised that
real effects could flow from monetary causes in the short run (e.g.
that inflation of the currency could stimulate trade and industry
and deflation might reduce output) and that conversely a growth
in output and trade would stimulate the volume of credit advanced and of currency in circulation. He described (without so
naming it) the increase in liquidity preference which results from
political 'consternation' or economic uncertainty and ascribed to
this the internal drains of 1793 and 1797. He noted the relative
rigidity of money wages and inferred that a scarcity of money
would raise unemployment.

Two things condition the character of monetary theory which
emerges at a given period – the nature of the existing monetary
institutions and the form in which the practical policy problems
present themselves. Thornton started, as did all the other
theoretical economists of his day, from Adam Smith's *Wealth of
Nations* but he did not find himself retaining much of the
Smithian foundations. For by the end of the century, the British
credit system had developed so significantly from the system
confronting Adam Smith that the latter's account was seriously
out of date. In particular, the numbers and importance of the
English note-issuing country banks had greatly expanded and
the Bank of England had acquired a central role in the credit
structure which made it the effective lender of last resort and

---

[2] The LSE edition edited with an introduction by F. A. v. Hayek and published
in 1939 contains in addition his evidence given before the Committees of Secrecy
of the Two Houses of Parliament on the Bank of England, March and April
1797, and reports his 1811 speeches on the 1810 *Bullion Report*.

custodian of the liquid reserves of all other banks in the system. Meanwhile the overseas trade was assuming a rapidly increasing direct importance in determining the level of British economic activity; and Britain's role in the international economy had so expanded as to become a dominating factor in the international exchanges. The long wars that broke out in 1793 accentuated these developments stemming from an industrial revolution based on an expansion both of overseas markets and of overseas sources of food and industrial raw materials. So, in contrast to Adam Smith who had assumed, for example, that all notes were automatically convertible into specie, that the typical source of paper credit was 'real bills' (i.e. bills backed by the sale of real commodities), that the effects of an increased issue of notes would have a local rather than national or international impact and that no special central significance attached to the role of the Bank of England in the credit structure, Thornton discussed a more complex and more integrated set of monetary institutions, where convertibility into specie was suspended, where the Bank of England's role was pivotal and where the effects of a divergence between the market price and the mint price of bullion worked themselves out on the international exchanges.

By the last decade of the eighteenth century British monetary problems were the problems of an economy already started on a process of unprecedentedly rapid economic expansion and change, faced with the need to finance a major war and to transfer massive subsidies to foreign allies, but lacking the institutions or the know-how to formulate and execute a consistent set of monetary policies at the national level. The Bank of England, originally set up in 1694 to meet the financial needs of the central government, enjoyed monopolistic powers (it was the sole joint stock bank in England and the only issuer of notes in the metropolis) but had not yet accepted the public responsibilities today assumed to attach to a Central Bank. In addition to the Bank of England, the Bank of Ireland, the three Scottish chartered banks and a multitude of country banks in England, Ireland and Scotland also exercised rights to issue their own bank notes, without any legal restraint other than the interest maximum of 5 per cent imposed by the Usury Laws (a limit which may have helped to check advances when money was scarce and borrowers pessimistic but which was a positive incentive to excessive borrowing during times of inflation). The credit system therefore lacked the kind of centrally dispensed discipline and

protection which emanates from a responsible Central Bank and
was endangered by the existence of numerous small and
financially weak links in the chain of confidence. The marvel was
not that such a vulnerable system was prone to severe financial
crisis but that it survived so many crises without more disastrous
consequences. Its remarkable stability probably resulted from the
buoyancy of the export trade associated with relatively large
reserves of bullion in the country generally and in the Bank of
England in particular.

The debate set off by the Bank's suspension of convertibility
in February 1797 began on a limited scale in the course of
parliamentary inquiries conducted by both Houses of Parliament
in March and April of that year. It gained general momentum
and political importance in 1800–1 when the value of commodities
in terms of gold and/or silver depreciated sharply on the foreign
exchanges[3] and when for the first time an essentially monetary
explanation for fluctuations in the exchange rate was accepted
by informed observers. It became a major issue of political
economy in the next decade leading up to the Bullion Committee's Report of 1810[4] and continued until the country went back
to convertibility and on to a formal gold standard after the ending
of the war. The 'bullionist controversy', as the debate has since
been labelled, hinged on a fundamental difference of opinion
between the bullionists, who attributed the rise in the price of gold
bullion primarily to an over-issue of paper-credit (i.e. to
monetary mismanagement by the Bank of England), and the
anti-bullionists, who found a sufficient circumstantial explanation in the effects of a major war – in particular to massive
overseas expenditures by the British Government accompanied
by a severe check to the expansion of British exports in the first
decade of the nineteenth century. The bullionist position was
taken by Thornton, Ricardo, Horner, Wheatley, Malthus,
Mushet and Huskisson and indeed by most of the leading
members of the early nineteenth-century community of economists. The essence of their view was that the main cause of the
depreciation of the pound in terms of bullion was the inflationary
policy of the Bank of England in issuing too much paper money;

[3] By May 1800 gold bullion was selling on the Hamburg exchange at 9 per cent
above the Mint price; by the autumn of that year the premium on gold bullion
had risen to 10 per cent.
[4] *Report of the Select Committee on the High Price of Gold Bullion*, Parliamentary
Papers (1810), III (349).

and that the only effective way of restoring monetary stability was to impose on the Bank the constraint of redeeming its notes in gold (i.e. of returning to convertibility) as soon as possible.[5] The opposite view was that taken by the Directors of the Bank and some leading Cabinet Ministers who denied that it was possible for notes to be issued in excess of needs: (a) because the credit-worthy borrowers to whom alone the Bank was ready to advance loans would not borrow more than they could profitably use; and (b) because most of the loans were extended on the security of 'real bills', thus ensuring that the notes would return to the bank in liquidation of these loans within a very few months, i.e. as soon as the goods in question were sold.

Thornton's *Paper Credit*, however, was written before the bullionist controversy had taken shape and is a more balanced exposition of fundamental economic principles than any of the pamphlets, speeches or letters-to-the-editor which flooded forth when political opinion polarised on these issues. It was also written at a time when the Suspension of Cash Payments was regarded as an abnormal restriction associated with a war that was not expected to last much longer and before the monetary reasons for rising prices evidently outweighed the combined effects of two bad harvests in rapid succession plus a war-caused shock to British exports. So far from castigating the Bank for a propensity to issue too much paper, Thornton began by criticising it for having, in the crises of 1793 and 1797, been too ready to contract its note issue on occasions when an abnormal demand for liquidity (for precautionary reasons) had led to hoarding and hence shortage of gold coin and a crisis of confidence in the banks which could easily have been rectified by a more liberal issue of banknotes.[6] Belief in discretionary monetary policy, however, inevitably hinged on confidence in the competence and skill of the monetary authority exercising it and Thornton was to lose much of his confidence in the ability of the Directors of the Bank to manage an inconvertible currency in the public interest. In 1809 the exchange value of the pound began to deteriorate again, a fact which was reflected in a widening of the divergence between the notional mint price of gold and the market

[5] There were of course differences of opinion about what was 'possible' in this context for it hinged essentially on a view of the fragility of business confidence. The bullionist view was stated formally in the Report of the 1810 Bullion Committee.

[6] H. Thornton, *Paper Credit, op. cit.*, p. 97 and p. 127.

price[7] and which stimulated Ricardo's first venture into print in the shape of an article on 'The Price of Gold' published anonymously in the *Morning Chronicle* of 29 August 1809.

This new rise in gold prices renewed the bullionist controversy and led to the formation of the Bullion Committee of the House of Commons which was appointed in February 1810 and reported later in the same year.[8] Thornton was himself a member of the Bullion Committee and as we may judge by his speeches when the Report was debated in the House of Commons, he was by then frankly dismayed by the inability of the Directors of the Bank to appreciate the link between the supply of paper money and the international value of the currency. He was then quite clear that a failure to arrest the over-issue of paper money would lead to a progressive depreciation of the currency which it might be impossible to reverse when peace came and made it possible to restore convertibility.

Ricardo joined the bullion controversy in 1809 with a series of articles and replies to critics in the *Morning Chronicle* and his position was crystallised in his 1810 pamphlet on *The High Price of Bullion, a Proof of the Depreciation of Bank Notes* which was reprinted in 1811 with an appendix dealing with some of the criticisms made by reviewers of the first edition.[9] In contrast to Thornton, who dealt as readily with the complex interaction between real and monetary causes and effects, that were the substance of the problems confronting practising bankers, as he did with the quantity theory and its international applications, Ricardo simplified the issues and went straight into an abstract theoretical exposition of the problem in a long-term framework of analysis.

The question at issue in the bullion controversy and to which Ricardo addressed himself in *The High Price of Bullion* was whether or not the fall in the international exchange value of the paper pound (the fall, that is in its gold value) reflected a corresponding fall in its domestic value and was a direct result of

---

[7] The mint parity price was £3. 17. 10½ and the market price did not diverge from it until 2 years after the 1797 Suspension when it began to rise, reaching £4. 6 in January 1801. Thereafter it was stable again until 1809 when it reached £4. 12. 10½.

[8] Report from the House of Commons, *Select Committee on the High Price of Gold Bullion* (1810). This was reprinted in 1919 and again in 1925 by P. S. King (London) with an introduction by Edwin Cannan. It has subsequently been republished by Frank Cass (1969).

[9] These are reprinted in Vol. III of the Sraffa edition of Ricardo's works.

an excess supply of money in the form of Bank of England notes. Was the wartime inflation, that is to say, simply an unavoidable consequence of the war (and the consequent disruption of overseas trade), aggravated from time to time by a poor harvest, or was it caused by monetary policy and was the depreciation of the currency on the foreign exchanges a fair reflection of the excess of the money supply over the demand for it?

Ricardo's answer to the question was a monetarist answer.

In saying... that gold is at a high price, we are mistaken; it is not gold, it is paper which has changed its value. Compare an ounce of gold, at £3. 17s. 10d to commodities, it bears the same proportion to them which it has before done; and if it do not, it is referrible to increased taxation, or to some of those causes which are so constantly operating on its value... In every market of the world I am compelled to part with £4. 10s in bank-notes to purchase the same quantity of commodities which I can obtain for gold that is in £3. 17s. 10d of coin.[10]

Much of his pamphlet repeated arguments already expounded in Thornton's *Paper Credit*; for example, his analysis of the factors governing the national and international distribution of the precious metals, or of the 'natural' limits on the money supply of a country adhering to the gold standard, or on the relation between the country bank note issues and the Bank's own note circulation. Characteristically, however, he swept aside, as unimportant or irrelevant, all qualifications which Thornton had noted to the simple monetary explanation. For example, he minimised the suggestion that the depreciation of the currency could have been due to a shift in the balance of trade, by a pseudo-statistical argument similar to that he was to use later to arrive at his labour theory of value:

Mr. Thornton has told us that an unfavourable trade will account for an unfavourable exchange; but we have already seen that an unfavourable trade, if such be an accurate term, is limited in its effects on the exchange. That limit is probably four or five per cent. This will not account for a depreciation of fifteen or twenty per cent.[11]

And he dismissed the notion that an increase in the note issue could ever add to the national stock of productive capital by

---

[10] D. Ricardo, *The High Price of Bullion, a Proof of the Depreciation of Banknotes,* reprinted in *The Works and Correspondence of David Ricardo,* ed. by P. Sraffa and M. Dobb, Vol. III, p. 80. Ricardo worked on the assumption that the *general* purchasing power of gold was invariable. See below p. 67.

[11] *Ibid*, p. 83. The rationale behind this opinion was that a shift in the balance of trade would have price effects which would raise the demand for exports but lower the demand for imports with only minor effects on the price of gold.

means of a somewhat circular reasoning: for having explained
that 'I am here speaking of an excess of their notes of that
quantity which adds to our circulation without effecting any
corresponding exportation of coin, and which, therefore, de-
grades the notes below the value of the bullion contained in the
coin which they represent',[12] he went on to assert that

> however abundant may be the quantity of money or of bank-notes;
> though it may increase the nominal prices of commodities; though it
> may distribute the productive capital in different proportions; though
> the Bank, by increasing the quantity of their notes, may enable A to
> carry on part of the business formerly engrossed by B and C, nothing
> will be added to the real revenue and wealth of the country...
> There will be a violent and an unjust transfer of property, but no bene-
> fit whatever will be gained by the community.[13]

In the end he laid the responsibility for the inflation and the
depreciating exchange rate squarely on the shoulders of the
Directors of the Bank, though he was prepared to allow that it
was not self-interest but too great a subservience to government
demands and a failure to appreciate the consequences of their
policy that accounted for their behaviour:

> If the Bank directors... *had acted up to the principle which they have avowed*
> *to have been that which regulated their issues when they were obliged to pay their*
> *notes in specie, namely, to limit their notes to that amount which should prevent*
> *the excess of the market above the mint price of gold, we should not have been*
> *now exposed to all the evils of a depreciated, and perpetually varying currency.*[14]

There was, of course, considerable force in Ricardo's monetary
explanation for the depreciating exchange rate after 1809. Napo-
leon's continental blockade was of course hindering exports as
well as imports, but the domestic output of consumer goods was
rendered more inelastic than usual by the relatively high
proportion of the adult male labour force caught up in the war
effort; and the denial on the part of the Bank's Directors and
their ministerial allies of any connection between its large loans
to the Exchequer, the suspension of cash payments and the
downward trend in the exchange rate, was evidence that the
nation's monetary authorities did not know what they were doing.
To most reputable economists (Thornton included) Ricardo's
analysis, and the Bullion Report which it closely resembled,
seemed entirely appropriate to the contemporary policy problem. Partly perhaps because it seemed at the time to hit the

[12] *Ibid*, p. 92, n.   [13] *Ibid*, p. 93.
[14] *Ibid*, p. 95 (Ricardo's italics).

contemporary nail so neatly on the head, and partly no doubt
because of Ricardo's 'staggering' authority among early nineteenth-century economists,[15] the doctrinaire monetarist line
became the basis of orthodox monetary theory and Thornton's
more qualified and subtle exposition of the complex interaction
betwen real and monetary factors, as set out in *Paper Credit*, fell
out of sight. What was thus lost from the subsequent legislation,
which leaned heavily on the Ricardian interpretation, was Thornton's vision of a discretionary note issue managed by a Central
Bank which adjusted its circulation, while giving explicit consideration to the real as well as the monetary effects of its
policies. What was lost from mainstream theorising was any
serious attempt to analyse the effects of variations in the demand
for money (changes in liquidity preference), and (at least until
Wicksell took it up at the end of the nineteenth century) any
attempt to integrate the monetary influences exerted on the rate
of interest by the banking system, and the 'real' influences on
the rate of profit on capital.

Superficially, the debate between the Currency and Banking
Schools which led up to the 1844 Bank Charter Act was a con-
tinuation of the earlier bullionist controversy. Actually, however,
the Currency School, following the Ricardian hard line, went
further than most of the bullionists, and the supporters of the
Banking School (Tooke in particular) echoed many of the arguments of Thornton's *Paper Credit*. For most bullionists it was
generally held sufficient to restore internal convertibility in order
to keep the supply of money broadly in line with the demand
for it, leaving the Bank some discretion to make certain that it
was dealing with a fundamental disequilibrium in the balance of
payments before contracting its note issue. For the Currency
School, mistrustful of giving any discretion to the Directors of
the Bank, it was essential to devise a technique of making the
paper circulation not merely redeemable in gold, but so rigidly
attached to the national stock of gold that the note issue would
automatically fluctuate with fluctuations in the stock. While recognising the virtues of a mixed currency as a means of economising
in monetary gold they insisted that the rules of the gold standard
demanded that the mixed currency should be made to behave
exactly as if it were a pure metallic currency.

On the other side of the fence, the Banking School developed
more sophisticated arguments than the anti-bullionists had used.

---

[15] See the quotation from Malthus on pp. 80–1 below.

Like some of the bullionists the Banking School were content to assume that convertibility would suffice to safeguard the note issue and to keep the balance of payments in long-term equilibrium. They emphasised the problem of defining money for the purpose of controlling the money supply and pointed out that bills of exchange and cheques were as much media of exchange in early nineteenth-century England as banknotes and coin; as a corollary they argued that it was the whole credit policy of the Bank and not merely the amount of cash in circulation that was relevant. They insisted on distinguishing between short-term disequilibria which called for a relaxed credit policy to sustain confidence, and long-term disequilibria which called for deflationary measures to stem an outflow of gold: the corollary of this argument was their advocacy of an adequate gold reserve which would permit the Bank to ride out temporary deficits without reducing its power to deal with more deep-seated problems. Finally they argued that the amount of money in circulation was as much a consequence of the demand for money as of the supply. In sum, their arguments had more in common with Thornton's approach than with Ricardo's.

The leading exponent of the Banking School side of the argument was Thomas Tooke[16] but, not being a theorist, he has had less attention from the historians of economic thought than the substance of his arguments deserved.[17] However, his analysis was less rigorous and less consistent than Thornton's had been and carried even less weight with most contemporary economists and politicians. In the event it was the 'currency principle' that prevailed and Sir Robert Peel's Bank Charter Act of 1844 owed more to Ricardo's prescriptions than to those of any other leading economist.[18]

The Act recognised the need to centralise the control of the nation's money supply (money being defined as metallic money plus a convertible note issue); and it formally established the Bank of England as the primary monetary authority. At the same

[16] See especially his *Inquiry into the Currency Principle* (1844).

[17] For a sympathetic modern interpretation of Tooke's argument see David Laidler, 'Thomas Tooke on Monetary Reform', in B. Corry (ed.). *Essays in Honour of Lord Robbins* (1972).

[18] The contemporary theoretical supporters of the Act were Robert Torrens, James Pennington and S. J. Loyd (Lord Overstone). Its leading theoretical opponent was J. S. Mill. By the 1830s the Directors of the Bank had ranged themselves on the side of the Currency Principle and were looking for a way of tying changes in the note circulation to changes in the gold stock.

time, however, it deliberately restricted the role of the monetary authority to that of protecting the nation's bullion reserves. Thus it set a maximum to the country bank note issues, which were eventually to be wholly absorbed by the Bank, and it divided the Bank itself into a Banking Department and an Issue Department.[19] The Issue Department was given the function of exchanging notes for coin or bullion (and *vice versa*) all notes in circulation being fully backed by gold apart from a fixed fiduciary issue covered by securities. The Banking Department was supposed to act as banker to the public, to other banks and to the government.

The importance of the Bank Charter Act for the evolution of monetary theory was that it determined, for a further 70 years at least, certain crucial features of the institutional framework within which British monetary policy was expected to operate. Its impact indeed went far beyond the British economy for it bound the monetary authority of the leading trading nation and the most advanced industrial state to abide by the rules of the international gold standard. For a generation and more the Bank of England, now recognised as the nation's Central Bank – though with a deliberately restricted role – turned firmly away from any notion that it ought to have some discretionary responsibility for controlling the money supply in favour of the view that its duty was to respond in robot fashion to the signals generated by the balance of payments. If gold showed a tendency to flow out of the country to finance a deficit on international account the Bank's duty was to raise its discount rate (so instantly checking the outflow of capital and eventually restricting the domestic credit supply if the disequilibrium proved at all persistent) and *vice versa* if gold flowed in. Beyond that it had no business to go and was expected to pursue its banking activities

[19] This separation of powers within the Bank reflects Ricardo's views expressed in his *Plan for the Establishment of a National Bank* (reprinted in the Sraffa edition of Ricardo's *Works* Vol. IV) which began: 'The Bank of England performs two operations of banking, which are quite distinct, and have no necessary connection with each other; it issues a paper currency as a substitute for a metallic one, and it advances money by way of loan to merchants and others.' Ricardo, however, proposed peeling off the note-issuing powers of the Bank altogether and giving them to a currency board – leaving the Bank to carry on its deposit business. In some respects, indeed, Ricardo's advice was more than a century ahead of its time, e.g. his proposal for the form gold convertibility should take (i.e. an exchange of bullion rather than coin against paper) – first advocated in a pamphlet entitled *Proposals for an Economical and Secure Currency* (1816) and reprinted in his *Principles* a year later – was not adopted in England until 1928.

in accordance with generally accepted principles of sound profit-maximising commercial banking, subject of course to the indirect limitation on its credit policy imposed by the ceiling on the fiduciary issues.

That the Bank Charter Act was able to establish the ground rules of British monetary policy for so long was due partly to the fact that it was not wholly inflexible; for example, in each of the three major crisis years 1847, 1857 and 1866, rising panic was contained when the legal limits on the fiduciary issue were temporarily lifted by Government directive so 'breaking the Bank Act'. But its persistence was largely due to the way the economic problem presented itself to policy makers in the mid and later nineteenth century. The notion of a fully automatic gold-backed currency fitted comfortably into the prevalent laissez-faire, free trade, economic philosophy: and the built-in limitations on domestic credit policy came under strain only rarely for an economy with a normally strong, secularly-expanding, surplus on international current account. It proved seldom, if ever, necessary to respond to an autonomous external drain of gold by pushing the appropriate credit restrictions through to an extent which could be seen to be seriously threatening the level of domestic economic activity. Conversely, when an expansion in domestic activity led to an internal drain on the Bank's gold reserves (often associated initially with an external drain due to rising imports) a relatively modest rise in interest rates was normally sufficient to offset the drain by attracting foreign short-term capital and gold inflows. However, in practice the limits on the money supply proved less rigid than the authors of the Act had intended, for the steady development of the use of cheques as a means of payment had the effect of circumventing the legal limits on the note issue.

With the day-to-day problems of monetary policy appearing less urgent and intractable than they had seemed in the war and immediate post-war era, and with the basic institutional framework operating in what was normally, if not invariably, a reasonably satisfactory manner, the need to innovate in monetary theory diminished in relative importance, and classical monetary thinking settled into a quiescent acceptance of a rather loose analytical framework. It was John Stuart Mill who best synthesised the classical orthodoxy in this as in so many other areas and who wrote the main textbook purveying the ideas developed in the first half of the nineteenth century to English (and often

American) readers embarking on a systematic study of economics in the second half.

The chief question on which the classical economists focused in this context was characteristically enough the question of value, viz 'what determines the value of money?' It was not a sharply focused question, for while it defined money in a very concrete sense (i.e. basically as a metallic cash currency plus convertible paper treated as a kind of *de facto* money) the yardstick by which its value might be assessed was left open and it was discussed in terms of ill-defined concepts such as 'purchasing power' and 'general prices'. Two theories of the value of money were conventionally distinguished – a short-run theory which was a (sometimes quite loose) variant of the quantity theory and a long-run theory which hinged ultimately on the cost of production of the precious metals. In neither case was much attempt made to establish strong causal links in the process of determination of the value of money. Most authors seemed content with an explanation which asserted that the value of money could be explained in the same way as the value of any other 'commodity', and that it depended on market supply and demand for the stock of money in the short run, and the cost of production of the newly-mined increment of the stock of metal in the long run. In effect, then, at this very superficial level of analysis the theory of money was merely a special case of the general theory of value.

However J. S. Mill, in his textbook synthesis of orthodox theory revealed more complexities in the special case of money in the context of a modern credit-based economy. For after stating the simple proposition that 'the value of money, other things being the same, varies inversely as its quantity; every increase of quantity lowering the value, and every diminution raising it in a ratio exactly equivalent',[20] and after introducing the concept of the 'rapidity of circulation' or 'the efficiency of money', he went on to admit that the simple demand and supply proposition 'must be understood as applying only to a state of things in which money, that is, gold or silver, is the exclusive instrument of exchange and actually passes from hand to hand at every stage, credit in any of its shapes being unknown'.[21] Indeed the qualifications to the proposition 'that the value of the circulating medium depends on the demand and supply, and is in the inverse ratio of the quantity' were such that 'under a

[20] J. S. Mill, *Principles of Political Economy*, Toronto edition, Vol. III, p. 512.
[21] *Ibid*, p. 514.

complex system of credit like that existing in England, render the proposition an extremely incorrect expression of the fact'.[22] Mill then went on to argue at some length that it is spending, not credit policy as such, which drives up prices and that the 'amount of purchasing power which a person can exercise is composed of all the money in his possession or due to him, and of all his credit...and the portion of it which he at any time does exercise, is the measure of the effect which he produces on price'[23] to explain the changes in the level of prices (value of money) associated with cyclical fluctuations in economic activity.

Similarly, Mill, after blandly expounding the classical doctrine of the long-term or 'natural' value of money as a function of the cost of production of the precious metals, went straight into the further admission that: 'this doctrine only applies to the places in which the precious metals are actually produced'.[24] The value of money 'considered as an imported commodity' was then explained in terms of the theory of international values, i.e. as dependent on the exchange values (after allowing for transport costs) between the exports of the countries importing bullion and the imports of the countries exporting it.

Mill's monetary analysis thus came closer to Thornton's realistic and broadly based interpretation and qualified Ricardo's narrowly abstract quantity theory in significant respects. His admissions and qualifications opened up the theory of money from the closed position in which Ricardo had left it more than he or his contemporaries seem to have thought worth discussing. For he diluted the traditional emphasis on the *supply* of money as the crucial factor determining prices in the short term; he adopted (implicitly if never explicitly) a wider concept of money as the relevant variable influencing price trends, and he recognised that the durability of bullion, and the vast world stock of non-monetary (as well as of monetary) gold or silver already in existence, greatly attenuated the link between the cost of production at the mines and the long-run value of money in England.

Given this degree of defection from the simple quantity-theory line of analysis it is not surprising to find that Mill was also highly critical of the rigidities of the Bank Charter Act,[25] quoting with

---

[22] *Ibid*, p. 516.   [23] *Ibid*, p. 540.

[24] *Ibid;* p. 523.

[25] On this he showed considerable foresight, e.g. *ibid*, p. 672: 'The function of banks in filling up the gap made in mercantile credit by the consequence of

approval some of Tooke's and other Banking School strictures on it, and drawing attention to the dangers to domestic confidence which might result from a too automatic and inflexible contraction of credit in response to a temporary disequilibrium in the balance of payments and which could actively precipitate a commercial crisis. On the other hand, he remained as blind as Ricardo had been (and less percipient than Thornton) towards the possibility that a deliberate expansion of credit might stimulate economic activity in times of depression and hence actually increase output rather than prices. This line of thought thus tended to fall out of the range of orthodox classical doctrine and with it went the prospects of developing any new ideas on the question of positive monetary management of the economy.

FURTHER READING

Primary literature

Edwin Cannan (ed.), *The Paper Pound of 1797–1821: The Bullion Report 8th June 1910*, 2nd edition reprinted (1969).

J. S. Mill, *Principles of Political Economy*, Toronto edn, Vol. III (1966).

David Ricardo, *The High Price of Bullion*, in Vol. III, *Works*, ed. Piero Straffa (1966).

Henry Thornton, *Enquiry into the Nature and Effects of the Paper Credit of Great Britain*, ed. F. A. von Hayek, LSE Reprint (1939).

Secondary literature

B. A. Corry, *Money Savings and Investment in British Economics 1800–50* (1962).

F. W. Fetter, *The Development of British Monetary Orthodoxy 1797–1875* (1965).

R. Harrington, 'The Monetarist Controversy', *Manchester School of Social and Economic Studies* (1971).

D. Laidler, 'Thomas Tooke on Monetary Reform', in B. Corry (ed.), *Essays in Honour of Lord Robbins* (1972).

R. S. Sayers, 'Ricardo's Views on Monetary Questions'; in *Papers in English Monetary History*, ed. T. S. Ashton and R. S. Sayers (1953).

J. Viner, 'English Currency Controversies', in *Studies in the Theory of International Trade, op. cit.*

undue speculation and its revulsion, is so entirely indispensable, that if the Act of 1844 continues unrepealed, there can be no difficulty in foreseeing that its provisions must be suspended, as they were in 1847, in every period of great commercial difficulty as soon as the crisis has really and completely set in.'

5

RICARDO ON VALUE, DISTRIBUTION AND GROWTH

The abnormal inflationary pressures associated with the Napoleonic Wars had shown up monetary theory as an area in which Adam Smith had clearly failed to provide the kind of theoretical framework appropriate to the analysis of urgent policy problems. The other economic policy issue dominating the early decades of the nineteenth century was the question of agrarian protection embodied in the Corn Laws. The issues raised here went to the heart of Smith's disciplinary framework for economics and inspired more fundamental attempts to revise orthodox economic theory. It was in this context that Ricardo turned his attention to a systematic study of the principles of political economy. His *Essay on the Influence of a Low Price of Corn on the Profits of Stock* appeared in 1815, the same year as Malthus' *Inquiry into Rent* and West's and Torrens' pamphlets on the same subject. In effect, the policy issues were beginning to hinge on questions relating to the distribution of the national product between rents, profits and wages and those who drew their economic theory from the *Wealth of Nations* found it inadequate for these purposes. Uppermost in Ricardo's mind when he focused on the price of corn and the level of profits was the danger that a high price of corn (the chief wage-good) would depress profits by pushing up the share of wages in the value of output and thereby reduce resources for investment and hence retard growth. The original preface of his *Principles of Political Economy and Taxation*, designed as an expansion and systematic elaboration of his *Essay on Profits*, stated categorically that the principal unsolved problem of political economy was to determine the laws which regulate the distribution of the national product between rent, profit and wages.[1]

[1] It was his friend James Mill who prodded him into expanding the Essay into a general theory. The first edition of Ricardo's *Principles* appeared in 1817 and there were two further editions in 1819 and 1821. The definitive variorum

The level of profits was crucial for Ricardo (as indeed for Smith) because it was what determined the level of capital accumulation and hence the rate of economic growth. Adam Smith, however, had explained the general level of profits in simple supply and demand terms which made it depend on the flow of savings into capital accumulation on the one hand and the opportunities for profitable investment on the other. Profits would then fall either if wages rose faster than prices or productivity, or if opportunities for profitable investment failed to keep pace with the rate of capital accumulation. For Ricardo this interpretation seemed incomplete. It led to some puzzling loose ends and some inconvenient circularities in the argument. One such loose end related to the effect of capital accumulation on profits. Smith's analysis had led to the conclusion that, unless opportunities for new investment expanded faster than available investible funds, increasing capital accumulation would lead to competition between capitalists and to a falling rate of profit. Yet the evidence did not suggest that interest rates were tending to fall in spite of a marked increase in the national level of capital accumulation in the late eighteenth and early nineteenth centuries. The question obscured by Smith's argument was the relation between profits (including interest) and rent in a growing economy, for returns in one kind of investment might rise at the expense of returns from another.

Another problem was that, although Smith's labour-commanded measure of value was a convenient index for one who was primarily interested in comparing total real income as between countries or over time, it contained an inconvenient circularity from the point of view of those concerned with trends in the relations between rents, profits and wages over time in a growing economy. As Ricardo pointed out in the first chapter of his *Principles*, which took issue at once with Smith's theory of value:

if the reward of the labourer were always in proportion to what he produced, the quantity of labour bestowed on a commodity, and the quantity of labour which that quantity would purchase, would be equal, and either might accurately measure the variations of other things; but they are not equal; the first is under many circumstances an invariable standard, indicating correctly the variations of other things; the latter is subject to as many fluctuations as the commodities compared with it.[2]

edition is contained in P. Straffa (ed.), *The Works and Correspondence of David Ricardo*, Vol. I (1951).

[2] Ricardo, *Principles*, Sraffa edn, Vol. I, p. 14.

Worse still, from Ricardo's point of view, Smith had argued that a rise in the price of corn would, by pushing up wages, raise the prices of all other commodities, for this line of argument left indeterminate the effects of a rise in corn prices, or wages, on profits.

The Ricardian theory of value and distribution was developed therefore to explain the principal unsolved problem of political economy as Ricardo then saw it, viz the way changes in the relative shares of land, labour and capital would interact with the process of capital accumulation and thus with the growth of output. Ricardo's theory had four distinctive though not necessarily original elements: it was their synthesis as the foundation of a single macroeconomic model of economic development and distribution that was original. The distinctive elements were: (i) a new theory of rent, (ii) a postulate connecting the impact of diminishing returns in agriculture with the rate of profit, (iii) a subsistence theory of wages and (iv) a labour measure of value. The analysis was conducted throughout in *real* terms – actually generally in commodity terms by the device of reducing all transactions to a single common denominator, corn.

(i) *Ricardo's Theory of Rent.* The theory of rent – a theory of differential rents in agriculture – was essentially the same as the theory propounded in 1815 by three other economists – Malthus, West and Torrens. Ricardo acknowledged his debt to Malthus and West in the preface to his *Principles*. It was a new theory in that it had not been elaborated by Adam Smith. It started from the assumption that land is specialised and in fixed supply but that it is not all in use. As population grows and capital accumulates new land is taken up. The cost of production of corn will vary with the fertility of the soil and its situation in relation to the market, but price must of course be high enough to cover the cost of production on the least productive piece of land in use – on the marginal land as we would now say. On this marginal land production will just cover costs and there will be no rent payable in the Ricardo model. On better land a surplus will be obtainable which will accrue directly to the owner of the land if he cultivates it himself or will be paid by tenants competing for the better pieces of land. In this model therefore rent is price-determined rather than price-determining and is a surplus over and above the basic cost of production determined by capital and labour inputs required by the marginal land. To quote Ricardo: 'Corn is not high because a rent is paid, but a rent is paid because corn is high'.[3] To the passage stating that 'rent does not and cannot enter in the least degree as a component part of its price', he added the footnote 'The clearly understanding this principle is, I am persuaded, of the utmost importance to the science of political economy.'[4]

The attraction of this theory from Ricardo's point of view was that it explained differences in the amount of rent yielded by different lands and at the same time simplified his theory of value and distribution by eliminating rent as a factor in the determination of value. Its attraction from the point of view of some of his followers – economists and politicians – was that it provided a rationale for policies which might be detrimental to the land-owning classes. Ricardo himself denies indignantly that he was the enemy of the landlords (having prudently converted most of his investments into land he was a substantial landed proprietor himself) but it is not difficult to find passages that served in the purposes of those who were: e.g. 'Independently of these improvements [in agricultural technology], in which the community have an immediate and the landlords a remote interest, the interest of the landlord is always opposed to that of the consumer and manufacturer'[5]; and later in the same paragraph: 'All classes, therefore, except the landlords, will be injured by the increase in the price of corn.'[6]

(ii) *Diminishing returns and the rate of profit.* Ricardo's theory of differential rent then, explained the way progressively less favourably situated or less fertile lands would be taken into cultivation as population grew and with it the demand for food. The same argument underlay the law of diminishing returns and Malthus' population theory. Ricardo carried the argument further, however. As population rises and poorer lands are taken into cultivation, or as additional units of labour are applied to existing scarce land, the share of wages tends to rise and the share of profits to fall. When the increasing difficulty of growing corn on land of progressively worsening quality has driven the wage share to the level where total wages equals total product minus rent, profits will be reduced to zero, and the stationary state will have been reached.

The natural tendency of profits then is to fall; for, in the progress of society and wealth, the additional quantity of food required is obtained

---

[3] *Ibid*, p. 74.   [4] *Ibid*, p. 77.
[5] *Ibid*, p. 335.
[6] *Ibid*, p. 336.

by the sacrifice of more and more labour. This tendency, this gravitation as it were of profits, is happily checked at repeated intervals by the improvements in machinery connected with the production of necessaries, as well as by discoveries in the science of agriculture, which enable us to relinquish a portion of labour before required, and therefore to lower the price of the prime necessary of the labour. The rise in the price of necessaries, and in the wages of labour is, however limited; for as soon as wages should be equal...to...the whole receipts of the farmer, there must be an end of accumulation; for no capital can then yield any profit whatever, and no additional labour can be demanded, and consequently population will have reached its higher point. Long indeed, before this period, the very low rate of profits will have arrested all accumulation and almost the whole produce of the country, after paying the labourers, will be the property of the owners of land and the receivers of tithes and taxes.[7]

(iii) *Subsistence theory of wages.* Ricardo took the view that wages as the price of labour were determined in the same way as that of any other commodity. Its 'natural price' is that 'which is necessary to enable the labourers one with another, to subsist and to perpetuate their race without either increase or diminution.' This in its turn depended on 'the quantity of food, necessaries and conveniences become essential to him from habit'.[8] A high rate of wages would stimulate an increase in population which would eat up more and more of the total product after payment of rent and reduce the proportion left for profit. The inducement to invest and hence the demand for labour would then decline and wage rates fall back to subsistence levels. Thus, taking explicit account of the influence of social and customary factors on the level of subsistence, he held the view that the market price of labour will always tend towards the subsistence price, though it might differ from it at particular times and places in relation to the short-term forces of supply and demand. The original Malthusian population theory had been formulated largely in terms of a kind of physical subsistence minimum. Ricardo's way of formulating it – treating the worker's subsistence level as a function of 'habit and custom' – made it possible to explain secularly rising real wages without having to abandon the theorem he found so useful for analytical purposes – that wages were supply-determined in the long run, independently of the demand for labour.

(iv) *The Labour Measure of Value.* Possibly the most distinctive and fundamental element in Ricardo's system, however, was the measure of value that he adopted. He distinguished as did Adam

[7] *Ibid*, pp. 120–1.   [8] *Ibid*, p. 93.

Smith between natural price (= value) and market price and he started explicitly from a cost theory of value which he also attributed to Smith. 'Utility then is not the measure of exchangeable value, although it is absolutely essential to it...Possessing utility, commodities derive their exchangeable value from two sources: from their scarcity, and from the quantity of labour required to obtain them.'[9] Scarcity, however, is a factor in natural price, or value, only for a few unique products like works of art or particular kinds of wine, i.e. for commodities in fixed supply or in conditions where competition is restricted. For all other commodities the real foundation of value is human labour. 'I confess it fills me with astonishment' he wrote in a letter to Malthus in 1818

to find that you think...that *natural price*, as well as *market price*, is determined by the demand or supply...In saying this do you mean to deny that facility of production will lower natural price and difficulty of production raise it?...If indeed this fundamental doctrine of mine were proved false I admit that my whole theory falls with it.[10]

His whole theory, that is to say, was developed in terms of the long-term or natural price (real value) of things and with this in view he settled on a cost-of-production theory of value.

Having successfully developed a theory which eliminated rent from cost of production he was left with the task of explaining value in terms of wages and profits. In the end he managed to reduce everything (or nearly everything) to its labour cost. He argued that in practice the long-term exchange value of goods would vary in proportion to the labour spent on producing them – including of course not only the direct labour cost but also the labour embodied in the fixed capital used up in their production.

Put like this of course it approximates to a simple labour theory of value and many writers have assumed that that was all the Ricardian theory of value amounted to. Actually it was more than that. In reducing capital to its embodied labour he divided it into two classes – circulating and fixed capital. There was no difficulty in measuring circulating capital in terms of labour; by generally accepted definition it was the amount of corn, or the wages fund, available to sustain the current labour force. Fixed capital, however, has another dimension, its durability: i.e. the fact that it increases the length of the productive process; and to the extent

---

[9] *Ibid*, pp. 11–12.   [10] Sraffa edn, Vol. VII, pp. 250–1.

that some commodities are produced with more fixed capital than others, their relative value will differ for another reason than their direct labour cost. 'It is hardly necessary to say that commodities which have the same quantity of labour bestowed on their production, will differ in exchangeable value, if they cannot be brought to market in the same time.'[11] He then illustrated his point with a numerical example showing that, at a given rate of profit, capital locked up in the production process for two years would require twice the profit accruing on the same amount of capital turned over in one year.

Ricardo thus recognised explicitly that differences in the durability of fixed capital and differences in the fixed capital/labour ratio introduce another factor into the determination of the long-term exchange values of commodities. There is a plaintive much-quoted passage for example in which he said: 'Mr. Malthus shows that in fact the exchangeable value of commodities is not *exactly* proportioned to the labour which has been employed on them, which I not only admit now but have never denied.'[12] And again in a letter to James Mill dated 1818 he insisted that there are only two causes 'at all stages of society' why exchangeable value varies: 'one the more or less quantity of labour required, the other the greater or less durability of capital' and that 'the former is never superseded by the latter but is only modified by it'.[13] But because he regarded variations in the input of fixed capital as representing in practice a mere fraction of variations in cost relatively to the input of labour,[14] he chose generally to ignore it and sometimes to write as though the input of labour was the sole measure of value that one need take into account. He did, however, explain that if one takes into account the fixed capital component one must recognise that a rise in wage rates relative to profit rates could raise the values of commodities made with low capital/labour ratios (or low fixed/circulating ratios – which amounts to the same thing) relatively to those made with high capital/labour ratios. To quote:

---

[11] Sraffa edn, Vol. I, p. 37.   [12] Sraffa edn, Vol. I, p. xxxviii.
[13] Sraffa edn, Vol. VII, p. 377.
[14] See e.g. Sraffa edn, Vol. I, p. 36: 'The greatest effects which could be produced on the relative prices of these goods from a rise of wages, could not exceed 6 or 7 per cent; for profits could not, probably, under any circumstances, admit of a greater general and permanent depression than to that amount.' Hence Stigler's description of Ricardo's theory as a 93 per cent labour theory of value. G. Stigler, 'Ricardo and the ninety-three per cent labour theory of value', reprinted in *Essays in the History of Economics*.

This difference in the degree of durability of fixed capital, and this variety in the proportions in which the two sorts of capital [fixed and circulating] may be combined, introduce another cause, besides the greater or less quantity of labour necessary to produce commodities, for the variations in their relative values – this cause is the rise or fall in the value of labour.[15]

Conscious therefore that he was simplifying, but convinced that he was not straying far from practical reality, Ricardo measured the relative value of a commodity in terms of the quantity (man-hours) of labour embodied in its production. This enabled him to explain profits as a residual after accounting for labour's share in national income net of rents. He differed from Adam Smith both in the form and in the objective of his measure of value. Smith – interested in growth more than in distribution of the national income – was looking for a kind of price deflator that would enable him to measure relative *real* incomes: so he adopted a labour-commanded measure of value (the amount of corn which would command a given quantity of labour). What Ricardo wanted was a measure of value which would be independent of changes in the division of the social product so that he could use it in a theory of distribution. For if a rise or fall in wages could of itself alter the value of total product it would be impossible to predict the effect on profits. With Ricardo's model however a rise in wages had no effect on prices or national product but was associated with a corresponding fall in profits. It was a theory which abstracted from differences in capital structure and was applied to the long-run pricing of reproducible goods under perfect competition.

Ricardo's basic model was formulated in real terms. Transforming it to money terms raised another set of problems, for it became necessary to distinguish changes which affected the relative *real* values of commodities from changes affecting their relative money values. In the end Ricardo cut through these difficulties with a characteristically bold simplification by assuming that the value of gold was invariant in relation to commodities. 'To facilitate, then, the object of this enquiry, although I fully allow that money made of gold is subject to most of the variations of other things, I shall suppose it to be invariable, and therefore all alterations in price to be occasioned by some alteration in the value of the commodity of which I may be speaking.'[16] The rationale (if it can really be so called) for this

---

[15] Sraffa edn, Vol. I, p. 30.　　　　　　　　[16] *Ibid*, p. 46.

proposition was the further assumption that gold was a 'standard' commodity in the sense that its conditions of production involved an input mix of labour and fixed capital which approximated to the average for most other commodities.[17]

However, Ricardo never solved to his own satisfaction the problems associated with devising a measure of value. In the *Principles* he was looking for a measure of relative variations in value and seems to have accepted that the problems of devising an absolutely invariable measure were insoluble. Towards the end of his life he was working on a paper on 'Absolute Value and Exchangeable Value' which remained unfinished. Ricardo's last letter to James Mill was indeed a characteristically modest critique of a paper written by the latter's son, John Stuart, on the measure of value.[18] The letter ends:

Beg him to consider this and to let me know if I am wrong in my critique on his paper. I have been thinking a good deal on this subject lately but without much improvement – I see the same difficulties as before and am more confirmed than ever that strictly speaking there is not in nature any correct measure of value nor can any ingenuity suggest one, for what constitutes a correct measure for some things is a reason why it cannot be a correct one for others.[19]

All of which makes it the more surprising to find John Stuart Mill's famous statement in his *Principles*: 'Happily, there is nothing in the laws of value which remains for the present or any future writer to clear up; the theory of the subject is complete.'[20] However, what this apparently complacent statement reflected was two things – first a shift of problem-focus and second a more eclectic, more realistic approach to economic theory on the part of the younger Mill. He was not concerned, as Ricardo had been, to explain the level and rate of profits as a function of wages in order to justify an anti-Corn Law policy. By the time Mill wrote his *Principles* the Corn Laws had been repealed and he was interested in analysing the wage-depressing effects of population growth. As far as profits were concerned, moreover, he had abandoned Ricardo's concept of them as a residual after determining wages and quoted approvingly Nassau

---

[17] *Ibid*, p. 45: 'May not gold be considered as a commodity produced with such proportions of the two kinds of capital as approach nearest to the average quantity employed in the production of most commodities?'

[18] Sraffa (ed.), *The Works and Correspondence of David Ricardo, op. cit.*, Vol. IX, pp. 385-7.

[19] Sraffa edn, *Works*, Vol. IX, p. 387. Ricardo died less than a week later.

[20] J. S. Mill, *Principles*, Vol III, *Collected Works*, p. 456.

Senior's view of them as a reward for abstinence; he went on to distinguish between net profits (which were a reward for risk taking) and interest, which was the reward for waiting and thus measured 'the comparative value placed in the given society upon the present and the future'. Finally, because Mill did not share Ricardo's propensity for abstract theorising and model building, his theory of value was expounded in a less rigorous way which permitted him fruitfully to explore various qualifications and exceptions to Ricardo's highly simplified framework of analysis. Thus he was among the first economists to analyse such questions as economies of scale, the effects of social status and education in setting up non-competing groups in the labour force, the applications of the labour theory of value to joint products, and the implication of alternative uses for land for the assumption that rent could be excluded from cost of production.

In sum then, Ricardo followed Adam Smith in adopting a cost-of-production theory of value but achieved greater rigour and consistency by process of abstraction. In the end he made value hinge ultimately on one factor of production – unskilled labour – and on this foundation constructed a general theory of the long-run relative exchange values of reproducible goods in a competitive exchange economy. Given the extreme simplicity of its assumptions the model described a complete and logically coherent set of relationships which were consistent with Ricardo's intuitive conclusions concerning the interdependence of profits and wages. However, whenever it became necessary to take into account the possibility that there might be more than one kind of labour, land or capital, or that there might be variable pro-portions in the input mix for different commodities, or that there might be variable periods of production, the model ran into insuperable difficulties. Its applicability that is to say was limited to a fairly narrowly defined analytical purpose.

FURTHER READING

Primary literature

D. Ricardo, *An Essay on the Influence of a Low Price of Corn on the Profits of Stock*, Vol. IV, *Works*, ed. Piero Sraffa (1966).

D. Ricardo, *Principles of Political Economy and Taxation* (ed. Sraffa), *op. cit.* (1970).

Secondary literature

M. Blaug, *Ricardian Economics* (1958).
M. Dobb, *Theories of Value and Distribution since Adam Smith* (1973).
R. L. Meek, *Studies in the Labour Theory of Value* (1973).
George J. Stigler, *Essays in the History of Economics* (1964).

6

SCOPE AND METHODOLOGY OF CLASSICAL POLITICAL ECONOMY

By the first decade of the nineteenth century, thanks to Adam Smith, the study of political economy had acquired recognition as a distinctive 'scientific' discipline.[1] His pupil Dugald Stewart was giving a named course on political economy in the University of Edinburgh in the 1800s and in 1805 T. R. Malthus was appointed Professor of Modern History and Political Economy to teach East India Company cadets at Haileybury College.

More important still, a self-conscious intellectual community of economists had begun to emerge in Western Europe. Its members were a fairly heterogeneous group, whose common ground lay in the fact that, having read the *Wealth of Nations*, they were concerned both to apply its analysis to current economic problems and to develop, criticise and extend its basic theory wherever necessary. Though two of the group's leading members – James Mill and J. R. McCulloch, both Scottish journalists – had been to Edinburgh University where Smith's pupil Stewart was lecturing on political economy, it is fair to say that they were all *qua* economists self-educated and mutually-educating men who had started from the same text-book. The British members in the first two decades also included Jeremy Bentham, an academic philosopher, a contemporary of Adam Smith whom he resembled in the sheer breadth of his intellectual interests; and there was Ricardo the Jewish stockbroker whose formal education had ended at the age of 14. On the continent, there was J. B. Say who published a two volume *Traité d'économie politique* (first edition 1803) expounding the Smithian paradigm to a Parisian audience until he had to carry on his work in Switzerland, when the Napoleonic regime made it politically unwise to advocate laissez-faire doctrines in France; there was

---

[1] It is of course open to question whether economics is, or was, a science. What is relevant here is that Adam Smith and his successors among the classical economists thought it was.

also J. C. L. Simonde de Sismondi, a Genevan by birth, who published his first major work on economics, *Richesse commerciale* in 1803, and that too was primarily an exposition of the doctrines of Adam Smith. These men formed the nucleus of an intellectual community whose members discussed, corresponded and debated in print about the application of the new theory to current economic problems in the first two decades of the century. By the end of the 1820s there were Chairs of Political Economy at Oxford (Nassau Senior was appointed to the Drummond Professorship in 1825) and at the newly-formed London University. McCulloch who had been giving the Ricardo memorial lectures to a distinguished audience of bankers, merchants and MPs since 1824[2] was offered the London Chair in 1827.

However, although political economy based on the Smithian paradigm had achieved a certain measure of academic recognition (it still had very little *status* within the universities) its fashionable appeal, and above all its attraction to active thinkers depended not on its academic reputation, but on its immediate relevance to contemporary policy problems. The problems which engaged the attention of the community of economists in the early nineteenth century were urgent and puzzling questions, related to such basic issues as economic growth (the population explosion), commercial policy (the corn laws) and inflation (the high cost of bullion). It was the conviction that political economy could provide a simple and effective method of analysing these complex problems, and hence a reasoned route to useful policy prescriptions that brought to McCulloch's lectures men such as the Chancellor of the Exchequer, the Lord Mayor of London and a bevy of Bank Directors, and that induced an acute mind such as Ricardo's to retire from a lucrative Stock Exchange practice to write a book on the principles of political economy and taxation.

So how did Smith's analytical framework stand up to the pressure of changing events in an industrialising economy and to the sustained critique of a group of lively intellects? In particular how did the views of the scientific community of economists on the scope and methodology of their subject change through

[2] McCulloch was lecturing in Edinburgh, Liverpool and London (twice-weekly in the West End and thrice weekly in the City in 1824). In 1825 the students at the City class alone numbered 240 and at the newly formed City of London Literary and Scientific Institution he had an audience of nearly 800. See D. P. O'Brien, *J. R. McCulloch, a Study in Classical Economics* (1970), pp. 52–3.

time? For although the formal qualifications of a professional economist were still extremely vague (they were far from precise even at the middle of the twentieth century) the existence of a self-conscious community of economists, dedicated to the scientific study of political economy, was illustrated by the establishment in 1821 of the Political Economy Club. This was a dining club whose members were pledged to 'regard their own mutual instruction and the diffusion among others of just principles of Political Economy as a real and important obligation', and which met several times a year to discuss 'some doubt or question on some topic of Political Economy' proposed in advance by its members.[3] Membership of the Club was limited and although not all its members would have thought of themselves as primarily economists, even in an amateur sense, all those who have made seminal contributions to English classical economic thought were active members at some time in their career.

For all the early members of the Political Economy Club, the acknowledged starting point was Adam Smith. According to McCulloch, it was in the *Wealth of Nations* that

the fundamental principles that determine the production of wealth were established beyond the reach of cavil and dispute. In opposition to the Economists, Dr. Smith has shown that labour is the only source of wealth; and that the wish by which all individuals are actuated, by augmenting their fortunes and rising in the world, is the cause of wealth being saved and accumulated.[4]

However, as McCulloch went on to point out, there were 'errors' in Smith's analysis which were rectified by subsequent economists. The most important of these (apart from the fact that Smith was not always doctrinaire enough for the taste of McCulloch who complained of his readiness to admit 'that individual advantage is not always a true test of the public advantageousness of different employments') related to his 'erroneous opinions' on rent and value. The 'true theory of rent' was elucidated by Malthus and West in pamphlets published independently of each other in 1815, though (again according to McCulloch) it had already been 'discovered and fully explained by Dr. James Ander-

---

[3] See *Political Economy Club Centenary Volume* (1921), for extracts from regulations, lists of members, of questions discussed and their proposers, and for extracts from the diary of one of its members, J. R. Mallet, covering the period 1823–37.

[4] J. R. McCulloch, *The Literature of Political Economy. A Classified Catalogue* (1845), LSE Reprints (1938), pp. 12–14.

son in a tract on the "corn laws" published in 1777'.[5] The theory
of value and with it the theory of distribution was worked out
by Ricardo in his *Principles* the appearance of which 'formed a
new era in the history of the science...Mr. Ricardo has traced
the source and limiting principle of exchangeable value, and has
extracted the laws which determine the distribution of the various
products of art and industry among the various ranks and orders
of society'.[6] It is fair to add that Ricardo also succeeded in
integrating the 'true theory of rent' into his theory of value and
in stamping his personal imprint on it so effectively that it has
come down to posterity as the Ricardian theory of rent.

   McCulloch's assessment, of Smith as the founder of the science
of political economy and Ricardo as the disciple who amended
and corrected the fundamental principles only in so far as they
related to the theory of value and distribution, was the accepted
contemporary view and accords with the account which Ricardo
himself gave in the Preface to his *Principles*. There Ricardo made
clear that he was not setting out to write a comprehensive treatise
on the principles of political economy which would replace the
Wealth of Nations, but to deal with a problem which the master
has left in some confusion mainly because he had failed to
appreciate the 'true doctrine of rent'. He was not, in other words,
creating a new paradigm, but offering a solution to a crucial
problem arising within the framework of the current orthodoxy.

To determine the laws which regulate this distribution [of the national
product], is the principal problem in Political Economy: much as the
science has been improved by the writings of Turgot, Stuart, Smith, Say,
Sismondi and others, they afford very little satisfactory information
respecting the natural course of rent, profits and wages.[7]

   Nevertheless the Ricardian analysis made a larger contribution
to the trend of economic thought, and to the methodology of the
discipline, than this modest claim might suggest. Of all the early
nineteenth-century economists none made a more powerful
impact on the minds of other economists[8] (then and after) than

   [5] The references are to James Anderson, *An Inquiry into the Nature of the Corn
Laws*, extensively annotated by McCulloch, *ibid*, pp. 68–70; T. R. Malthus, *An
Inquiry into the Nature and Progress of Rent and the Principles by which it is Regulated*
(1815); and Sir Edward West, *An Essay on the Application of Capital and Land* (1815),
annotated *ibid*, p. 33.   [6] McCulloch, *op. cit.*, p. 16.
   [7] D. Ricardo, *On the Principles of Political Economy and Taxation* (1819), Sraffa
edn, Vol. I, p. 5.
   [8] Unlike Adam Smith, Ricardo did not score a popular success – his analysis
was too abstract, too little polemical to catch the popular imagination.

did Ricardo. McCulloch saw the publication of the *Principles* as opening 'a new era in the history of the science'.[9] Ricardo was the mentor of Karl Marx who described him as 'the last of the scientific economists' and the main inspiration attracting the young Alfred Marshall to the systematic study of economics in the 1860s. Modern economists differ widely in their evaluation of him but there is no doubt that he made, and still makes a powerful direct impact on his professional readers. The controversy as to whether Ricardian economics 'conquered England as completely as the Holy Inquisition conquered Spain' (which was the way Keynes described it) or whether 'the Ricardians were always in a minority in England' (which was Schumpeter's interpretation), or whether (according to Marx) the year 1830 marked the end of Ricardian economics, is more a reflection of the differences in the way economists have interpreted the essential nature of the Ricardian message than of any doubt about his fundamental importance in setting the course not only of mainstream classical economics but also of Marxian and neo-classical economics. For it was not in suggesting a new total vision of the way the economic order operated (he was content to accept without argument Adam Smith's basic philosophical assumptions), or in advocating any specific economic theory or policy, that Ricardo put his distinctive stamp on his professional successors; it was in developing a new technique of economic analysis.

In effect Ricardo was the first specialist economist. Most of the other leading economists had been philosophers, students of society in the round. Their economics was embedded in philosophical disquisitions and long historical digressions which may have leavened them for the contemporary general reader but which obscure the message for the modern reader interested in the essential structure of the economic analysis. Ricardo, however, started and finished with the economic problem and refused to be side-tracked by philosophical, sociological or historical considerations. In this undoubtedly he over-simplified the practical economic problems which he considered, by abstracting them from their social and political context. And it is arguable that he helped to narrow the scope and significance of economic thought by giving it a rationale for developing independently of the other social sciences. In so doing, however, he laid the foundations of a distinctively economic technique of

[9] J. R. McCulloch, *op. cit.*, p. 16.

analysis which represented the beginnings of modern economic science – the beginnings of economics as a technique of analysis rather than as a collection of philosophical axioms and historical or pseudo-historical generalisations.

His first serious excursion into print (apart from some short pieces in the *Morning Chronicle*) was in January 1810 when he published a short pamphlet on wartime inflation entitled *The High Price of Bullion*. As an active participant in the money market one might have expected Ricardo to have based his argument on facts rather than on generalisations. But he began by an explicit attempt to formulate 'the laws that regulate the distribution of the precious metals throughout the world'; and starting from the simple postulate that merchants are always out to maximise their money gains he propounded the law that 'a depreciation of the circulating medium is the necessary consequence of its redundance' and that 'this depreciation is counteracted by the exportation of the precious metals'. From these first principles (which he illustrated by reference to the events in Britain since 1797 when the Bank of England was permitted to issue unconvertible notes), he went on to develop a theory of interest in opposition to the prevailing view 'that the rate of interest and not the price of gold or silver bullion is the criterion by which we may always judge of the abundance of paper money; that if it were too abundant interest would fall and if not sufficiently so interest would rise'. Against this he set what came to be the typical classical argument 'It can I think be made manifest that the rate of interest is not regulated by the abundance or scarcity of money but by the abundance or scarcity of that part of capital not consisting of money.' His remedy for inflation, based on this very general reasoning process (which his Bank of England opponents derided as 'wholly theoretical'), was the remedy that eventually prevailed as the financial orthodoxy of the nineteenth century and as the basis of the international gold standard, viz 'The remedy which I propose for all the evils of our currency, is that the bank should gradually decrease the amount of their notes in circulation until they shall have rendered the remainder of equal value with the coins which they represent.'[10]

Ricardo's characteristic approach to the urgent economic issues of his day was thus to begin by trying to formulate the laws underlying the relevant categories of economic behaviour, to develop a theory based on a few precisely stated assumptions and

[10] See below, Chapter 4, for a fuller exposition of his line of analysis.

to illustrate it by reference to the facts of the contemporary world. From this essentially abstract reasoning process he deduced practical policy conclusions. He went his own way in his professional as in his private life, owing little to any other writer, except of course to the extent that a critique of Adam Smith formed the starting point for much of what he wrote, and that his arguments with contemporary economists, especially with James Mill and with Malthus, helped to clarify and crystallise his own thoughts. His first major pamphlet outside the financial controversy in which he became involved while still a practising stockbroker was the *Essay on the Influence of a Low Price of Corn on the Profits of Stock* (1815) written to oppose the prevailing orthodoxy that low corn prices would lead via lower agricultural profits to a fall in profits generally. The *Principles* was originally planned as an enlarged version of this *Essay* but in October 1815 he announced in a letter 'his determination "to concentrate all the talent" he possesses upon the subject on which his opinions "differ from the great authority of Adam Smith, Malthus etc." namely "the principles of Rent, Profit and Wages".'[11]

It was his talent for consistent economic logic, severe in its simplifications but unrivalled in its capacity for synthesis, that won the unstinted admiration of his major contemporaries and was imitated by his successors – most effectively by those whose training enabled them to use the mathematical short-cuts which this simple logic facilitated. Schumpeter has analysed vividly the virtues and the vices of this methodology. Ricardo's interest, he wrote

was in the clear-cut result of direct, practical significance. In order to get this he cut that general system to pieces, bundled up as large parts of it as possible, and put them into cold storage – so that as many things as possible should be frozen and 'given'. He then piled one simplifying assumption upon another until, having really settled everything by these assumptions, he was left with only a few aggregative variables between which, given these assumptions, he set up simple one-way relations, so that, in the end the desired results emerged almost as tautologies.[12]

This, Schumpeter went on to say, is exactly the same method as that adopted a century later by Keynes – although their results and views on economic policy were poles apart.

When Ricardo began to rethink in his own terms the Smithian

[11] Sraffa, *Ricardo Works*, vol. I, p. xiii.
[12] J. Schumpeter, *History of Economic Analysis*, pp. 472–3.

orthodoxy he took for granted the *general* analytical model of the economic system that Adam Smith had worked out and focused his attention on certain sectors of this model which he found particularly unsatisfactory – originally with the forces determining the distribution of the national product between rent, profits and wages, and then with the theory of value which he found he had to work out before he could deal effectively with his starting-problem.[13] Having in effect accepted Smith's view of capital accumulation as the prime motive force in the growth process he was primarily concerned to explain the trend in profits which by providing both the resources and the incentive for new investment provided the key to the problem of how and whether the growth of output would be maintained indefinitely. Where he diverged from Smith was in recognising that in order to explain why profits rose or fell it was necessary to develop a theory of the distribution of the national product between profits, wages and rent. The reason why he had to grapple first with the concept of value was that he needed to be able to explain the value of the national product independently of the sum of profits, wages and rent, if he was to explain how it came to be distributed between these components.

Current economic conditions helped to shape the research priorities of the invisible college of economists. It was not altogether surprising that distribution began to assume a special importance in the first half of the nineteenth century. For Adam Smith, writing on the threshold of the industrial revolution, before the escape from economic stagnation became an accepted fact of life in the latter decades of the eighteenth century, the problem of sustaining growth had dwarfed all others. In the relatively rapidly expanding, industrialising and transforming economy of the period following the Napoleonic wars, the problem of the associated changes in distribution of the national income between the different income or power groups of social classes in the community assumed a major importance. Robert Torrens expressed the rationale for the classical interest in distribution in practical rather than theoretical terms in the preface to the 1829 edition of his *Essay on the External Corn Trade*:

[13] Sraffa notes, in p. xiv of his introduction to Vol. I (1970) of *The Works and Correspondence of David Ricardo* (ed. P. Sraffa and M. H. Dobb), that in the early correspondence with Mill, when Ricardo (under Mill's pressure) was beginning to rough out an outline for the *Principles*, there was no reference to Value. That came first somewhat obliquely in a letter to Mill dated 30 December 1815 saying: 'Before my readers can understand the proof I mean to offer they must understand the theory of currency and of price.'

The study of Political Economy, if it did not teach the way in which labour may obtain an adequate reward, might serve to gratify a merely speculative curiosity, but could scarcely conduce to any purposes of practical utility. It claims the peculiar attention of the benevolent and good, mainly because it explains the causes, which depress and elevate wages, and thereby points out the means, by which we may mitigate the distress, and improve the condition, of the great majority of mankind.[14]

This was also a crucial problem for Karl Marx. And the debate between Malthus and Ricardo reflected the shift in the political and economic power structure between the landed gentry and the manufacturing interests as industrialisation gathered momentum.

However, if one were to try to account for the importance of Ricardo in the development of economic thought – an importance which would be admitted by admirers and detractors alike – one does not find the answer either in the 'topical' character of his message, or in the originality of his ideas or concepts, nor even in the superiority of his theoretical analysis. It lies rather in his capacity to construct out of familiar conceptual materials a simple, consistent, and (within its limits) logically satisfying macroeconomic system which, though severely simplified, seemed to contemporary economists to establish the essential 'landmarks' needed for the analysis of complex real-world problems.[15] He inspired Marx as well as Marshall, both of whom were seduced by the internal consistency of his system and sought to make it more general. He showed for the first time how a simple *analytical* model of the economy, operating with a very few, precisely defined, readily intelligible, strategic variables, could be employed to analyse complex economic processes and justify unambiguous policy prescriptions.

His methodology in effect was mathematical rather than his-

---

[14] R. Torrens, *On Wages and Combination* (1834) p. 1. Quoted in Lionel Robbins, *Robert Torrens and the Evolution of Classical Political Economy* (1958), p. 249. Lord Robbins notes that this passage was repeated in at least three other of Torrens' publications.

[15] See, for example, McCulloch's note on Ricardo's *Principles* in his *Literature of Political Economy*, p. 17: 'Mr. Ricardo's is not a practical work... It is not even a systematic treatise, but is principally an inquiry into an elucidation of certain fundamental principles, most of which had previously been undiscovered. And though it be often exceedingly difficult, or, it may be, all but impossible, to estimate the extent to which these principles may in certain cases be modified by other principles and combinations of circumstances, it is obviously of the greatest importance to have ascertained their existence. They are so many land-marks to which to refer; and can never be lost sight of even in matters most essentially practical.'

torical or philosophical. I have suggested that the debate between
Malthus and Ricardo reflected the power struggle between the
landed gentry and the manufacturing interests. It was also a
reflection of a methodological issue of some importance in the
development of economic thought – viz the problem of whether
economics should draw its characteristic techniques of analysis
from the moral or philosophical sciences or from the mathematical or rational sciences. McCulloch has referred to 'the
mathematical cast he [Ricardo] has given to his reasonings'.[16]
Malthus, who wrote his *Principles of Political Economy* (1820) as a
reply to Ricardo's *Principles*, took up the methodological issue in
the opening sentence of his introduction: 'The science of political
economy resembles more the sciences of morals and politics than
the science of mathematics.'[17] And he went on to say that: 'The
principal cause of error, and of the differences which prevail at
present among the scientific writers in political economy, appears
to me to be a precipitate attempt to simplify and generalize.'[18]
His own objective was to steer a judicious middle course between
those who 'seem to be satisfied with what has already been done
in political economy' and those who having questioned certain
aspects of the Smithian orthodoxy had allowed their predilection
for 'simplification and generalization' to lead them to erroneous
conclusions. However he followed Ricardo's lead in focusing on
'some important yet controverted points' in the current orthodoxy rather than in attempting 'to frame a new and complete
treatise' and most of his *Principles* was devoted to a discussion
of the theoretical issues which Ricardo had raised, viz the nature
and measure of value, and the theory of rent, wages and profit.
It was only in the final section that he came back to what he along
with most of the other classical economists accepted, following
Smith, as the *primary* objective of political economy, viz 'to trace
the causes which are most effective in calling forth the powers
of production in different countries'.[19]

It is worth noting, however, that even while preparing to
demonstrate Ricardo's errors, Malthus frankly recognised his
importance as the leading authority among the contemporary
community of economists: 'I have so very high an opinion of
Mr. Ricardo's talents as a political economist, and so entire a
conviction of his perfect sincerity and love of truth, that I frankly
own I have sometimes felt almost staggered by his authority,

[16] *Op. cit.*, p. 17.
[17] T. Malthus, *Principles of Political Economy* (1820), from the Sraffa edition of
Ricardo's *Works* Vol. II, p. 5.
[18] *Ibid.*   [19] *Ibid*, p. 300.

while I have remained unconvinced by his reasonings.'[20] Certainly no other economist who followed Adam Smith in the classical school had quite the authority and influence on his colleagues that Ricardo had, and it was his methodological bias rather than that of Malthus which set the pattern for the 'science' of economics (as opposed to the 'art' or practical applications of economics) for mainstream English economic thought. Henceforth economics was to be regarded by the leading theoretical economists as a primarily deductive abstract, rather than inductive historical science.

In spite of their common origin as disciples of Adam Smith, Malthus and Ricardo started with two basic differences of attitude – (a) radically different ideological preconceptions which led them to widely divergent conclusions on policy, and (b) differing intellectual approaches which so shaped the routes by which they reached these conclusions as to make them at times virtually incapable of getting on the same wavelength of discussion. Living as they did in a period of transition to modern economic growth one represented the old world and the other the new. Parson Malthus the Professor reached back for inspiration beyond Adam Smith to the Physiocrats. He accepted that land was the ultimate source of economic progress and that the national interest depended on maintenance of the traditional social structure in which the landed interest was the keystone. Ricardo, the city businessman saw no escape from stagnation except through active development of domestic and international trade and believed that 'the strength of England and the well-being of its people proceeded from the abundance and cheapness of British capital'.[21]

In the debate between them Ricardo, in spite of his practical stockbroker background, emerges as the abstract and *a priori* theorist, concerned to identify the basic long-term trends and equilibrium conditions of the economic system, while Malthus, in spite of his mathematical academic training was preoccupied by the causes and consequences of day-to-day changes in the real world. A letter from Ricardo in January 1817 identified this difference:

It appears to me that one great cause of our difference of opinion, on the subjects we have so often discussed, is that you have always in your mind the immediate and temporary effects of particular changes –

[20] *Ibid*, p. 12.
[21] J. Hollander and Gregory (eds.), *David Ricardo's Notes on Malthus' Principles of Political Economy*, pp. xxiii–xiv.

whereas I put these immediate and temporary effects quite aside, and fix my whole attention on the permanent state of things which will result from them.[22]

To which Malthus responded a few days later

I really think that the progress of society consists of irregular movements, and that to omit the consideration of causes which for eight or ten years will give a great *stimulus* to production or population, or a great *check* to them, is to omit the causes of the wealth and poverty of nations – the grand object of all enquiries in Political Economy.[23]

Their contemporary, Robert Torrens summed up the difference more tersely as follows:

If Mr. Ricardo generalizes too much, Mr. Malthus generalises too little. If the former occasionally erects his principles without waiting to base them upon a sufficiently extensive induction from particulars, the latter is so occupied with his particulars, that he neglects that inductive process which extends individual experience throughout the infinitude of things, and imparts to human knowledge the character of science.[24]

In the end the winner in the battle for dominance over English economic thinking was Ricardo. Perhaps it was because Malthus, in spite of his gift for identifying and formulating the crucial economic problem of his day, was less clearheaded and logical than Ricardo. Perhaps it was because Malthus failed – except on the population problem and then originally only by accident[25] – to appreciate as clearly as Ricardo the structural changes taking place in the industrialising economy and failed accordingly to appeal to the decision takers who were gradually taking over economic and political power. Perhaps it was because, as Blaug

22 P. Sraffa and M. H. Dobb, *The Works and Correspondence of David Ricardo*, Vol. VII, p. 120.

23 *Ibid*, p. 122.

24 Robert Torrens, *An Essay on the Production of Wealth* (1821), pp. iv–v.

25 Malthus' first *Essay on Population* was published as an anonymous pamphlet in 1798 to refute the rosy predictions of the philosopher-idealists (e.g. Rousseau, Condorcet and Godwin) who argued that all that stood in the way of an ideal egalitarian organisation of society was private ignorance and public inertia. When the first Census (1801) results became available to confirm conclusively the views of the pessimistic side in the perennial population debate, Malthus, who had shared the view of most of his contemporaries, when the first edition was published, that *in fact* the population of England had increased little during the eighteenth century, found himself a kind of prophet without having prophesied. His 'principle of population' suddenly assumed urgent topical importance and he set about expanding the pamphlet into a book (1803) which became the bible of the pessimistic school and a justification for those who wanted to rationalise a tightening up of the relatively generous system of Poor Relief opened up by the Speenhamland system.

has suggested, Ricardo happened to win aggressive disciples. Whatever the reason it was Ricardo the amateur political economist not Malthus the academic who was the effective successor of Adam Smith in establishing a school of economics and in providing the text to which professional economists referred constantly for nearly half a century.[26]

A little over a century later the fashion cycle in economics had turned full circle again when Maynard Keynes launched his celebrated attack on classical economics and claimed direct descent from Malthus, lamenting the fact that 'it was Ricardo's more fascinating intellectual construction which was victorious and Ricardo who, by turning his back so completely on Malthus's ideas; constrained the subject for a full hundred years in an artificial groove'.[27] And again: 'If only Malthus instead of Ricardo had been the parent stem from which nineteenth century economics proceeded, what a much wiser and richer place the world would be today.'[28]

Ricardo's technique of abstract reasoning from *a priori* postulates, his propensity for logical–mathematical rather than philosophical–historical theories had important implications for the methodology of orthodox economic theory. In the first place, it helped to draw theoretical economics away from the real world by encouraging the theorist to depend on a type of theory which called for logical refutation rather than empirical verification.[29] To the extent that succeeding economists adopted this technique they could (and often did) explore, develop and even test their theories without reference to any empirical data other than the 'stylised facts' embodied in generally accepted starting postulates. One of Malthus' persistent objections to the Ricardian

[26] For further discussion of the methodology and impact of Ricardian economics see M. Blaug, *Ricardian Economics: A Historical Study* (1958); F. W. Fetter, 'The Rise and Decline of Ricardian Economics', *History of Political Economy* (Spring 1969); and N. B. de Marchi 'The Empirical Content and Longevity of Ricardian Economics', *Economica* (1970).

[27] J. M. Keynes, *Collected Writings* Vol. x. *Essays in Biography*, p. 87.

[28] *Ibid*, pp. 100–1. The passage quoted from Malthus on p. 80 above reflects Keynes' own view of the nature of economic science.

[29] Cf. K. Popper, 'On the status of science and of metaphysics', in *Conjectures and Refutations* (1963), p. 197: 'Whenever we find a mathematical theory of which we do not know whether it is true or false we test it, first superficially and then more severely, by trying to refute it. If we are unsuccessful we then try to prove it or to refute its negation. If we fail again, doubts as to the truth of the theory may have cropped up again, and we shall again try to refute it, and so on, until we either reach a decision or else shelve the problem as too difficult for us.'

method was that it failed to pay sufficient attention to the facts of experience:

> The tendency to premature generalization among political economists occasions also an unwillingness to bring their theories to the test of experience. The first business of philosophy is to account for things as they are. A comprehensive attention to facts is necessary, both to prevent the multiplication of theories, and to confirm those which are just.[30]

In the second place, the use of the Ricardian technique permitted economic theory to develop independently of other social sciences. For although the stylised facts adopted as starting assumptions by economic theorists often contained an element of social psychology or sociology there was no longer an incentive to require that these any more than the economic facts were empirically verified in any scientific sense. Exceptions to the starting postulates could be put aside in a *ceteris paribus* clause and subsequently ignored.

Nassau Senior was the first major classical economist to exploit this technique after Ricardo. In his *Outline of the Science of Political Economy* published in 1836 he postulated four propositions which could be substantiated 'empirically' from the personal observation of any armchair theorist and from which an integrated economic theory could be deduced by a logical reasoning process.[31] His four propositions were as follows:

(1) That man desires to obtain additional wealth with as little sacrifice as possible [i.e. an income-maximisation principle].
(2) That the Population of the world, or, in other words, the number of persons inhabiting it, is limited only by moral or physical evil, or by fear of a deficiency of those articles of wealth which the inhabitants of each class of its inhabitants lead them to require [i.e. a modified Malthusian population principle].
(3) That the powers of Labour and of the other instruments which produce wealth, may be indefinitely increased by using their Products as means of further production [i.e. a principle of capital accumulation].
(4) That agricultural skill remaining the same, additional Labour employed on the land within a given district produces in general a less proportionate return, or, in other words, that though, with every increase of the labour bestowed, aggregate return is increased, the

[30] T. R. Malthus, *Principles of Political Economy*, reprinted in Vol. II of *The Works and Correspondence of David Ricardo*, ed. Sraffa and Dobb, p. 10.

[31] The four 'fundamental propositions' had been developed in his introductory lecture at Oxford in 1826. See Marian Bowley, *Nassau Senior and Classical Economics* (1937), pp. 42–52. They are listed and discussed in Nassau W. Senior, *An Outline of the Science of Political Economy*, 1938 edn, p. 26.

increase of that return is not in proportion to the increase of the labour [i.e. a principle of diminishing returns].

From these 'empirically induced' postulates or axioms Senior set out to develop the analytical apparatus of an exact science with universal validity. He also moved in the direction of a deliberate narrowing of the scope of so-called scientific economics by making a distinction (which McCulloch rejected as too narrow but which the neo-classical theorists were to lean heavily upon) between the 'science' of economics and the 'art' of economics.

The business of a Political Economist is neither to recommend nor to dissuade, but to state general principles, which it is fatal to neglect, but neither advisable, nor perhaps practicable, to use as the sole, or even the principal, guides in the actual conduct of affairs... To decide in each case how far those conclusions are to be acted upon, belongs to the art of government, an art to which Political Economy is only one of many subservient Sciences.[32]

Later Senior was to concede that an 'art' of political economy was a possibility, but not until the 'science which states the laws regulating the production, accumulation, and distribution of wealth, or in other words the science (as distinguished from the art) of Political Economy itself' had been much more comprehensively and clearly elaborated.[33]

However, according to Senior, the premises on which the whole of the science of political economy depended were not derived by observation (as in the natural sciences) or by hypotheses (as in the logical–mathematical sciences) but by a process of introspection. This is how what Senior chose to call the 'mental sciences' could base their principles on *positive* premises in spite of the fact that it was not open to them to verify their hypotheses by formal experiment. 'When we direct our attention to the workings of our own mind, that is to say, when we search for premises by means of consciousness instead of by means of observation, our powers of trying experiments are much greater.'[34] In effect Senior was seeking to lay the foundations of a positive science of economics – a science based on positive premises analogous to those of the natural scientist rather than on the *a priori* hypotheses of the logician.

[32] Nassau Senior, *An Outline of the Science of Political Economy*, 1938 edn, p. 3.

[33] See Bowley, *op. cit.*, pp. 49 *et seq.*, for a discussion of Senior's views on this issue.

[34] *Lectures 1847–52*, p. 31.

The consequence, however, of this narrowing of the scope of 'pure' or 'scientific' economics was to confine it to such problems as could be solved by applying a process of logical–mathematical reasoning (based on a few simple introspectively derived postulates) to a handful of strategic variables, and to limit the range of economic problems which economists *qua* economists would consider themselves competent to study. Two of the principal problems which have traditionally preoccupied political economists – the economics of welfare and of development – were effectively excluded on this specification from the central core of 'scientific' economics and were relatively neglected by the mainstream theorists until well into the twentieth century.

It was John Stuart Mill, however, who formalised the Ricardian methodology and who wrote the systematic treatise on political economy which was designed to bring the *Wealth of Nations* up-to-date. In so far as English classical political economy fashioned a new paradigm out of the Ricardian innovations it was J. S. Mill who expounded it explicitly and comprehensively in a text book which remained for almost half a century the authoritative starting point for students of political economy, in much the same way as Adam Smith's *Wealth of Nations* had been over the previous half century or so. This was the textbook with which Alfred Marshall began his study of economics and from which he moved on to Ricardo and it had no serious rival either in Britain or the USA until Marshall's *Principles* appeared in the 1890s.

Actually Mill must have been one of the first major nineteenth-century economists not to begin the study of political economy from the *Wealth of Nations*. His father James Mill, who had acted as midwife to Ricardo's *Principles* over the years 1815–17, began to teach his 13 year old son political economy in 1819 by lecturing him daily and making him write and rewrite these lectures until they met with parental approval.[35] Not that John Stuart was altogether unprepared for the discipline. His father had started teaching him Greek at the age of 3 (he had read the whole of Herodotus before he was 8), then went on to arithmetic, history, Latin, mathematics (he was grappling with the calculus at 11) and then logic (at 12). By the time he was 15 he was privileged to spend

---

[35] See J. S. Mill's own account of this process in his *Autobiography*: 'In this manner I went through the whole extent of the science, and the written outline of it which resulted from my daily *compte rendu* served him afterwards as notes from which to write his *Elements of Political Economy*.'

a summer at Ricardo's Gatcomb house discussing political economy on walks with the master himself. After that formidable
father, Ricardo 'who by his benevolent countenance and kind-
liness of manner, was very attractive to young persons'[36] must
have exerted a deep impression on this highly intelligent and
over-educated lad. Ricardo's critique of a paper written by John
Stuart Mill (then aged 17) on the difficult problems of
principle involved in measuring value has already been
referred to above,[37] and illustrates the quality of their
intellectual relationship. On the other hand, the younger
Mill also came under the influence of Jeremy Bentham (another
close friend of his father's); and this early contact, plus
the sheer breadth of his education, helped to ensure that
John Stuart would inherit an eighteenth century approach to
political economy as a branch of social philosophy.

J. S. Mill's definition of the scope and methodology of economics is contained in an essay 'On the Definition of Political
Economy' which was written in 1831 and subsequently published
among his *Essays on Some Unsettled Questions of Political Economy*
in 1844. He began by making the point that the definition of a
science (a branch of knowledge) depends (1) on what its practitioners actually do:

The definition of a science has almost invariably not preceded, but
followed, the creation of the science itself. Like the wall of a city it has
usually been erected, not to be a receptacle for such edifices as might
afterwards spring up, but to circumscribe an aggregation already in
existence;[38]

and (2) on their philosophical preconceptions:

The definition of a science must indeed be placed among that class of
truths which Dugald Stewart had in view, when he observed that the
first principles of all sciences belong to the philosophy of the human
mind...If we open any book, even mathematics or natural philosophy,
it is impossible not to be struck with the mistiness of what we find
represented as preliminary and fundamental notions, and the very in-
sufficient manner in which the propositions which are palmed on to us
as first principles seem to be made out, contrasted with the lucidity of
the explanations and the conclusiveness of the proofs as soon as the
writer enters upon the details of his subject.[39]

[36] J. S. Mill, *Autobiography* (1873), p. 54.
[37] See above, p. 68.
[38] J. S. Mill, *Essays on Economics and Society. Collected Works of J. S. Mill*, Vol.
IV, p. 310.
[39] *Ibid*, p. 311.

By the 1830s, however, political economy could be regarded as a relatively well-established science in the sense that its practitioners shared a common set of concepts (though they were not always able to agree on their definitions), common rules of procedure and scientific values (in spite of their methodological disputes) and were broadly agreed on what were the problems political economy ought to be trying to solve (though they might differ on the order of priorities to attach to the catalogue of problems). The proceedings of the Political Economy Club to which all leading nineteenth-century British economists and some of their continental contemporaries belonged at one time or another, bear witness to the existence of a community of economists and illustrate their common and disputed ground. J. S. Mill did not become a member himself until 1840 but he knew the leading economists of the day and was well-equipped to express their views. He made the distinction between a 'science' and an 'art', for example, in the same terms as Senior did.

Science is a collection of *truths*; art, a body of *rules*, or directions for conduct...Science takes cognizance of a *phenomenon*, and endeavours to discover its *law*; art proposes to itself an *end* and looks out for *means* to effect it. If, therefore, Political Economy be a science, it cannot be a collection of practical rules; though, unless it be altogether a useless science, practical rules must be capable of being founded on it.[40]

Having divided the whole of human knowledge into two divisions – physical science and moral or psychological science – Mill set economics firmly in the camp of the latter and further defined it as one of the social sciences. However, it is distinguished from the other social sciences in that it starts from the premise that men are motivated solely by the desire to acquire and consume wealth[41] 'and aims at showing what is the source of action into which mankind, living in a state of society, would be impelled, if that motive...were absolute ruler of all their actions' except to the extent that it is modified by what he called the 'two perpetually antagonizing principles to the desire of wealth' viz 'aversion to labour and desire of the present enjoyment of costly indulgences'. Not of course that economists really believe that men are solely motivated by economic aims 'but because this is the mode in which science must necessarily proceed. When an effect depends upon a concurrence of causes, those causes must be studied one at a time.'[42]

---

[40] *Ibid*, p. 312.   [41] Hence Mill's use of the abstraction the 'economic man'.
[42] *Ibid*, pp. 321–2.

On Mill's definition, political economy was characterised as essentially an abstract science, reasoning from 'assumptions not facts' analogously to other abstract sciences like geometry.

Geometry presupposes an arbitrary definition of a line 'that which has length but not breadth'. Just in the same manner does Political Economy presuppose an arbitrary definition of man, as a being who invariably does that by which he may obtain the greatest amount of necessaries, conveniences and luxuries, with the smallest quantity of labour and physical self-denial with which they can be obtained in the existing state of knowledge.[43]

It is worth noting that the same technique is common in some of the natural sciences using mathematical methods.[44]

Except to the extent that facts open to the observation or introspection of any educated observer provide the basis for some of the fundamental postulates of economics, empirical evidence was relevant to the science of political economy as defined by Mill only for the purpose of *verifying* theories. It played no part in the discovery of scientific truth in economics because experimentation is simply not possible and because real life is too complex to throw up 'general laws'. To those who advocated a historical method of approach he replied: 'History, by itself, if we knew it ten times better than we do, could...prove little or nothing: but the study of it is a corrective to the narrow and exclusive views which are apt to be engendered by observation on a more limited scale.'[45] And finally to the Malthusian objection to the Ricardian technique he answered: 'The error...does *not* arise from generalizing too extensively...but in making the wrong *kind* of assertion', i.e. in predicting

an actual result when he should only have predicted a *tendency* to that result – a power acting with a certain intensity in that direction...What is thought to be an exception to a principle is always some other and distinct principle cutting into the former; some other force which impinges against the first force and deflects it from its direction.[46]

[43] *Ibid*, p. 326.
[44] See E. Nagel, *The Structure of Science* (1961), p. 131: 'It is common, if not normal for a theory to be formulated in terms of ideal concepts such as the geometrical one of straight line and circle, or the more specifically physical ones of instantaneous velocity, perfect vacuum, infinitely slow expansion, perfect elasticity and the like. Although such "ideal" or "limiting" notions may be suggested by empirical subject matter, for the most part they are not descriptive of anything empirically observable.'
[45] J. S. Mill, *Essays on Economics and Society, op. cit.*, p. 333, n.
[46] *Ibid*, p. 337–8.

Nevertheless, although Mill shared Senior's view of the narrow limits of 'scientific political economy', and indeed originally propounded a somewhat more abstract definition of its methodology than Senior, his *Principles of Political Economy with Some of their Applications to Social Philosophy* (1848) was, as its title suggests, more in the tradition of Adam Smith than of Ricardo. He began writing it in 1845 – as a spare time activity when he was a full-time civil servant, and in competition with other writings – and finished it in under 2 years. It was a conscious attempt to produce a synthesis of classical economic theory, for a lay rather than a professional audience, to apply it to current socio-economic problems and to link it explicitly to its sociological–philosophical context of ideas.

The 'Wealth of Nations' is in many parts obsolete and in all, imperfect. Political Economy, properly so called, has grown up almost from infancy since the time of Adam Smith; and the philosophy of society, from which practically that eminent thinker never separated his more peculiar theme, though still at a very early stage of its progress, has advanced many steps beyond the point at which he left it. No attempt, however, has yet been made to combine his practical mode of treating his subject with the increased knowledge since acquired of its theory, or to exhibit the economical phenomena of society in the relation in which they stand to the best social ideas of the present time, as he did, with such admirable success, in reference to the philosophy of his century.[47]

This was the lacuna which Mill set out to fill in his *Principles*.

In spite of (perhaps because of) its long-standing success as a textbook Mill's *Principles* has had a bad press from the economics profession generally. Much has been written about the inconsistencies and the lack of rigour in his argument some of which can be traced back to his persistent effort to reconcile conflicting or disparate theories. The section on 'The Noxious Influence of Authority' with which Jevons concluded his *Theory of Political Economy* (1871) was clearly aimed at Mill: 'I protest against deference for any man, whether John Stuart Mill, or Adam Smith, or Aristotle being allowed to check inquiry. Our science has become too much a stagnant one, in which opinions rather than experience and reason are appealed to.'[48] And in similar vein Foxwell complained that his influence was 'distinctly

---

[47] Preface to J. S. Mill, *Principles of Political Economy*, p. xcii.
[48] W. S. Jevons, *Theory of Political Economy* (1871), ed. R. D. Collison Black (1970), p. 261.

soporific'. Marx disliked him heartily.[49] Later economists have been less openly hostile or more sympathetic, but they seem to feel a need to explain away the success of the *Principles*.[50]

The fact is that the community of professional economists was no more ready to grapple with the wider social and philosophical issues raised by Mill in what he saw to be a natural development of the Ricardian paradigm than to stomach Marx's theoretical reformulation of it. There were some authorities who (in more Malthusian tradition) were attracted by a historicist methodology of the kind currently fashionable in Germany (e.g. Ashley, Cliffe Leslie and Ingram) and the historical school of economists enjoyed a considerable prestige in the later decades of the nineteenth century. But the mainstream theorists chose to pursue the narrower path opened up by Ricardo, to follow the goal of logical consistency, to sharpen their mathematical tools and to limit their attention (in their professional, or as they preferred to call it 'scientific', capacity) to the kind of economic problems that were soluble in these terms. In so doing, however, they revolutionised the classical methodology.

J. S. Mill was the last in the line of major English philosopher–economists in the tradition of Adam Smith, economists for whom economics was merely one of the moral sciences (though the most highly developed of the social sciences) and only part of the wider field of knowledge over which they felt themselves competent to practice.[51] He prefaced his *Principles* with the declaration that 'for practical purposes Political Economy is inseparably intertwined with other branches of social philosophy. Except on matters of mere detail, there are perhaps no practical questions, even among those which approach nearest to the character of purely economical questions, which admit of being decided on economical premises alone.'[52] When he distinguished the 'art' of economics from the 'science' and insisted that economics was an

[49] 'Whenever Marx mentions Mill's name (which does not happen very frequently) he never forgets to add some derogatory comment.' Bela Balassa, 'Karl Marx and John Stuart Mill', *Weltwirtschaftsliches Archiv* (1959), p. 117.

[50] See e.g. J. Viner, *The Long View and the Short*, p. 329; J. Schumpeter, *History of Economic Analysis*, p. 380; L. Robbins, *Evolution of Modern Economic Theory*, pp. 167–8.

[51] Until Marshall persuaded the University of Cambridge to establish a separate Economics Tripos in the early 1900s, political economy was merely one option in the Moral Sciences Tripos. When Jevons was appointed Professor at Manchester in 1866 it was as Professor of Logic and Political Economy.

[52] Mill, *Principles*, *op. cit.*, p. xci.

abstract system of *a priori* reasoning based on the hypothetical assumption of an 'economic man' he did not intend either to confine his own studies to economic problems within these narrow limits, or to imply that the 'scientific' problems of political economy were any more prestigious than its normative or prescriptive aspects. However, even those classical (and neo-classical) economists who did not share Mill's range of scholarship and who regarded themselves as professional economists in the narrowest contemporary sense of that term would have taken it for granted that the normative and prescriptive aspects of the subject were as much (for some more so) their business as the abstract, 'pure' or 'scientific' aspects. It was *theoretical* economics that was progressively to narrow its scope in the neo-classical era.

FURTHER READING

Primary literature

T. R. Malthus, *Principles of Political Economy*, reprinted with Ricardo's Notes, Vol. II of *Works and Correspondence of David Ricardo*, ed. Piero Sraffa (1951).

J. S. Mill, 'On the Definition of Political Economy', *Essays on Economics and Society*, Vol. I of *Collected Works of J. S. Mill*, Toronto edition (1967).

David Ricardo, *Principles of Political Economy and Taxation, op. cit.*

Nassau Senior, *Principles of Political Economy with some of their Applications to Social Philosophy* (1848).

Secondary literature

M. Blaug, *Ricardian Economics: A Historical Study* (1958).

Marian Bowley, *Nassau Senior and Classical Economics* (1937).

A. W. Coats, 'The Role of Authority in the Development of British Economics', *Journal of Law and Economics* (1964).

F. W. Fetter, 'The Rise and Decline of Ricardian Economics', *History of Political Economy* (1969).

J. M. Keynes, 'Thomas Robert Malthus', in *Essays in Biography*, reprinted for the Royal Economic Society, Vol. x, *Collected Writings of John Maynard Keynes* (1972).

N. B. de Marchi, 'The Empirical Content and Longevity of Ricardian Economics', *Economica* (1970).

D. P. O'Brien, *The Classical Economists* (1975).

Alan Ryan, *J. S. Mill* (1975).

Pedro Schwartz, *The New Political Economy of J. S. Mill* (1972).

7

THE MARGINAL REVOLUTION AND THE NEO-CLASSICAL TRIUMPH

It is generally accepted that the British classical economists of the first half of the nineteenth century constituted an identifiable school of economic thought. They shared a distinctive framework of economic ideas, shaped by a particular set of axioms and theories and generally characterised by a strong bias towards economic policies favouring economic individualism and laissez-faire. Whether this school of thought constituted a 'scientific community' in the sense that T. S. Kuhn uses the term in his analysis of the structure of scientific revolutions or whether it is better described as a 'pre-paradigm school' may be open to question. In Kuhn's view a scientific community consists of the practitioners of a scientific specialty who share a common paradigm. 'To an extent unparalleled in most other fields they have undergone similar educations and professional initiations; in the process they have absorbed the same technical literature and drawn many of the same lessons from it. Usually the boundaries of that standard literature mark the limit of a scientific subject matter.'[1]

Certainly nineteenth-century economists drew their basic assumptions and techniques from the same textual sources – Adam Smith, David Ricardo, Nassau Senior and John Stuart Mill being the main links in a clearly perceptible continuity of thought – though there was as yet no *formally* recognised education as an economist. The doubt, however, is not whether the nineteenth-century community of economists shared 'similar educations and professional initiations' but whether they were the practitioners of a *scientific* specialty. The doubt remains in the twentieth century, in spite of the fact that economists rarely now debate the question 'is economics a science?' which typically provided the opening lecture of university courses in economic theory as

[1] T. S. Kuhn, *The Structure of Scientific Revolutions* (1969), p. 177.

recently as the 1930s. The basic problem of identifying the scientific community of economists is that economics was (is) not the exclusive preserve of a group of academic theorists and empirical research workers (amateur or professional) but the active concern of a heterogeneous collection of journalists, bankers, civil servants, politicians and others whose attempts at the objective explanation and/or prediction of economic behaviour give them as much claim to form part of the intellectual community of economists as the academics. An intellectual or scientific revolution in economics involves converting this wider group to the new orthodoxy as well as the academic teachers and the researchers labouring under their supervision. This indeed is what is implicit in the term, the marginal revolution, applied by historians of economic thought to the methodological changes that took place in orthodox economics in the fourth quarter of the nineteenth century.

The 1850s and the 1860s were a period of relative prosperity for the British economy and of relative consensus (or complacency) in British economic thought. Although the Ricardian theories of value and distribution had come under influential attack, Ricardo's analysis of the benefits of international trade, his views on monetary policy and the ideological bias in favour of an individualist free market economy which he had inherited from Adam Smith still dominated orthodox economic thinking. The Political Economy Club had begun debating questions which began 'Was Ricardo right...?' within a few years after the master's death, but the leading economists – Nassau Senior, John Stuart Mill and even Karl Marx – accepted his original 'authority' while often dissenting from him in detail and sometimes quite extensively. With hindsight one can perceive the widening cracks in the doctrinal facade of classical political economy. Nassau Senior had already brought the notion of utility squarely back into his theory of value in the 1840s. Stanley Jevons presented his 'Brief Account of a General Mathematical Theory of Political Economy' to the British Association for the Advancement of Science in 1862. But little notice was taken of either of these shifts of emphasis away from an exclusively cost-of-production theory of value, nor indeed of the work of Gossen the German theorist who had published in 1854 a book which elaborated two basic laws – (1) the principle of diminishing utility; and (2) maximisation of satisfactions as the aim of all human conduct – and formulated them in full geometrical and algebraic terms.

It seems as though the time had to be ripe for the acceptance of a new paradigm and when the time was ripe it emerged independently in several places at once. In 1871 Jevons published his *Theory of Political Economy* which was an attempt to produce an explicitly mathematical theory of economic science inspired by Bentham's felicific calculus.[2] In the same year the Austrian economist Menger produced his *Principles of Economics* also elaborating a subjective theory of value. Like Jevons, Menger made his theory of value hinge on marginal utility as the determinant of the ratios at which goods were exchanged, though he was no mathematician and relied on a careful precise verbal logic. Finally, in 1874, again independently, the French economist Walras published the first part of his *Elements of Pure Economics* which presented marginal utility analysis in formal mathematical terms as a set of demand and supply functions with a determinate equilibrium: three years later he published the second part of this work – a theory of production which applied the same techniques of general equilibrium analysis to the problem of pricing factors of production. Meanwhile in Cambridge, Alfred Marshall who was then teaching political economy to Cambridge students reading for the Moral Sciences Tripos in the 1870s had already begun to graft marginal utility analysis on to the Ricardian system.

The so-called marginal revolution involved a wide-ranging transformation of the characteristic methodology of analytical economics by means of what was essentially a mathematical tool derived from the calculus. 'The Theory of the Economy thus treated' wrote Jevons in the Preface to the first edition of his *Theory of Political Economy*

presents a close analogy to the science of Statical Mechanics, and the Laws of exchange are found to resemble the Laws of Equilibrium of a lever as determined by the principle of virtual velocities. The nature of Wealth and Value is explained by the consideration of indefinitely small amounts of pleasure and pain, just as the Theory of Statics is made to rest upon the equality of indefinitely small amounts of energy.[3]

For Walras also the conscious analogy with physical science and the central concept of equilibrium were essential features of a

---

[2] R. D. C. Black, 'Jevons, Marginalism and Manchester', *Manchester School* (March 1972), p. 7, describes it as 'a pure theory of economic science with the aid of the differential calculus of De Morgan and the felicific calculus of Bentham'.

[3] W. S. Jevons, *Theory of Political Economy* (1871), 4th edn, 1911, p. vii.

new kind of methodology which helped to determine not only the techniques of analysis appropriate to economic theory but also, in the end, the kind of questions on which the theorist normally focused. He defined pure economics (i.e. theoretical economics as distinguished from applied economics or social economics) as an ideologically neutral, 'physico-mathematical' science primarily concerned with the 'theory of the determination of prices under a hypothetical regime of perfectly free competition'.[4] He carried the marginal apparatus to its logical–mathematical conclusions by applying it to markets in general – not merely to consumer behaviour – thus linking the markets in commodities with the factor of production markets in a mutually dependent system of equations relating prices and quantities. His original contribution was to demonstrate mathematically the conditions for general equilibrium of the market economy. Menger too, though he rejected the artificial construct of a unique and determinate market equilibrium and was concerned primarily with consumer goods markets, was also trying to evolve a *general* economic theory based on marginal analysis and focused on the problems of price determination in competitive markets.

It is easy to over-dramatise the concept of a 'marginal revolution' in economic theory by attributing it primarily to three innovative thinkers, each of whom exploded independently into print at roughly the same time (early 1870s) and by dating from this 'multiple discovery' a transformation in the 'entire constellation of beliefs, values, techniques and so on, shared by the members' of the scientific community of economists.[5] Those who interpret the marginal revolution of the 1870s as a paradigm change in this sweeping sense usually fall into one of two schools of thought. Either they believe that the paradigm-shift represented a disastrous evasion of the real problems facing economists – a retreat from socially 'relevant' political economy into sterile formalism. Or they believe that it was the crucial stage in the creation of a genuinely scientific unified theory of economic behaviour which became for the first time a testable theory – not only logically verifiable in the most rigorous mathematical sense of the term but also empirically testable. Both

[4] L. Walras, *Elements of Pure Economics*, translated by W. Jaffé (London 1954), p. 40.

[5] See T. S. Kuhn, *op. cit.* (1969), p. 175.

schools of thought may be fortified in their convictions by con-
trasting ideological preconceptions which they tend to project
freely on to the agents in the 'multiple discovery' and, even more
freely, on to their disciples.

On the face of it, the marginal revolution in economics fits
rather uneasily into the grand role of a total *Gestalt* shift. For one
thing the three agents in the so-called revolution – Jevons, Walras
and Menger – did not share the same constellation of beliefs,
values, techniques etc. Menger in particular stood apart from the
other two. It is debatable indeed whether Menger and his
followers were even marginalists in the sense in which this term
is generally applied to Jevons, Walras and the neo-classical school
generally.[6] For another thing their direct influence on the subsequent development of orthodox economists' views on the scope
and methodology of economics was clearly rather limited. Jevons
died before he was 50, he was better known to his contemporaries
as an applied economist than as a theorist and his *Theory of
Political Economy* never became as widely accepted as a text as did
either Mill's *Principles* or Marshall's *Principles*. Walras proved too
mathematical to be accessible to the majority of economic
theorists until relatively recent times. His *Elements* did not even
get into an English translation until 1954. Finally and in the third
place it took more than twenty years for the methodological
innovations associated with the marginal revolution to make
sufficient impression on the current economic orthodoxy to justify the view that a substantive new paradigm was taking over.

On the other hand, the reality of a revolution does not depend
on all its agents being cast in the same mould – the mould being
that to which the heirs of the revolution subscribe – and it
remains true that the work of Jevons, Walras and Menger
marked the beginnings of a major change in economists' views on
the scope and methodology of their discipline. The change can
plausibly be categorised as a paradigm-shift in the narrower
sense of Kuhn's concept, i.e. as a pervasive change in the typical
criteria, exemplars and procedural rules accepted as normal by
professional economists, which brought with it new ways of

---

[6] Erich Streissler, 'To what extent was the Austrian School marginalist', in
Black, Coats and Goodwin, *op. cit.*, pp. 160–75. Cf. also Blaug in the same sym-
posium, p. 9: 'Whichever version we adopt [of the new paradigm implicit in the
"marginal revolution"], it is difficult to sustain the thesis that Jevons, Menger
and Walras were really occupied with the same paradigm.'

formulating, ranking and tackling the critical unsolved problems on the academic research agenda. The key to the paradigm-shift thus interpreted was the application of marginal analysis.

The characteristic techniques of marginal analysis were applied first to value theory in terms of the concept of utility, a concept with which the classical economists were thoroughly familiar, but which, because they had not yet devised a way of quantifying it, they had tended to leave out of their theories of value and exchange. It was then found applicable to theories of production and distribution as well as to theories of value and exchange and a wide area of theoretical economics was thus brought within its range. In essence, as Boulding has pointed out, the marginal analysis was no more than a 'detailed spelling out of the theory of maximisation – that is the theory that the optimum position of the variables of any economic organisation is that given by the maximum position of that variable which measures desirability or preference',[7] i.e. utility or output.

The marginal revolution had significant implications for both the scope and methodology of orthodox economic theory. For in providing the theorist with a convenient set of analytical tools that were easily and effectively applied over a wide range of uses it changed the problem orientation of economic orthodoxy and (in the process though not necessarily by design) associated with that orthodoxy significant philosophical and ideological tendencies. Briefly, the marginal analysis is designed to find the most efficient allocation of competing resources, of scarce means with alternative ends. At the optimum position marginal values are equalised, i.e. the gains to be derived from putting a unit of a resource to one use exactly equal the losses involved in withdrawing it from another. This can be applied right across the board – to the allocation of a fixed income among a range of consumer goods, or of a fixed outlay among a set of factors of production, or of time between work and leisure. Wherever diminishing returns are obtainable from putting a given unit of income or time or productive resources to a particular use the optimum result is obtained when values are equalised at the margin. Within the conventional assumptions of the marginal analysis it can be logically shown that perfect competition leads to equimarginal allocation of expenditures and resources.

Armed with this technique the neo-classical economists were

7 K. Boulding, *The Skills of the Economist*, p. 34.

able to produce a logically consistent explanation of the determination of commodity and factor prices in a market system and to define the conditions for maximising consumer satisfactions. They were even capable in principle of quantifying inputs and outputs into the economy at micro and macro levels, for by defining value as equivalent to price in a perfectly competitive market they could measure the value of consumers' satisfactions and the marginal product of labour or capital in objective additive terms. The analytical power and range of the new technique, the plausible simplicity of its basic assumption – that consumers and producers would naturally behave so as to maximise their satisfactions or profits in a competitive market – was immensely attractive to students of 'pure' economics, i.e. to the academic theorists who were more dedicated to scientific truth, defined as abstract theory, than to political programmes. Not surprisingly then, the half century before the First World War, when the neo-classical orthodoxy – the heir to the marginal revolution – was effectively established in Britain and the USA, was also the period when the leaders in the discipline tended more often to be academics than otherwise.[8]

In spite of their mathematical origins the marginal techniques developed in this period were fully accessible to non-numerate economists; but they did lend themselves readily to mathematical expression and abstraction – a quality that then (as now) helped to attract to the profession distinguished graduates in mathematics who went on to make major contributions to economic theory.[9] As economics became more professionalised and more academic, its innovating theorists tended more and more to focus on abstract theoretical problems and to abstract their models from the real world. The focus of the marginal analysis was the market and the neo-classical theorists accordingly narrowed the scope of their subject matter so as to be almost exclusively confined to a study of market processes. Consequently, although individual neo-classical theorists may have been, and some certainly were, as strongly activated by political and social objectives as any of their predecessors among the classical economists, they

[8] See George J. Stigler, 'The adoption of the marginal utility theory', in Black, Coats and Goodwin, *op. cit.*, for evidence to support the hypothesis that 'Economics became primarily an academic discipline in the last decades of the nineteenth century'.

[9] Neither Marshall nor Keynes had formal academic qualifications in economics. Both were Cambridge Wranglers, i.e. first class honours graduates in Mathematics.

concentrated most of their attention *qua* economists on abstract
theoretical issues which had no immediate connection with the
urgent contemporary questions of practical policy.

Among the reasons which Kuhn in his study of scientific
revolutions in the natural sciences has identified as typically
important in inducing a scientific community to reject one disciplinary matrix in favour of another are: (i) the emergence of
a 'methodological crisis' due to the failure of the current
orthodoxy to deal effectively with problems that have come to
be regarded as crucially important; (ii) the ability of the new
paradigm to resolve the problems that led its predecessor into
crisis; and (iii) its superior quantitative precision. Reference has
already been made to the relatively precise mathematical
techniques and (in principle) quantifiable concepts associated
with the new marginal analysis and in the following Chapters we
shall consider some of the problems that the neo-classical
economists could be said to have solved more effectively than
their classical predecessors.

As for the incidence of 'methodological crisis', there is plenty
of evidence for a sharpening of the debate on the scope and
methodology of mainstream economics in the 1870s and 1880s.
Jevons referred in his *Theory of Political Economy* to 'the mono-
tonous repetition of current questionable doctrines' and in an
article published in 1876 lamented that 'one hundred years after
the first publication of the *Wealth of Nations* we find the state of
the science to be almost chaotic. There is certainly less agreement
now about what political economy is than there was 30 or 50 years
ago'.[10] A year later, in 1877, the Professor of Political Economy
at Oxford, Bonamy Price, was so disenchanted by the scientific
pretensions of the discipline that he proposed dropping its
annual contribution to the British Association for the Advancement of Science.[11] No doubt it is arguable that the differences
between the supporters of competing paradigms (e.g. the historicists and the marginalists) were similar to the earlier differences
between Malthus and Ricardo or between Senior and McCulloch.
But they were on a different scale, the area over which the
protagonists would admit agreement was generally narrower, the
loss of professional prestige was greater and the resolution of

[10] W. S. Jevons, 'The Future of Political Economy', *Fortnightly Review* (1876),
p. 620.
[11] A. W. Coats, 'The Historicist Reaction in English Political Economy
1870–90', *Economica* (1954).

the conflict had wider implications for the orthodox view of the methodology and scope of economic science.

One might, of course, expect that methodological crises – divisive methodological controversies polarising opinion among the leading practitioners in the discipline – would be a frequent occurrence for economics. In the changing social, institutional and economic context in which the policy problems arise, the need for revolutionary new ways of interpreting and analysing reality must appear more often than in the natural sciences simply because the shape and content of the economic policy problems that successive generations of policy makers regard as fundamental change constantly. It is surprising indeed, and may reflect the strength of ideological constraints on social scientists' freedom of intellectual manoeuvre, that revolutions in the disciplinary matrix of economic thinking do not take place more often than they apparently do.

In the event, the fact that the neo-classical economists of the period up to 1914 were able to retain unimpaired the classical bias towards economic individualism and laissez-faire, and the ideological overtones which this gave to the policy conclusions deducible from their analyses, may have had more to do with the success of the neo-classical paradigm than its problem-solving qualities. The problems of value and distribution which had preoccupied the Ricardians were solved, or, more accurately, one might say swept under the carpet, by simple process of definition. The problems of growth were outside the effective range of marginal analysis and further consideration of them was consciously postponed.[12] At the same time, the very jargon of pure economic theory, e.g. the notions of 'rationality', or 'perfect' competition, of an 'optimum' allocation of resources, helped to accentuate its ideological overtones and to lend ostensible 'scientific' support to a political *status quo* which depended on accepting a philosophy of economic individualism and harmony.

It took a couple of decades or so before the neo-classical

---

[12] See e.g. Jevons, in the preface to the first edition of his *Theory, op. cit.*, p. 44: 'But I believe that dynamical branches of the Science of Economy may remain to be developed, on the consideration of which I have not at all entered.' Marshall was possibly more far-sighted in envisaging a theory of economic growth which would escape from the more static analogies of equilibrium theory, e.g. in an article on 'Distribution and exchange', *Economic Journal* (March 1898), p. 43: 'And therefore in the later stages of economics when we are approaching more nearly to the conditions of life, biological analogies are to be preferred to mechanical, other things being equal.'

paradigm began to supplant its classical predecessor in the textbooks and so to overcome the challenge of its chief contemporary
rivals – the historicists. The new leader however was not Stanley
Jevons, who had launched the first successful attack in England
with his *Theory of Political Economy* (1871), but Alfred Marshall.
Marshall did not publish his *Principles of Economics*, the bible of
the English neo-classical school, until 1890; but by then he had
been teaching economics for twenty years in Cambridge, Bristol
and Oxford, and he had indoctrinated the inhabitants of half the
economic chairs in England.[13] The formal and explicit definition
of the new orthodoxy's position with regard to the methodology
and scope of the discipline appeared in John Neville Keynes'
Scope and Method of Political Economy[14] which was published,
appropriately enough, in the same year as Marshall's *Principles*.
Neville Keynes was one of Marshall's earliest pupils and a col-
league at Cambridge: he was also the father of John Maynard.

The tone of J. N. Keynes' methodological treatise reflected the
success of the revolution, it was the tone of a peacemaker rather
than a disputant, judicious rather than declamatory, expository
rather than argumentative. 'I have endeavoured' he wrote in the
Preface

to avoid the tone of a partisan and have sought in the treatment of
disputed questions to represent both sides without prejudice. Whilst
making no attempt to bring about a complete reconciliation between
opposing views, I have been able to show that the nature of the opposition between them has sometimes been misunderstood and its extent
consequently exaggerated.[15]

Neville Keynes distinguished three concepts of political economy in order to bring into focus the interpretation which he
clearly regarded a fundamental:
(1) a positive science, i.e. 'a body of systematized knowledge'
   ...'concerned purely with that *is*'...'the whole province of
   which is to establish economic laws or uniformities'. This is
   what he equated unequivocally to 'economic science'.[16]

---

[13] Keynes, in his Memoir on Marshall published in the 1924 *Economic Journal*,
quoted a newspaper report on Marshall to the effect that: 'half the economic
chairs in England are occupied by his pupils and the share taken by them in
general economic instruction in England is even higher than this'.
[14] J. N. Keynes, *Scope and Method of Political Economy*, went through four
editions: 1890, 1897, 1907 and 1917 and was reprinted in 1930 as a classic. The
references which follow are to the 1930 reprint.
[15] *Ibid*, p. vi.
[16] J. N. Keynes, *op. cit.*, p. 53, n.

(2) a normative or regulative science: 'a body of systematized knowledge relating to criteria of what ought to be and concerned therefore with the ideal as distinguished from the actual'.

(3) 'an *art*, a system of rules for the attainment of a given end'.

He did not have a great deal to say about (2) which seems to have been defined largely to distinguish (and exclude it explicitly from) positive economics: though it is significant that he was prepared to call it a 'science'. An appendix on (3) effectively dismissed this concept from the discipline with the conclusion that 'a definitive art of political economy, which attempts to lay down absolute rules for the regulation of human conduct will have vaguely defined limits and *be largely non-economic in character*'[17] (my italics).

Thus, while deliberately refraining from drawing exclusive boundaries and while freely admitting that political economy shades off into other social sciences and draws heavily on the moral sciences, Neville Keynes stressed again and again the need to distinguish *sharply* between what he called positive economics, i.e. economic science, and all other conceivable aspects of political economy. It was positive economics that he regarded as the prime function of the professional economist, the logical starting point and essential prerequisite for any normative or policy-making considerations or for any related empirical enquiry (such as economic history). It was only behind the barrier of abstract and restrictive assumptions which marked off positive economics that the economist could hope to conduct precise, rigorous, analysis and come up with universal, (in principle) quantifiable laws. Outside its well-defined limits economic laws turned into tendencies and non-economic factors could be at least as important as economic factors in determining actual economic behaviour. In effect, then, the historical school was politely relegated to a sort of interdisciplinary no-man's-land, as being more concerned with ethics and policy precepts (i.e. with the second and third concepts of political economy) than with pure, universally valid (rather than historically relative) economic science.[18]

The other recurrent methodological controversy which Neville

[17] *Ibid*, p. 82.
[18] *Ibid*, p. 26: 'if it be granted that political economy is directly concerned with what ought to be then most of the rest may be said logically to follow'; 'the rest' in this context being the historical school's insistence on realism, historical method, social and ethical standpoints, relativity of economic doctrine, etc.

Keynes effectively disposed of was the argument about whether inductive or deductive techniques were appropriate to political economy: this was an issue which had greatly exercised nineteenth-century economists who were anxious to establish the scientific credentials of their discipline, and its re-emergence could perhaps be regarded as evidence of a sharpening of the sense of professional insecurity which Kuhn finds characteristic of periods of methodological crisis. It was then generally accepted that the natural sciences relied largely on inductive techniques and the historicists (claiming their authority from Bacon) took an extreme position in insisting that economic laws could achieve scientific validity only to the extent that they were originally derived from, as well as verified by, empirical observation. This was a reaction against the deductive method of the Ricardians who had deliberately reasoned *a priori* rather than *a posteriori* in basing their theory on a handful of assumptions about the propensities guiding human behaviour – assumptions verified, if at all, only by introspection.[19]

Characteristically Neville Keynes wrapped up this controversy by seeing room for both inductive and deductive techniques in economic science. He categorised it as a quantitative science, heavily dependent on mathematical methods in its deductive (abstract) methods and on statistical methods in its inductive (concrete) aspects. However, although agreeing in principle with the view that the theorist should base his reasoning on realistic principles[20] he effectively gave equal weight to 'generality and simplicity' as criteria for the economist's choice of assumptions. In effect, he claimed deductive theory and objective positive economics as the heart and core of the *scientific* discipline of economics, while fully recognising the appropriateness of testing theory against historical fact and of developing the kind of theory which could be applied to the solution of current policy problems.

Finally, Neville Keynes dealt with the ideological issues that

---

[19] See, for example, J. S. Mill 'On the Definition of Political Economy' (written in 1831), in Vol. I of the *Collected Works of J. S. Mill* (Toronto edition), p. 326: 'Political Economy therefore reasons from *assumed* premises which might be wholly without foundation in fact and which are not pretended to be universally in accordance with it.'

[20] E.g. he quotes (*op. cit.*, p. 231) with approval Bagehot's assertion that 'Nothing but unreality can come of political economy till we know when and how far its first assertions are true in matter of fact and when and how far they are not.'

were involved in the methodological debate by absolving classical and neo-classical economic theory from ideological bias. The classical economists had based their normative judgments on traditional English philosophical foundations which embodied a mixture of eighteenth-century natural law doctrine and Benthamite utilitarianism. They had been totally frank about their ideological commitment to laissez-faire. Keynes had noted that 'independently of differences ĩn regard to the scope and method of political economy, the dominant German school [i.e. the historicists] is distinguished from the older English economists by a difference of attitude towards *laisser faire* and government interference'[21] However, he referred back to methodological pronouncements of the classical school economists to demonstrate that they too regarded political economy as 'a science, not an art or a department of ethical enquiry. It is described as standing neutral between competing social sciences. It furnishes information as to the probable consequences of given lines of action, but it does not itself pass moral judgments, or pronounce what ought or ought not to be.'[22] And in an Appendix to this chapter Neville Keynes went on to justify the characteristic classical assumption of laissez-faire on non-ideological grounds, pointing out that even among English economists their traditional adherence to laissez-faire was subject to numerous qualifications and exceptions and giving two ostensibly 'value-free' reasons for the free-competition assumption: (a) because free competition and the absence of government interference represented what was theoretically the 'simplest' case; and (b) because 'in modern economic societies *laisser faire* has been as a matter of fact the general rule'. Nevertheless he went on to claim ideological neutrality for positive economics, insisting that 'neither *laisser faire* nor any other maxim of conduct can form an integral portion of its teaching'. This claim to ideological neutrality came to constitute one of the main characteristics of the neo-classical school.

One of the characteristics that a successful new orthodoxy might reasonably be expected to exhibit is a greater measure of success with the problems that its predecessor had stumbled over.[23] However, it is not easy to identify the specific problems

[21] J. N. Keynes, *op. cit.*, p. 25.　　　　　　　　[22] *Ibid*, p. 13.
[23] Cf. Kuhn, *op. cit.*, p. 153: 'Probably the single most prevalent claim advanced by the proponents of a new paradigm is that they can solve the problems that have led the old one to a crisis.'

that may have precipitated a methodological crisis – if only because the failures of the old orthodoxy tend to have a cumulative effect in discouraging its practitioners. More important still for economics is that its practitioners are never the exclusive judges of its success, and when economists fall into popular disrepute for having failed to come up with patently useful policy prescriptions, which the narrower scientific community would admit to be outside its professional competence, the resulting sense of professional insecurity may sow its own seeds of methodological doubt.

The puzzle that persistently teased the classical economists was of course the problem of value. Adam Smith found it necessary to devote Chapters v–vii of the first Book in his *Wealth of Nations* to 'the principles which regulate the exchangeable value of commodities'. Ricardo had to produce a theory of value before he could begin to grapple with his target problem of the distribution of incomes; and as we have seen, he was still struggling with value theory when he died. True J. S. Mill found the theory of the subject 'complete'.[24] But his readers might have been forgiven for remaining unconvinced by this assertion for Mill himself both affirmed and rejected Ricardo's labour theory of value and referred to the effects of demand and supply without making it at all clear how these might interact to *determine* actual value.[25]

One way in which the leaders of an intellectual revolution can establish their position, however, is to reformulate the problems troubling the traditional orthodoxy and provide answers to what are really a different and apparently more relevant set of questions. The marginal revolution drew its inspiration from mathematical rather than philosophical techniques of analysis and it had the effect of diverting the attention of economists from their search for the meaning of value – a search which had deep philosophical implications – and to focus instead on the determinants of market price. Jevons, for example, set *intrinsic value*

---

[24] See, e.g. the passage quoted on p. 68 above.

[25] *Ibid*, p. 477: 'The value of commodities...depends principally...upon the quality of labour required for their production'; p. 479: 'the value of a commodity is not the name of an inherent and substantive equality of the thing itself, but means the quantity of other things which can be obtained in exchange for it'; and on p. 471: 'The value at any particular time is the result of supply and demand; and is always that which is necessary to create a market for the existing supply.'

aside as a nonentity: 'the word value, so far as it can be correctly used merely expressed *the circumstances of its exchanging in a certain ratio for some other substance*', and focused instead on the concept of utility 'as the subject-matter of economics'.[26] He thus went on to develop a theory of exchange rather than of value. He adopted a mathematical tool – the differential calculus – to analyse the behaviour of the utility-maximising individual and was inspired by mechanical analogies in developing his concepts. With these analogies in mind he explicitly set out to develop a theory of political economy which used the concepts and analytical techniques of 'the science of statical mechanics.'[27]

Jevons had hit on the crucial innovation contained in the 'marginal revolution' by demonstrating that it was the marginal increment of utility on which exchange-value or price depended, but it was Alfred Marshall who, by jettisoning Jevons' philosophical hedonism and by bringing supply as well as demand into the equation of price, fathered the neo-classical paradigm. The Marshallian theory of value is discussed below in Chapter 8. For the moment what needs to be said is that the mature neo-classical school replaced the fragmented, often vaguely-defined, philosophically-oriented analysis of the classical school with an integrated theory of value-in-use and value-in-exchange in which market price was mathematically determined by the intersection of the schedules of supply and demand. The framework was set out in Book v of Marshall's *Principles* the section which he regarded, with reason, as containing the real nub of his own special contribution to economic theory.[28]

In the event, the neo-classical theory of value (really a theory of market prices more than anything that the classical economists would have defined as value) became more than a theory of price, it became a theory of the allocation of scarce resources to specific uses under the dual incentives of utility maximisation for the consumer and profit maximisation for the producer, using con-

[26] W. S. Jevons, *Theory of Political Economy*, Penguin edn ed. R. D. Collison Black (1970), p. 127 (Jevons' italics). See also W. S. Jevons, *Principles of Economics*, ed. H. Higgs (1905), p. 49.
[27] See the quotation on p. 95 above.
[28] See his introduction to the second edition of his *Principles of Economics*; 'To myself personally, the chief interest of the Volume centres on Book v: it contains more of my life's work than any other part: and it is here more than anywhere else that I have tried to deal with *the unsettled questions of the science*' (my italics).

cepts, criteria and techniques of analysis that could be applied analogously throughout the economic system. In the Marshallian system then, to quote one of its later disciples:

> The principle of mutual determination everywhere supersedes the idea of a single determinant or a one-way chain of causes. The conditions of demand are everywhere given equal status with those of supply. The determination of 'market' values and 'natural' value, of value under monopoly and value under competition, of value under constant and under diminishing returns, of rent, wages and profit, is no longer seen as a series of separate problems, sharply distinguished from each other and each with a separate 'law' appropriate to itself – all are subsumed under the single unifying idea of the balance at the margin, a balance of small increments of receipts and outgoings, payments and costs, differing in its manifestations and giving different results in different cases, but common to them all, with the principle of substitution acting everywhere as a master-key. All this is entirely foreign to Ricardo's manner of thinking and to Mill's.[29]

The explicitly mathematical orientation of the new school and its claims to quantitative precision may indeed have contributed to its success not only directly but by adding to its aesthetic qualities – its greater generality, for example, and the fact that the same tools and concepts could be applied over virtually the whole range of the problems on which the neo-classical economists elected to concentrate, viz the problems associated with the allocation of scarce resources to given ends. Finally it can be said that the neo-classical approach illuminated an important aspect of the economic process which had only dimly been perceived before. By demonstrating mathematically the total interdependence of the economic system – the fact that everything depends on everything else – the new school revealed new regularities and interconnections and suggested new and more fruitful techniques of analysis. Even for the non-mathematical economist there was a special attraction in its unrivalled effectiveness as a technique of analysis over an important, if restricted, range of economic problems. Efficient economic decision making (at the macro or micro level) depends to a considerable extent on a clarification of the relationship between alternative ends and scarce means. The notion of an integrated system in which changes in prices and quantities, in demand and supply, could be interpreted as a system of opposing forces and handled with the techniques of static mechanics provided a remarkably

---

[29] G. F. Shove, 'Marshall's *Principles* in Economic Theory', *Economic Journal* (1942), p. 303.

effective technique of analysis and generated a whole range of fruitful though simple tools (e.g. the concept of elasticity) which enabled the academic conceptual apparatus to be put to direct practical use in sorting out the crucial issues involved in many real-world policy problems.

There is thus no shortage of explanations for the attraction of the marginal techniques of analysis which distinguished the neo-classical school that emerged from the marginal revolution and began to dominate mainstream economic thought in the later decades of the nineteenth century. It effectively bypassed the problem of value which had most persistently bogged down its predecessor; it offered superior quantitative precision to either the classical or the historicist system of thought; it revealed more effectively than either alternative the phenomenon of economic interdependence; it had special qualities of generality and simplicity which were peculiarly satisfying to the more mathematically minded economist; and it opened up new analytical horizons for even the mathematically untrained economist with an interest in the public policy problems of resource allocation. There are interesting analogies here with the reasons suggested by Kuhn as being commonly responsible for the success of a new paradigm in the natural sciences.

But the problems faced by the social sciences have intimate political affiliations to a degree that is not true of the natural sciences and there is another factor to be taken into account in evaluating a new paradigm – its ideological implications. It may be that this was more important than any other single factor in accounting for the neo-classical triumph. For although the new disciplinary matrix had special attractions for the mathematical economists, the majority of practising economists were more at home in a philosophical or logical or historical than in a mathematical framework of analysis. Moreover the new matrix was a particularly powerful medium only in relation to one set of economic problems – the allocation problems – with the result that the problems of choice, of 'economising', rapidly became the primary problem for the professional economist. With some distinguished exceptions[30] the new school detached itself progressively from questions of welfare and income distribution (which were laden with normative implications) and confessed itself defeated by the problem of growth and development which had been the

---

[30] e.g. A. C. Pigou, *Economics of Welfare*, (1920) and J. A. Schumpeter, *Theory of Economic Development* (1912).

leading questions for most classical economists from Adam Smith to J. S. Mill.

One can see the reflection of this shift of emphasis for example, in Neville Keynes' readiness to concede the position of the historical school on the question of economic development. For example he admitted that: 'The theory of economic progress is exceptional in its almost entire dependence upon an historical method of treatment, and...it is more distinctly subordinate than are other portions of economic doctrine to general sociology'.[31] And he went on to conclude:

> This accords with the view...that when we come to deal with problems of economic growth and progress, the appropriate method becomes less and less deductive and more and more inductive. For it is to be observed that mechanical analogies (dynamical as well as statical) naturally suggest deductive methods of investigation while biological and evolutionary analogies suggest inductive methods.[32]

He returned to this theme in the chapter dealing with the connections between economics and economic history. E.g.: 'In more general problems relating to economic growth and progress the part played by abstract reasonings is reduced to a minimum and the economist's dependence upon historical generalizations is at a maximum. Theories of economic growth and progress may indeed be said to constitute the philosophy of economic history.'[33]

This narrowing of the range of their discipline was a high price for the broader scientific community of economists to pay (however well it might fit in with the predilections of the more mathematically minded among them) and it needed some very special justification to convert the applied economists as well as the theoreticians to this relatively restrictive framework. One attraction no doubt was the fact that the ideological implications of the neo-classical paradigm were more palatable than any conceivable alternative. English economists, nurtured in a tradition whose philosophical premises included the doctrine of social harmony and whose political bias was in favour of free trade and a minimum of government intervention found their laissez-faire, economic individualist ideology under increasing strain in the 1870s and 1880s. There were various reasons for this: British industry was faced with intensifying international competition abroad and increasing labour problems at home; the social and economic problems associated with an urbanised industrial

---

[31] *Op. cit.*, p. 145.   [32] *Ibid*, p. 149.   [33] *Ibid*, p. 283.

economy seemed to call for a revision of traditional dogma concerning the role of government in the economy; the process of constitutional reform was extending the vote to the working classes at a point in time when the incomes gap between rich and poor was becoming, if not wider, at least more obvious. In these difficult circumstances, a methodology which took as its central examplar a demonstration of the optimal allocation of scarce resources in a perfect market and substituted a 'scientific' concept of equilibrium for the out-dated philosophical assumption of the 'natural law' was well worth some narrowing in the scope of the discipline. For it permitted economists to justify an ideological bias towards the *status quo* of income distribution on ostensibly non-political grounds.[34]

The alternatives open to them were much less attractive. The Marxian alternative which is discussed below in Chapter 9 lay too far outside their cultural tradition to be a serious competitor. A less heretical development of the Ricardian tradition might also have led in dangerous directions. Some of Ricardo's own statements for example carried some disturbing implications for those disposed to pursue them to socio-political conclusions: e.g. his statement in the *Essay* that 'the interest of the landlords is always opposed to the interest of every other class in the community'.[35] Then there was his labour theory of value which by putting wages and profits in inverse relation to one another suggested the rationale for an inherent capital–labour conflict.[36] Even J. S. Mill's bland efforts to broaden the horizons of economic philosophy by bringing it into relation with other social sciences, and his tendencies towards a kind of liberal socialism, carried some uneasy potential when looked at from the point of view of the laissez-faire economic individualist. Finally, the historicists who took their inspiration from Germany shared the German historicists' bias towards a state-directed economy which was anathema to most English and American economists.

In the event, although the marginal revolution was in no sense exclusive to English-speaking economists, the basic textbook for the new paradigm was not Walras' mathematically rigorous

---

[34] Cf. G. Myrdal, *The Political Element in the Development of Economic Theory* (1953 edn), p. 192: 'The perpetual game of hide-and-seek in economics consists in hiding the norm in the concept.'

[35] See also the passages quoted on p. 63 above.

[36] According to H. S. Foxwell, for example, 'it was Ricardo not Owen who gave the really effective inspiration to English socialism'. See his introduction to A. Menger, *The Right to the Whole Produce of Labour* (1899), p. lxxxiii.

Elements of Economics but Marshall's *Principles of Economics*, readily comprehensible to the intelligent layman with no mathematical expertise.[37] For in reading Marshall's *Principles* the English or American economist, reared on a diet of Adam Smith, Ricardo and Mill would soon find himself on familiar ground. For Marshall, though a mathematician by training and intellectual approach, deliberately kept his mathematics in the background of his economics, insisted that his theory was subordinate to its applications and wrapped it all up in a mass of descriptive and historical material that was aimed more at laymen than at academic economists. Even his demand and supply curves were relegated to a footnote where the mathematically squeamish economist could conveniently ignore them.

Moreover, although the Marshallian analysis was conceived within a general equilibrium framework, it was brought into relation with the real world by Marshall's special technique of partial equilibrium analysis. Instead of seeking a solution to the problem of how the economy *as a whole* brought its demand and supply into equilibrium, as Walras had done, Marshall proceeded to look at a series of cross-sections. He considered, for example, how an individual firm in an industry would find its equilibrium price or output if one assumed away the complications arising outside its own special conditions of demand and supply. Partial equilibrium analysis thus explains the determination of prices in a particular market assuming all other markets frozen (*ceteris paribus* that is to say). By starting from an analysis of the demand and supply conditions of an individual producer Marshall tried to bring economic theory into relation with the practical problems of actual business situations. By adopting the theoretical device of the 'representative firm' he was able to go on to state the conditions for the equilibrium of the output of a whole industry without having to make the assumption that all the individual firms in the industry were in equilibrium.[38] From there he went

[37] It is not difficult to explain the failure of Walras' book to convert the scientific community of English speaking economists to a new framework of analysis. The mathematical superstructure of his general equilibrium theory – his rigorous solution to the problem of the mutual interdependence of all prices and quantities in producing a general market equilibrium – was tough enough to daunt all but the mathematically expert theorist. The virtually total detachment of his idealised economic system from concrete economic problems or data would deter the applied economist from taking it at all seriously.

[38] The rationale for the assumption was by analogy with the biological variety of trees in a forest – some growing, some dying, some static – so that it was convenient to think in terms of a representative unit, e.g. a 'representative firm'

on to provide his explanation of prices in long-run equilibrium which became the lynch-pin of neo-classical theory. Whatever business men might say about the relevance of the neo-classical simplifying assumptions relating to their actual motives and decision-making processes, they were able to recognise their own concepts and problems in the economist's interpretation of them: they were operating, that is to say within the same categories and in the same kind of language.

For the economists in his audience, as well as for the under-graduates who had a reading-list of classical economists to digest, Marshall's *Principles* had the supreme advantage that it did not pretend to overturn the classical orthodoxy – merely to complement and modernise it. Moreover, it may be relevant in evaluating the impact of the Marshallian system on contemporary economists to recall the strength of the historical tradition among the rank and file of British and American economists in the latter decades of the nineteenth century,[39] and Marshall's high respect for the role of economic history as a branch of applied economics. Book I of the *Principles* was a broad historical survey which ran to 120 pages in the 4th edition: and although it had been slimmed by the 8th edition to less than 50 pages Marshall never lost his strong interest in economic history. It was easier for those who had some sympathy with the historicist viewpoint to be seduced by Marshall's *Principles* than to accept either Jevons' *Theory* or Walras' *Elements*.

whose cost conditions approximated to the average for the industry and whose profits in equilibrium approximated to the industrial norm. The problem effectively sidestepped by this theoretical abstraction was that in the real world the existence of economies of scale could be expected to lead to a disproportionate growth in the size of the more successful firms, thus destroying the competitive conditions on which the whole analysis was based.

[39] According to Blaug 'The dominant view among English economists in the seventies and eighties was that of the Historical School (M. Blaug, *Economic Theory in Retrospect*, 2nd edn, p. 305). J. B. Parrish, 'The rise of economics as an academic discipline', *Southern Economic Journal* (July 1967), documents the dependence of American universities on economists who had had their post-graduate study in Germany where the historicist school was dominant. By 1900 however 'Interest of American scholars had shifted to the leading British economists whose theoretical contributions became widely adopted in this country' (p. 5).

FURTHER READING

Primary literature

H. S. Foxwell, 'The Economic Movement in England', *Quarterly Journal of Economics* (1888).

W. S. Jevons, *Theory of Political Economy* (1871).

J. N. Keynes, *The Scope and Method of Political Economy*, LSE Reprints (1930).

Alfred Marshall, *Principles of Economics*, 8th edn (1952).

A. C. Pigou (ed.), *Memorials of Alfred Marshall* (1925).

Leon Walras, *Elements of Pure Economics*, translated by W. Jaffé (1954).

Secondary literature

R. D. C. Black, 'Jevons, Marginalism and Manchester', *Manchester School of Social and Economic Studies* (1972).

R. D. C. Black, A. W. Coats, Craufurd D. W. Goodwin, *The Marginal Revolution in Economics* (1973).

A. W. Coats, 'The Historicist Reaction in English Political Economy, 1870–1890', *Economica* (1954).

R. S. Howey, *The Rise of the Marginal Utility School 1870–1889* (1960).

T. W. Hutchison, *'Positive' Economics and Policy Objectives* (1964).

T. W. Hutchison, *A Review of Economic Doctrines 1870–1929* (1953).

J. M. Keynes, 'Alfred Marshall', in *Essays in Biography, op. cit.*

J. M. Keynes, 'William Stanley Jevons', in *Essays in Biography, op. cit.*

G. Myrdal, *The Political Element in the Development of Economic Theory* (1953).

L. Robbins, 'The Place of Jevons in the History of Economic Thought', *Manchester School of Social and Economic Studies* (1936).

G. F. Shove, 'Marshall's *Principles* in Economic Theory', *Economic Journal* (1942).

8

THE NEO-CLASSICAL THEORY OF VALUE

As we have seen, Ricardo had been concerned by two shortfalls in his theory of value. The first was that a labour theory of value did not seem able to explain changes in value *through time*: for as soon as one admits the possibility of capital with differing degrees of durability (different lives that is) being involved in the production process, then a general rise in the share of wages could alter relative prices independently of relative labour inputs by raising the prices of labour-intensive products relative to capital-intensive products. The second was that he had no answer to the question of what determined absolute value, for there was no commodity whose value was not dependent on its own costs of production: 'that is, there is none which is not subject to require more or less labour for its production'.[1] As far as the founders of the marginal revolution were concerned, Ricardo's problems in both of these respects were of his own making. His labour-embodied theory of value had led English classical economics into a *cul de sac* from which there was no escape unless one were prepared to start from a new set of premises and with a new set of analytical tools.

Jevons fired the opening broadside in the attack on the classical orthodoxy. The Preface to the second (1879) edition of his *Theory of Political Economy* ends with the following peroration:

When at length the true system of Economics comes to be established, it will be seen that that able but wrong-headed man, David Ricardo, shunted the car of Economic science on to a wrong line – a line, however, on which it was further urged towards confusion by his equally able and wrong-headed admirer, John Stuart Mill. There were Economists such as Malthus and Senior, who had a far better comprehension of the true doctrines (though not free from the Ricardian errors) but they were driven out of the field by the unity and influence of the Ricardo–Mill school. It will be a work of labour to pick up the fragments of a

---

[1] Ricardo, *Principles*, Sraffa edn, *op. cit.*, Vol. I, p. 44.

shattered science and to start anew, but it is a work from which they must not shrink who wish to see any advance of Economic Science.[2]

The way out of the Ricardian *impasse* was to reformulate the problem of value in terms quite different to those the classical economists had in mind. To begin with, for example, it was necessary to abandon the search for a definition of absolute or intrinsic value. Value, according to Jevons, implies a relation. 'A student of Economics has no hope of ever being clear and correct in his ideas of the science if he thinks of value as at all a *thing* or an *object*, or even as anything which lies in a thing or an object. Persons are thus led to speak of such a nonenity as *intrinsic value*.'[3] The marginalists then shifted the whole emphasis of their enquiries from value to exchange, from 'natural' price which had been the focus of interest for classical economists to 'market' price. Significantly, for example, Jevons did not attempt a theory of value. He set out instead to expound a theory of exchange.

Having thus disclaimed all interest in value as such, the marginal utility theorists had no further use for the abstractions involved in the classical cost-of-production theories of value. Ricardo's labour theory of value was promptly jettisoned on three main grounds, viz its failure to explain *either* (a) the prices of goods in fixed supply (such as works of art or vintage wine) *or* (b) the prices of goods in excess supply *or* (c) differences in prices due to the heterogeneity of labour (the wages of labour of differing skills can be explained only in terms of the value of their products). They then proceeded to argue that in Jevons' words 'value depends entirely upon utility', and in particular on marginal utility. To quote Jevons again:

In order that there may be no possible mistake about this all-important series of relations, I will restate it in a tabular form as follows:-
Cost of production determines supply;
Supply determines final degree of utility:
Final degree of utility determines value.[4]

It was left to Alfred Marshall to develop these seminal ideas into a more extensive framework of analysis which opened up a whole new way of thinking about economics. Whereas the classical school, obsessed by the problem of defining 'natural' price, or long-term equilibrium supply price, had fallen back exclusively on a cost-of-production theory, and whereas Jevons

---

[2] Jevons, *op. cit.*, Pelican edn, ed. R. D. Collison Black, p. 72.
[3] *Ibid*, p. 127.   [4] *Ibid*, p. 187 (Jevons' italics).

had swung in the opposite direction and asserted dogmatically that 'value depends entirely on utility', Marshall produced a theory which took both aspects into account simultaneously. 'We might as reasonably dispute whether it is the upper or the underblade of a pair of scissors which cuts a piece of paper as whether value is governed by utility or cost of production', he wrote.[5] The scissors analogy is Marshall's own but it does not really do justice to the quality of his synthesis. For it implies that the two blades of the scissors move, in a sense, independently of one another and the beauty of the Marshallian solution was that it showed the total interdependence of demand and supply on each other. The components of cost, for example, are all determined by an interaction between cost and utility. The result was a completely integrated theory of value in use and value in exchange, applying similar criteria and similar techniques of analysis to an impressively wide range of economic problems. Starting from the analogous assumptions of utility maximisation for the consumer and profit maximisation for the producer he constructed interdependent theories of (a) demand, based on marginal utility analysis and (b) production, based on marginal productivity analysis.

Of course, in emphasising the interdependence of prices throughout the system and in defining the equilibrium price in a competitive market at the point of intersection of the demand and supply curves, Marshall was following much the same line of argument as Walras. Indeed Walras went further than Marshall by defining a general equilibrium system for the economy as a whole. He showed that it was possible to construct a comprehensive set of simultaneous equations, one equation for each unknown, by which in principle all unknown prices and quantities in the system could be solved. The result was a rigorously formal mathematical model which no one, not even Walras, seemed able to relate to the daily decisions taken by real people. Marshall by contrast was actively interested in the causes and consequences of the behaviour of consumers and firms in the real world. His partial equilibrium analysis enabled him to focus on cross sections of the total economy, to analyse the determination of price in a particular market, for example, while assuming all other markets frozen and thus to fix attention on the behaviour of the individual firm or the individual consumer.

[5] A. Marshall, *Principles of Economics*, 8th edn, (1952), p. 290.

His theory of value, moreover, exhibits a constant preoccupation with the element of time, a problem wholly excluded from the timeless general equilibrium solution. For example he noted in Book v that 'The element of time is a chief cause of those difficulties in economic investigations which make it necessary for man with his limited powers to go step by step; breaking up a complex question, studying a bit at a time, and at last combining his partial solutions into a more or less complete solution of the whole riddle.'[6] In effect then, by breaking down the problem of price determination into more manageable proportions Marshall introduced into it a time dimension which no previous ecónomist had been able to take into account. He distinguished explicitly but theoretically between four periods of time relevant to the problem of price determination: (1) the market period in which supplies are absolutely fixed; (2) the short period in which supply can be increased only within the limits of the existing stock of capital; (3) the long period in which capital can be replaced; and (4) the secular period in which normal price is affected 'by the gradual growth of knowledge, of population and of capital and of the changing conditions of demand and supply from one generation to another'.[7] His own price theory was primarily concerned with the third of these periods.

In sum, then, the Marshallian theory of value and distribution turned away from the macro problems posed by the classical economists to focus on the problem of analysing market prices in long-term competitive equilibrium. In this essentially micro theory of market prices the behaviour of consumers and producers was analysed in terms of their marginal utility and cost functions. The individual parties to an exchange transaction were assumed to adjust the quantities offered or demanded to the point where their marginal preferences and costs coincided with given market prices and these in turn were assumed to reflect the combined preferences and costs over the economy as a whole. Value was thus equated to the price determined by this balance at the margin and could therefore be *measured* by the normal, i.e. the equilibrium, price. The problem of distribution was solved by the same kind of mechanism. Profit-maximising entrepreneurs were seen as engaged in a continuous process of substitution as between factors of production – machinery for labour, skilled labour for unskilled labour, etc. – weighing up the costs and

[6] *Ibid*, p. 304.   [7] *Ibid*, pp. 314–15.

returns of alternative combinations; the most profitable technique being that which equated costs and returns at the margin.

As a theory of distribution, however, Marshall's solution was less than satisfactory for it made the normal returns to factors of production depend on their marginal costs and rewards in conditions of long-term competitive equilibrium. Labour fitted fairly readily into the marginal cost/marginal revenue system of equations. 'Wages tend to equal the net product of labour; its marginal productivity rules the demand price for it; and, on the other side, wages tend to retain a close though indirect and intricate relation with the cost of rearing, training and sustaining the energy of efficient labour.'[8] Land, Marshall allowed, was different, being in fixed supply: 'the stock of land (in an old country) at any time is the stock for *all* time'.[9] The loose end in the system was capital which Marshall tried to dispose of by adopting the device already used by Nassau Senior and J. S. Mill, of treating interest as a reward for abstinence or 'waiting'. The trouble was, however, that this glossed over the distinction between capital accumulated by past generations (what kind of cost or sacrifice is involved in lending inherited capital?) and capital accumulated out of current savings. Characteristically Marshall identified the loose end himself by recognising that the return to the stock of capital already in existence was analogous more to rent of land (he dubbed it a quasi-rent) than to the wages of labour:

the income that is derived from a factory, a warehouse, or a plough (allowance being made for wear-and-tear, etc.) is governed in the same way as is the income from land. In each case the income tends to equal the value of the marginal net product of the agent: in each case this is governed for the time by the total stock of the agent and the need that other agents have of its aid.[10]

To make the net return to capital a function of the flow of savings was to adopt a simplification that might serve well enough for a theory of prices but was not very helpful in a theory of distribution.

This, however, was the device Marshall adopted – though expressing some doubts and qualifications. That he was aware of the ideological implications of the stratagem is apparent from his remarks on the labour theory of value. 'If we admit that it is the product of labour alone, and not of labour and waiting, we can

[8] *Ibid*, p. 442.   [9] *Ibid*, p. 445.
[10] *Ibid*, p. 444.

no doubt be compelled by inexorable logic to admit that there
is no justification for interest, the reward of waiting; for the
conclusion is implied in the premise.'[11] He then went on to rebut
the Marxian case as being based on 'a series of arguments in a
circle' with a circular argument of his own illustrating only too
well how the conclusions of economic analysis may be determined
by its assumptions:

if it be true that the postponement of gratifications involves *in general*
a sacrifice on the part of him who postpones, just as additional effort
does on the part of him who labours; and if it be true that this
postponement enables man to use methods of which the first cost is great;
but by which the aggregate of enjoyment is increased, as certainly as
it would be by an increase of labour; then it cannot be true that the value
of a thing depends simply on the amount of labour spent on it.[12]

The advantage, however, of explaining profits as a price (for
a combination of waiting, risk-bearing, entrepreneurial skill etc.)
was to make it possible to apply to the factor markets a similar
range of techniques to those applied to the commodity markets
and to merge the theory of production and distribution into an
integrated theory of prices. Marshall's successors went on to
develop this technique on lines that he would almost certainly
have regarded as too far-fetched, for there are many passages
in which he refers to the limitations of the method which he
describes as 'The statical theory of equilibrium' and which he
thought of as being fully applicable only on the assumption of
a stationary state, e.g.

when pushed to its more remote and intricate logical consequence, it
slips away from the conditions of real life. In fact we are here verging
on the high theme of economic progress; and here therefore it is
especially needful to remember that economic problems are imperfectly
presented when they are treated as problems of statical equilibrium and
not of organic growth.[13]

There were losses as well as gains involved in the re-structuring
and re-orientation of value theory associated with the adoption
of the neo-classical paradigm. On the credit side was the consistency, precision and elegant simplicity of analysis permitted
by the use of the marginal technique and the new tools that
developed within its ambit (e.g. elasticity and rate of substitution
concepts and, later, indifference curves and production functions). For those who could tolerate the assumptions involved in

[11] *Ibid*, p. 487.   [12] *Ibid*, p. 488.
[13] *Ibid*, p. 382.

treating capital as a factor of production complementary to labour and conceptually independent of the labour embodied in it, it became possible to explain the processes of production and distribution in marginal productivity terms analogous to the marginal utility analysis of consumers' behaviour; and thus to develop a two-dimensional concept of value measurable in terms of the price resulting from the totality of transactions in a competitive market. Perhaps also there was a net advantage in having diverted the attention of theoretical economists from the insoluble, metaphysical problem of measuring absolute value. It could also be argued (though this is more debatable) that it related the economist's pure theory of economic behaviour to the actual behaviour of decision makers in a real market.

On the debit side of the account was the way it narrowed the scope not only of value theory but of economic theory generally. Certain problems which might reasonably be expected to come within the range of a satisfactory theory of value were not so much solved as shelved out of sight, e.g. the theory of distribution or the role of expectations in determining values. The problem of distribution which had so preoccupied the classical economists was allowed to drop out of the theoretical economist's research agenda as being somehow out of range. Thus the pattern of income distribution was assumed *given* and the assumption frequently forgotten, so that the strong normative implications of the neo-classical theory concerning the optimum allocation of economic resources were able to carry as illicit baggage the presumption that the closer the economic system conformed to the operations of a perfectly competitive market the nearer it would come to an optimal distribution of *incomes*. By refusing to confront the problem of value in terms wider than those of market prices and by postulating that economic theory was value-free and hence objective, the neo-classical economists effectively prejudged a considerable area of economic policy.

Actually, however, not all neo-classical economists carried the notion of a value-free economics to its logical conclusions. The pragmatic Marshallian tradition of partial equilibrium analysis, inspired by constant concern with real world problems and conditions, permitted a less rigid kind of theorising to thrive on the strength of the neo-classical theory of value. Pigou, for example, Marshall's disciple and successor, went on to work out a welfare theory which fully faced up to the possibility of divergences between marginal private social cost or benefit and social cost or benefit. Joan Robinson, another pupil from the same stable, developed a theory of imperfect competition from a Pigovian starting point, using and indeed extending the full paraphernalia of the marginal analysis.

In line with the growing trend towards a more positive formulation of economic theory, however, Hicks and Allen succeeded in emptying the Marshallian demand curve of some of its classical heritage of armchair psychology by making it unnecessary to assume that consumers were capable of measuring utility in a cardinal (additive) sense. They demonstrated by means of the indifference curve technique that to explain the downward slope of the demand curve it was sufficient to assume that consumers were capable of choosing between products, and hence of ranking them, i.e. of measuring the strength of their desires for different commodities in an ordinal (relative) sense. They thus offered an alternative criterion to the principle that a consumer maximises his satisfaction from a given income by laying it out in such a way that the marginal utility of his expenditure on each good is proportionate to its price.[14] Given an indifference curve which describes the consumer's preferences for different combinations of any pair of goods, and a price line which reflects the price ratio between the goods in question it can be shown that a consumer maximises his satisfaction at their point of tangency, i.e. where the marginal rate of substitution between the two products is exactly equal to their price ratio. Finally, the positive economists took a further step away from the subjective, introspective assumptions underlying traditional demand theory by adopting the 'revealed preference' approach to analysing consumer behaviour.

In sum, the key to the shift from a classical to a neo-classical value theory can be interpreted in terms of another shift in problem focus. Whereas Ricardo had been primarily concerned to explain the share of profits in the national product – essentially because he regarded profits as the engine of growth for a capitalist economy – the neo-classical economists were content to let the answer to the question of what determined the factor distribution of incomes come out as a logical by-product of their assumptions about the prices of factors in long-term

---

[14] The concept of indifference curves can be traced back to Edgeworth and Pareto but it was the article by R. G. D. Allen and J. R. Hicks, 'A reconsideration of the theory of value', *Economica* (1934), which first used the technique as a criterion for maximisation of consumers' satisfactions.

competitive equilibrium. In a perfectly competitive private enterprise economy where the agents have full knowledge and perfect foresight it is a condition of equilibrium that the returns to labour and capital will equal their marginal products. However, for the benefit of those who persisted in asking what determined the rate of profits at a particular point of time they provided answers which represented a natural extension of the marginal supply and demand analysis on which their theory of exchange was based. Thus they interpreted the return to capital as a reward to the capitalist for postponing consumption (just as the return to labour was a reward for the disutility of effort) and defined the long-term rate of profit (not distinguished from the long-term rate of interest) in terms of the intersection of the marginal productivity schedule of capital facing investors and the marginal rate of time preference for savers. The difficulties of defining the marginal product of capital (or of labour for that matter), the problems arising from the fact that both capital goods and labour are heterogeneous inputs, and the influence on the distribution of factor incomes of the bargaining situation in factor markets, could conveniently be ignored as beside the point if the object of the model was to explain the values at which commodities and factors exchanged in a perfectly competitive market and to draw implications for an optimum allocation of scarce resources with alternative uses.[15] Consequently, although the neo-classical theory of prices fell short of a theory of value and had little of substance to contribute to a theory of distribution, it was not empty of significance even for those whose practical interests lay in the problems of planning for a socialist or a mixed, rather than a private enterprise, economy – as was evidenced by the lively debate on the economics of socialism in the inter-war period.[16]

[15] Cf. Keynes' discussion in his chapter on 'the marginal efficiency of capital' of the Marshallian theory; 'It is evident from the above that Marshall was well aware that we are involved in a circular argument if we try to determine along these lines *what the rate of interest actually is*' (*General Theory*, p. 140, my italics). In a footnote to this passage however Keynes asks 'But was he not wrong in supposing that the marginal productivity theory of wages was equally circular?'

[16] See C. J. Bliss, 'Prices, Markets and Planning', *Economic Journal* (March 1972), for an account of this debate in the course of an article reviewing twentieth-century progress in price theory.

FURTHER READING

Primary literature

W. S. Jevons, *Theory of Political Economy, op. cit.*
Alfred Marshall, *Principles of Economics, op. cit.*

Secondary literature

M. Friedman, 'The Marshallian Demand Curve', in *idem, Essays in Positive Economics* (1949).
Tapas Majumdar, *The Measurement of Utility* (1958).
G. J. Stigler, *Essays in the Theory of Economics, op. cit.*

9

THE MARXIAN ALTERNATIVE

In 1867 while Alfred Marshall the young mathematician was busy transcribing the basic theory of Mill and Ricardo into abstract mathematics there was published in Germany the first volume of Karl Marx's massive reconstruction of political economy – *Das Kapital*.[1] Marx had been working his way through 'the confounded ramifications of political economy' in the British Museum Reading Room since 1850 and had already published (again in Germany) a substantial sample of his new theory, illustrating his distinctive methodological approach, in 1859 under the title: *Zur Kritik der Politischen Oekonomie*.[2] Like both J. S. Mill and Marshall he was an innovative follower of Ricardo. Unlike Mill and Marshall he deliberately set out to replace the classical system of thought with a new integrated set of theories, concepts and analytical techniques – a new disciplinary matrix. However, he remained throughout his life outside (and virtually ignored by) the English-speaking community of economists and had little or no influence on the subsequent evolution of mainstream economic thought.

Yet Marxian economics descended directly from the English classical school. Marx shared the classical interest in growth and began, as Ricardo had done, by recognising value and income distribution as the key to understanding growth. He accepted Ricardo's labour-quantity theory of value and his theory of the falling rate of profit and snapped up his hints on technological unemployment. Following the classical example he classified the

[1] Marx, after completing a conventional doctorate in philosophy at the University of Berlin in 1841 spent a stormy few years as a political journalist, moving between Paris, Brussels and Cologne, pursued incessantly by continental police, before settling in London in 1849 to be pursued by bailiffs rather than police and to earn a spare living as economic correspondent for the *New York Tribune*.

[2] Published in English under the title *A Contribution to the Critique of Political Economy* (1904). Now available in an edition introduced and edited by Maurice Dobb and published in 1971 by Lawrence and Wishart.

economy into three socio-economic groups – landlords, capitalists and workers – and focused on an analysis of the movements
in rents, profits and wages as between the three classes of income
recipients: like Ricardo he set rent on one side and expounded
a labour theory of value in terms of equilibrium prices in long-
period perfect competition leading to a uniform and eventually
declining rate of profit. He took over Ricardo's assumption of
a capital-using bias in technical change. But he came to totally
different conclusions. How? How, given what was apparently the
same conceptual starting point and the same analytical tools, did
he manage to produce a theory of the evolution of the capitalist
system that was right outside the mainstream of English economic
theory fathered by Ricardo and Smith?

The answer to this question has three main facets – first that
he did his thinking in a different philosophical context and hence
with different philosophical premises, second that he had a
different scientific objective – different problems to solve, that is
to say – and third that he adopted a different methodological
approach to political economy.

The salient characteristic which Marx shared with Adam
Smith, Jeremy Bentham and J. S. Mill and which distinguished
him from Ricardo (and most subsequent economists) was that
he was a philosopher first and an economist second – a social
scientist rather than a 'pure' economist. For Marx, political
economy was merely one branch (if the most important) in the
study of human social behaviour in the round. He came to the
study of economics with a rigorous training in philosophy, history
and law, and strong political motivation and an insatiable appetite
for empirical knowledge.[3] However, Marx's continental upbringing plus his uncompromisingly critical approach to orthodox
doctrine of all kinds (philosophical, historical or economic) ensured that he would move off in a direction totally divergent from
the mainstream of economic ideas. Like Adam Smith he set out
to analyse the conditions of human progress, particularly human
progress in the material sphere. But whereas Adam Smith's
philosophical preconceptions led him to adopt an analytical framework based on the assumption that progress tended to evolve
'naturally' out of a god-given harmony of individual sentiments
and motives in human society, Marx started from the framework

---

[3] See e.g. his letter dated 1868 to his daughter Laura: 'I am a machine
condemned to devour books and then to hurl them transformed on to the
dunghill of history.'

of the Hegelian dialectic which envisaged progress as a product of continuous conflict – revolution and counter-revolution. Even so, Marx deliberately inverted the orthodox Hegelian dialectic,[4] bringing the material world (rather than the world of spirit) to the fore and explaining the progress of human society in terms of man's struggle with nature and of the changing pattern of human relationships (conflict and combination) associated with man's struggle to improve his material conditions of life.

Marx's study of political economy thus grew out of his political interests and was, according to his own account, a corollary of his critical re-examination of the Hegelian philosophy of law which he undertook in 1843–44.

My inquiry led me to the conclusion that neither legal relations nor political forms could be comprehended whether by themselves or on the basis of a so-called general development of the human mind, but that on the contrary they originate in the material conditions of life, the totality of which Hegel, following the example of English and French thinkers of the eighteenth century embraces within the term 'civil society': that the anatomy of this civil society, however, has to be sought in political economy.[5]

From then on he and his collaborator, Frederick Engels, concentrated on an intensive study of political economy. When the continental political reaction that came to a head at the end of the decade of the 1840s cut short his career as a political journalist he resumed his studies in London in 1850. As he wrote in 1859 in the preface to his *Critique of Political Economy*:

The enormous amount of material relating to the history of political economy assembled in the British Museum, the fact that London is a convenient vantage point for the observation of bourgeois society, and finally the new stage of development which this society seems to have entered with the discovery of gold in California and Australia, induced me to start again from the very beginning and to work carefully through the new material.

Political economy – in the sense that contemporary classical economists would have defined it – constituted the heart and core of the Marxian message. Like Adam Smith and J. S. Mill, Marx related his economics explicitly to the broader framework of his philosophical, social and political thinking, of which it was always

---

[4] 'My dialectic method is not only different from the Hegelian, but is its direct opposite' (Afterword to the 2nd German edition of *Das Kapital*, reprinted by R. C. L. Tucker, in *The Marx–Engels Reader*, p. 197).

[5] Preface to *A Contribution to the Critique of Political Economy*, ed. Maurice Dobb (1971), p. 20.

an integral part; like most of the classical economists he adopted a hypothetical–historical style of exposition when describing the essential characteristics of a *modern* economic system; and like Ricardo (and the later macro-economists) he saw the process of production (rather than of exchange or consumption) as the fundamental determinant of the character of an economy and the main subject of study for an economist. 'We have proceeded from the premises of political economy', he wrote in 1844, 'We have accepted its language and its laws.'[6] However that was before he developed his own version. He went on in subsequent decades to mount a systematic critique of orthodox political economy, beginning with an essay on Sir William Petty,[7] and to produce an analysis which differed from mainstream economic analysis as it developed in the second half of the nineteenth century in two main respects: (a) in confronting a different primary objective; and (b) in adopting a different methodology.

Marx's objective as he described it in the Preface to Volume 1 of *Das Kapital*, was to discover the laws of motion of the modern economic system: 'it is the ultimate aim of this work to lay bare the economic law of motion of modern society'.[8] This was an even more ambitious target than Adam Smith had confronted in his 'inquiry into the nature and causes of the wealth of nations', for it was an attempt to analyse a dynamic social system by developing an organic and not merely a mechanical interpretation of human society. For Marx the analogy of a machine was not helpful in explaining the historical process of socio-economic change in which the capitalist mode of production was merely one stage in a continuously developing system of social and economic relationships. He drew his inspiration, the philosophical orientation which determined his view of human society, from the Hegelian dialectic with its dramatic sequence of conflict, contradiction and revolutionary change, each new stage in the sequence carrying its own seeds of dissolution and replacement. In explaining how his critique of the Hegelian interpretation of

6 *Economic and Philosophical Manuscripts of 1844*, reprinted in R. C. Tucker, *The Marx–Engels Reader*, p. 56.

7 Most of his history of economic theory (originally designed to constitute Vol. IV of *Das Kapital*) did not appear in print until the twentieth century. It is now available under the title *Theories of Surplus Value*, published in English in 3 Parts by Lawrence and Wishart (1968–72).

8 K. Marx, *Capital. A Critique of Political Economy*, Vol. 1, Lawrence and Wishart (1970), p. 10. This is the edition (translated from the 3rd German edn by Samuel Moore and Edward Aveling) that is referred to in this book.

'civil society' led him to a reconstruction of orthodox political economy Marx wrote:

The general conclusion at which I arrived and which, once reached, became the guiding principle of my studies can be summarized as follows. In the social production of their existence men inevitably enter into definite relations, which are independent of their will, namely relations of production appropriate to a given stage in the development of their material forces of production. The totality of these relations of production constitutes the economic structure of society, the real foundation, at which arises a legal and political superstructure and to which correspond definite forms of social consciousness.[9]

The result was a new kind of political economy, conforming to a paradigm unique of its kind, impressive in the sheer range of its explanatory ambitions. Engels put the Marxist assessment succinctly in his speech at the Highgate graveside in 1883: 'Just as Darwin discovered the law of development of organic nature, so Marx discovered the law of development of human history... But that is not all. Marx also discovered the special law of motion governing the present-day capitalist mode of production and the bourgeois society that this mode of production has created.'[10]

So when Marx settled down in the British Museum to make a systematic study of classical political economy he was armed with a set of premises and a set of questions which had emerged out of his training in political philosophy and his interest in political science. He approached Ricardo, for example, as he did Adam Smith and the Physiocrats, with the intention of working out for himself the laws of motion of contemporary capitalist society (as typified more particularly in England and America) but with his mind made up about which were the crucial variables and links in the whole process of social evolution. Naturally he found Ricardo's analysis particularly useful, for Ricardo, by focusing on the question of the distribution of the total national product, provided exactly the right starting point for Marx's central economic problem – the origins of the surplus.

But Marx did not intend to stop there. He differed from Ricardo in that he looked forward as well as backward, that he took a dynamic view of contemporary society and that he regarded its organisational relationships not as given constants but as *endogenous* to his model of economic change. He was interested not merely in *how* the national product was distributed

[9] *Contribution to the Critique of Political Economy, op. cit.*, p. 20.
[10] Reprinted in Tucker, *op. cit.*, p. 603.

but also in *why* it was so distributed and especially in how it arose. He accepted the conventional classical assumption of competition as a distinctive characteristic of the contemporary economic system, but he embodied in his model an explanation of the way it developed inevitably out of past systems of economic organisation and the way it would, equally inevitably, merge into the monopoly-capitalism of the mature capitalist economy. He criticised orthodox political economy for having failed to explain the laws of *motion* of capitalist organisation, e.g. 'The only wheels which political economy sets in motion are *avarice* and *the war among the avaricious – competition.*'[11] He reacted vigorously against the tendency of contemporary economists to present 'production, as distinct from distribution, etc. . . . as governed by eternal natural laws which are independent of history, and at the same time *bourgeois* relations are clandestinely passed off as irrefutable natural laws of society *in abstracto*'.[12]

Marx therefore saw the task of the political economist as being primarily an investigation into the long-term development of modern economic society; and since he saw its organisational developments and corresponding social relationships as both cause and effect of economic growth in the material sense there was no reason to bottle up the social aspects of change in a set of *ceteris paribus* assumptions. The production relationship that he identified as being both the most distinctive and the most significant feature of the contemporary economic scene, *and* the key to its further development was the capital–labour relationship, i.e. the separation of producers into two social classes, those owning the instruments of production (and extracting the profit) and those actually producing physical output in return for wages. It was this basic relationship of the capitalist economy that made it capable of generating increases in production and productivity on a scale unknown in previous epochs and also sowed the seeds of the class struggle and social revolution which would eventually transform the capitalist economy into a communist economy.

Ricardo with his rather narrow unemotive approach to economic analysis provided Marx with a skeleton that called strongly for some social flesh and blood: and with a skeleton of the right formal shape for Marx's needs. For Ricardo, who was not concerned with the broader social implications of his analysis, far

[11] From *Economic and Philosophic Manuscripts of 1844*, reprinted Tucker, *op. cit.*, p. 57.
[12] *Critique of Political Economy*, ed. Dobb, p. 192.

less conscious of its revolutionary implications, wrote in simple abstract language and was astonished when people drew obvious socio-political conclusions from it. He was particularly annoyed, for example, with Malthus and others who called him the enemy of the landowners. It seemed absurd to him that anyone could take his precise economic logic, based on simplified carefully-defined premises, as a critique of the social order or the capitalist system, both of which he took as given, outside his terms of reference. So he could write, for example:

Each year the capitalist begins his operations, by having food and necessaries in his possession of the value of 13,000 *l.* all of which he sells in the course of the year to his own workmen for that sum of money, and, during the same period, he pays them the like amount of money for wages; at the end of the year they replace in his possession food and necessaries of the value of 15,000 *l.*, 2,000 *l.* of which he consumes himself, or disposes of as may best suit his pleasure and gratification.[13]

Which was a perfect springboard for Marx's exploitation theory of profits.

It is fair to say that Ricardo never had a theory of the determination of profits. Indeed this is not what he had in mind. He was trying to understand what determined the way the national product was distributed, and having dealt with rent on the basis of a theory which enabled him to explain it separately he proceeded to construct a theory of the relation between profits, wages and total product. His successors then dealt with the resulting gap in economic theory in ways which matched their ideological preconceptions on the one hand and their intellectual interests on the other. The direct classical succession developed a theory of profit (not at all clearly distinguished from interest) which made it a reward for the role played by the capitalist in the productive process. According to Mill for example: 'The gross profits from capital, the gains returned to those who supply the funds for production, must suffice for three purposes. They must afford a sufficient equivalent for abstinence, indemnity for risk, and remuneration for the labour and skill required for superintendence.'[14] The neo-classical economists as we have al-

[13] Ricardo, *Principles*, Sraffa edn, Vol. 1, p. 388.
[14] J. S. Mill, *Principles*, Toronto edn, Vol. 1, p. 401. But see also, p. 411, a passage which harks back to the Ricardo interpretation and supports the Marxist route: 'The cause of profit, is that labour produces more than is required for its support.'

ready seen were less interested in explaining the distribution of
the national product than in developing a theory of market prices
and resource allocation. Accordingly they extended the classical
line of thought implied in Mill's definition by treating profits
(analogously to wages) as determined by demand and supply for
a factor of production. This permitted them to exclude as
irrelevant the socio-political considerations that were unavoidable in an extended consideration of the distribution problem.

Here the route followed by Marx diverged sharply and significantly from the orthodox classical route. For Marx never lost
sight of the socio-economic distribution problem, and, following
the trail suggested by Ricardo's treatment of rent – as a surplus
attributable to the institutional fact of property ownership –
proceeded to explain profits in terms of the class structure of
capitalist society in which a proletarian wage-earning class
confronted the classes owning the capital and land which constituted the means of production. That this was the crucial difference between the Marxian alternative and the classical
orthodoxy was recognised plainly by Marshall who pointed
out that the conclusions of 'William Thompson, Rodbertus,
Karl Marx and others' flowed inexorably from their initial
assumptions.

They argued that labour always produces a 'Surplus' above its wages
and the wear-and-tear of capital used in aiding it: and that the wrong
done to labour lies in the exploitation of this surplus by others. But this
assumption that the whole of this Surplus is the produce of labour,
already takes for granted what they ultimately profess to prove by it;
they make no attempt to prove it; and it is not true.[15]

Neither the notion that the development of economic relationships is the main determining factor in history, nor that the
historical process can be fruitfully analysed as a continuous
conflict between the classes in possession of society's economic
resources and the classes dependent on them for subsistence,
were new ideas. Karl Marx had found a similar approach in the
French writer Saint-Simon (himself a leading eighteenth-century
aristocrat dispossessed by the Revolution) and in the Swiss
economist Sismondi who had predicted that the class struggle
which would eventually emerge from the over-production crises
of capitalist society would be catastrophic in its effects. The dis-

---

[15] Alfred Marshall, *Principles of Economics*, 8th edn. (1952), p. 487. Of course
the orthodox neo-classical route also stemmed from its particular package of
assumptions as Marshall went on to illustrate. See above p. 120.

tinctive feature of Marx's treatment of these ideas was that he embodied them in a socio-economic model of economic development in which everything followed logically from that single central hypothesis. It was the capital–labour relationship that permitted large-scale accumulation of capital and technical progress, that produced economic growth *and* economic cycles, that determined both the structural characteristics of the economy and the lines of its further development.

Marx thus went on to adopt in a much more complete sense than Ricardo had ever done, the labour-quantity theory of value, which he developed into a theory of profits or surplus value. Whereas Ricardo had introduced this theory as a convenient hypothesis, a deliberate simplification, which permitted him to explain relative variations in the long-run natural prices of commodities in terms of variations in their labour inputs, to Marx the labour embodied in commodities was the essence as well as the measure of their values. Under the capitalist system labour power itself becomes a commodity which worker sells to employer at a market value determined by its supply cost, i.e. the amount of socially necessary labour time required to maintain the labourer. 'The labour-time materialised in the use-values of commodities is both the substance that turns them into exchange-values and therefore into commodities, and the standard by which the precise magnitude of their value is measured...Regarded as exchange-values all commodities are merely definite quantities of *congealed labour-time.*'[16] The difference, however, in the value of the labour embodied in a commodity (including the cost of labour embodied in capital and other inputs used up in the production process) and the value of the labourer's product was 'profit, the specific mark characterizing the form of surplus-value belonging to the capitalist mode of production'. Here then was the key to the whole process of capitalist development, for surplus value provided both the resources for capital accumulation (and hence growth) and the motive power for the inherent conflict between classes by which capitalism would eventually be destroyed.

Marx developed his own theory of value, then, in a historic and social frame of analysis distinguishing three essentially abstract stages of development, three basic types of economic system. In

---

[16] *Contribution to the Critique, op. cit.,* p. 30. Marx repeated the last sentence of this passage in Vol. I of *Capital, op. cit.,* p. 40.

a pre-capitalist society where producers own their own means of production and there are no distinct classes of capital owners (or landowners), the exchange value of a commodity depends quite simply on the quantity of labour required for its production – including the labour embodied in the capital stock and raw materials used up by the process of production. Thus far he followed lines of argument indicated by Smith and Ricardo. In the early stages of capitalism, with the emergence of a social class enjoying a monopoly of the factor of production capital (or analogously land) the privileged class can use its monopoly powers to 'compel the working class to do more work than the narrow round of its own life-wants prescribed',[17] and to extract a new form of income via profit on capital: at this stage the exchange values of commodities are still strictly proportionate to the quantities of labour embodied in them, but the capitalists (e.g. the medieval master craftsmen or farmers employing paid labour) have been able to divert to themselves the value of the additional working time they have coerced the labourers into putting out. Finally in a fully developed capitalist society, where the application of capitalistic methods of production has changed not only the distribution of incomes but the organisation of the productive process itself, the exchange value of commodities is determined by their fixed capital as well as their direct labour costs of production and the whole of this surplus value is transformed into profits. So as technological progress increasingly hinges on replacing men by machines, the share of living labour in the national product (the wage-bill) falls and the share of dead labour (labour embodied in capital equipment) rises, and the system becomes less and less capable of maintaining full employment of the labour force.

The social frame is set by the relations between the factors of production. The *value* of commodities arises out of a chain of socially cooperative activities – production, distribution and exchange. To quote: 'If...we bear in mind that the value of commodities has a purely social reality, and that they acquire this reality only insofar as they are expressions or embodiments of one identical social substance, viz human labour, it follows as a matter of course that value can only manifest itself in the social relation of commodity to commodity.' Labour power itself is transformed into a commodity in the fully developed capitalist

[17] *Capital*, Vol. 1, pp. 309–10.

system as envisaged by Marx. Thus the source of surplus value is the fact that in a developed capitalist economy where labour power itself is transformed into a commodity, its purchaser can sell its output at a higher price than he has paid for the embodied labour time.[18]

Marx thus classified the expenditures generating the annual gross product of the capitalist economy (i.e. its annual value-added) as consisting of three components – variable capital (equivalent to the wage-bill), constant capital (equivalent to depreciation plus raw materials i.e. to outlays on capital and other inputs used up in the production process) and surplus value (which accrued to the capitalist property-owner). He was able to explain why the competitive capitalist entrepreneur seeking to maximise his total profits did not bid up wages, by postulating the existence of an industrial reserve army of the unemployed providing increasing competition for vacancies. The classical economists would no doubt have justified this postulate by an appeal to the Malthusian principle of population, but Marx's ideological preconceptions did not sit easily with a theory which could be held to imply that poverty could be alleviated by greater chastity on the part of the poor and more extravagant consumption on the part of the rich. In effect the Malthusian approach ran counter to the whole thrust of the Marxian argument that modern (capitalist) growth hinged on the ability of the working classes to produce a surplus to their subsistence needs, and on the power of the capitalist class (landlords and industrialists) to appropriate the whole of that surplus and convert it into productivity-promoting capital investment. Indeed Marx started from the assumption of a persistent bias towards labour-displacing technical progress in mature capitalist economies. Like Ricardo he assumed that wages were determined by the level of subsistence of the labourer (i.e. that they were supply-determined) the mechanism being as follows: first that as capitalist enterprise grows at the expense of pre-capitalist enterprise it creates an unemployed fringe, and second (more importantly) that the process of capitalist accumulation involves a continuous change in the 'organic

[18] Marx did not distinguish analytically between rent and profit and rejected Ricardo's theory of rent as falling 'into a two-fold historical error: on the one hand, he assumes that the productivity of labour in agriculture is *absolutely the same* as in industry, thus denying a purely *historical* difference in their actual stage of development. On the other hand, he assumes an *absolute decrease in the productivity of agriculture* and regards this as its law of development' (*Theories of Surplus Value*, Pt 2, *op. cit.*, p. 244).

composition of capital' away from variable capital, which main-
tains the labour force, and in favour of constant capital, i.e. that
part of capital expenditure which is devoted to raw materials and
fixed capital. In other words, productive outlays in a capitalist
economy are increasingly spent on 'dead labour' rather than
'living labour'. When the industrial reserve army begins to
diminish, the capitalists respond to the emergence of labour
scarcities by investing in capital-using technical innovations which
raise output per head.[19]

In effect, Marx adopted the classical cost-of-production explanation for the long-term exchange value of commodities and
made cost of production a function of their labour inputs. In so
doing he ran into the same sort of problem as Ricardo had faced
in accounting for the possibility of variations in the composition
of inputs. For if the proportion of constant to variable costs varied
as between industries the factors determining commodity prices
could also vary, since capitalists would seek a price that covered
total costs and not merely variable costs, and equilibrium market
prices would not necessarily be equivalent to the value of labour
inputs, however these were defined.

It was crucial to Marx's thesis, however, that 'the only source
of surplus value is living labour' and he had therefore to face
the implication that the competitive pressures which tended to
equalise the rate of profit on capital put to different uses in a
capitalist economy, would bring variations in the rate of surplus
value. Indeed, if the prices at which goods were marketed in a
capitalist economy depended solely on their variable capital costs,
and if there was a uniform rate of profit on *total* capital outlays,
then the rate of profit per man employed would be higher in
labour-intensive industries than in capital-intensive industries –
which was not a realistic outcome.

To simplify the exposition of Volume i of *Capital* Marx explicitly set aside this problem (or rather postponed it to Volume
iii) by assuming that the prices of commodities would match the
value of the labour time embodied in them.[20] In Volume iii he
relaxed the assumption that prices of production were always

---

[19] E.g. in a footnote on p. 407 of *Capital* Vol. i, Lawrence and Wishart (1970):
'It is one of the greatest merits of Ricardo to have seen in machinery not only
the means of producing commodities, but of creating a "redundant
population".'

[20] See *Capital*, Vol. i, p. 220, n.: 'We have in fact assumed that prices = values.
We shall, however, see in Book iii that even in the case of average prices the
assumption cannot be made in this very simple manner.'

equivalent to real (i.e. to labour-embodied) values and argued that although aggregate surplus value and aggregate profit both depended solely on labour input, actual profits were shared out among capitalists in proportion to their total capital outlays. Commodities produced by relatively capital-intensive methods were accordingly sold at prices which were typically above their labour values and commodities produced by relatively labour-intensive methods sold below their values. Overall (and for commodities produced with a capital composition which matched the national average), however, the sum of the prices of production would equal the sum of the labour values embodied in their production process.

An enormous volume of literature has grown up around Marx's solution to the so-called 'transformation problem', i.e. the problem of relating prices of production to real values. In the end, however, the assumption that the value of output and amount of the social surplus stemmed basically from the labour time embodied in the production process remained a matter of faith rather than of falsifiable fact or logic.[21] All that the solution was designed to achieve was to explain, in terms of the specific historical characteristics of the capitalist system, why the classical 'natural price' of a commodity was not necessarily a faithful reflection of the amount of labour time embodied in it. Competition among capitalists ensured that commodities would be sold at cost of production, including an average profit, and this price could be above or below 'value' if the cost of production of particular goods included a larger or smaller element of constant capital. Value itself was determined by the starting assumption in the analysis and the rate of surplus value (the rate of exploitation) could then be explained by the historically specific characteristics of mature capitalism in which the owner of the means of production typically bought the worker's labour power and thus diverted to himself the social surplus of the community.

The theory of surplus value represents the most significant difference between the Marxian alternative and the orthodox classical succession. It is here that we find expressed most clearly and unambiguously the 'dreadful heresy' of a necessary conflict between the interests of capital and labour. It is of course an

[21] See e.g. *Capital*, Vol. I, p. 186: 'We know that the value of each commodity is determined by the quantity of labour expended on and materialised in it, by the working-time necessary, under given social conditions, for its production.'

inevitable corollary of the assumptions on which the problem is formulated, just as the role assigned to the industrial reserve army is a corollary of Marx's assumptions about the character of technical progress. Whether these opening postulates are more analytically useful than other simplifying assumptions depends on whether they are *either* more realistic, *or* more helpful in illuminating the crucial forces at work within the economic system. And this again depends on the objective of the analysis. Marx was using this theory as a tool for historical explanation and for prophesy, i.e. as a means of explaining the evolution of the capitalist system through time, real historical time. So one way of assessing its usefulness is to consider how effectively it explained the way the economic system was developing at the time he wrote, and how accurately it predicted its further evolution.

Marx's vision of capitalism as an exchange economy with private ownership of the means of production, and with the population divided into two parts, one part owning the means of production, and the other compelled to sell to that part its labour, was a realistic enough description of the industrial organisation that emerged from the first industrial revolution. The classical economists, though they would not have emphasised the institutional aspects of this set-up in quite the terms Marx did, were saying much the same thing when they described the class structure. What was special, however, about the Marxian analysis was that it treated these institutional characteristics of the system not as a static datum but as a crucial factor, *the* crucial factor in its evolution. Because techniques of production in the industrial economy were leading to economies of scale, because capitalists were obliged by competition to maximise the size of their units of production (rather than their short-run profits) in order to reap the fullest economies of scale, they were forced to keep reinvesting their profits in larger and larger enterprises. When the economy's productive resources had been sufficiently concentrated to remove the necessity for competitive accumulation by the successful few, the stage of 'monopoly capitalism' would be reached in the Marxian model and the system would become more and more vulnerable to economic crises arising from an imbalance in the demand for capital goods and consumption goods. Capitalists faced by a persistent tendency to overproduction and a falling rate of profit, would find it more and more difficult to extract a surplus, to fund either consumption or further investment; and intensifying economic crises would lead inexorably to social revolution. In the Marxian model, therefore, accumulation is stimulated not by an innate psychological propensity on the part of entrepreneurs, but by the social pressures of competitive society. These same pressures drive the capitalists to hold down wages where they can and to innovate by introducing labour-saving equipment where they cannot. Again, from the vantage point of the middle of the nineteenth century, the assumption that technical change was labour-displacing and capital-intensifying was a realistic enough assumption on the face of it.

So Marx offered a vision of an economy expanding under competitive pressure, increasing its fixed capital stock at the expense of the labour force, concentrating the nation's capital in fewer and fewer hands, steadily increasing the scope of the large-scale, capital-intensive enterprise, running into successive crises as opportunities for technical progress accelerate the pace of capital formation, so that the resulting overproduction drives prices down and the rate of capital formation then contracts; and so generating a situation of chronic underemployment punctuated by severe depressions. It was a remarkably accurate set of prognostications.[22] For the first time economists were presented with a model which explained both growth *and* fluctuations of the economy in terms of the reactions between the institutional environment and the technique of production that emerged from the industrial revolution.

Of course Marx's predictions did not always come out right in the event. His theories of the steady worsening of the living conditions of the labour force, of progressively worsening capitalist crises and of the falling rate of profit have not all been borne out by events. If the rate of profit has now sunk to unprecedentedly low levels in modern capitalist societies it is for reasons other than those envisaged in Marx's theory. The class struggle between proletariat and capitalists no longer ranks as the main source of socio-economic conflict in modern mixed capitalist societies. Where workers are sufficiently well-organised to withdraw their labour, ownership of the means of production no longer guarantees to the capitalist command over the social

[22] For an admiring assessment of Marx's predictive powers see the article by W. W. Leontief, *American Economic Review Supplement* (March 1938). Reprinted in Leontief, *Essays in Economics* (1966), e.g. 'Marx was the great character reader of the capitalist system' (*ibid*, p. 78).

surplus. The fact is that Marx failed to envisage *either* the institutional changes which were to improve the bargaining position
of the labour force and replace the capitalist economy by a mixed,
semi-socialist type of economy, *or* the technological changes
which were as often capital-saving (or neutral) as capital-using,
or the demographic changes which were to ensure that the labour
force would grow more slowly than the stock of capital. However,
detailed, accurate predictions of long-run economic change are
subjects for economic astrology rather than economic science,
and the original Marxian economic categories and socio-economic
relationships have a limited relevance in a twentieth-century
context. What Marx was trying to do was to predict – within a
historically specific framework of institutional, technological and
demographic change – where the capitalist system was going.
Given his mid nineteenth century starting point his logical
sequences were cogent and, even where the reasoning was
faulty, often his gift for direct observation and his extraordinary
erudition kept the end-product convincing.

Given the real qualities and range of the Marxian analysis,
the interesting question, of course, is why did it make so little
impression on mainstream economics? It has to be remembered
first that it was none of Marx's intention to convert the scientific
community of economists to a new research programme. He was
not an applicant for membership of the Political Economy Club
and the audience for which he wrote was the continental socialist
intellectuals and the literate working classes. His ultimate objective was not to prescribe policies that would enable the capitalist
system to work more efficiently, but to assist the proletariat to
transform a system of productive relations that had immensely
advanced the material potential of mankind but was now out-
running its usefulness and moving towards catastrophe. 'No
social order is ever destroyed before all the productive forces for
which it is sufficient have been developed, and new superior
relations of production never replace older ones before the
material conditions for their existence have matured within the
framework of the old society.'[23] His scientific work was published
in German in a turgid, diffuse, often vituperative prose (largely
posthumously published and possibly for that reason repetitious
and disorganised) and presented an economic theory expressly

[23] Preface to his *Contribution to the Critique of Political Economy*, ed. Dobb, *op.
cit.*, p. 21.

designed to stimulate the revolutionary movement that would eventually and inevitably destroy the capitalist system.

It is difficult to imagine any of the leading nineteenth-century British and American economists (reared in a philosophical tradition which assumed a natural social harmony and in an economic tradition which trusted laissez-faire), finding enough common ground with this continental philosopher (starting from the premise of natural social conflict and determined to assist in the inevitable social revolution), to follow his argument beyond its fiercely polemical preface. Had any of them done so he would have found himself grappling at once, not only with an unpalatable set of premises but with a new set of concepts, an unfamiliar technique of analysis and a totally new language.

No doubt the fact that neither Marx nor Engels nor any of their more distinguished followers were at all concerned to convert the intellectual community of economists to their way of thinking helped to prevent a school of Marxian economists from developing in Western Europe or in the USA in the late nineteenth or early twentieth centuries. There must be some direct persuasion in the process of conversion to a new paradigm. Possibly also the fact that the 'invisible college' of economists had already developed a disciplinary solidarity militating against any criticism that did not involve acceptance of certain fundamental principles, also had something to do with the failure of the Marxian model to have even the most diluted impact on mainstream economic thought. But it is difficult to escape the conclusion that the main factor was ideological. The neo-classical attempt to develop a value-free economic science seemed right because the totality of 'bourgeois economists' as Marx would have called them accepted certain implicit commitments – a bias towards the *status quo* in property institutions, laissez-faire and economic individualism – without serious question. True, it constrained positive economics within a restricted scope – leaving economic development virtually outside its range and producing a disproportionate emphasis on micro-economics. But the areas where neo-classical economics scored its greatest triumph, e.g. in the realm of allocation theory, were regarded as important by the community of economists when the neo-classical paradigm assumed its dominance over mainstream economic thought: and in these areas Marxian economics had nothing to contribute.

When, in the inter-war period, advanced capitalist economies were confronted with problems of persistent unemployment and trade depression, so that increasing government intervention began to seem not only acceptable but actually desirable and the ideological commitments that had seemed so unquestionable in the pre First World War era began to crack; and when in the post Second World War era the problems of economic development in the underdeveloped countries were found to be conditioned at least as much by political and social as by economic factors; then it became easier for bourgeois economists to examine the Marxian model on its scientific merits.[24] By that time however the organisational structure of capitalist society had changed completely, the structure of developing countries was something different again and the communist countries faced problems that could never have been foreseen in the nineteenth century, so that the original Marxian model was no more relevant than the Marshallian model.

FURTHER READING

Primary literature

Karl Marx, *Contribution to the Critique of Political Economy*, ed. Maurice Dobb (1971).
Karl Marx, *Capital*, Vols. I–III (1970).
Karl Marx, *Theories of Surplus Value*, Pts I–III (1962–72).
R. C. Tucker (ed.), *The Marx–Engels Reader* (1972).

Secondary literature

M. Dobb, *On Economic Theory and Socialism: Collected Papers* (1955).
G. Duncan, *Marx and Mill: Two Views of Social Conflict and Harmony* (1973).
D. Horowitz (ed.), *Marx and Modern Economics*.
M. C. Howard and J. E. King, *The Political Economy of Marx* (1975).
R. L. Meek, *Economics and Ideology* (1967).
J. Robinson, *An Essay on Marxian Economics* (1942).
Paul A. Samuelson, 'Understanding the Marxian Notion of Exploitation: A Summary of the So-Called Transformation Problem between Marxian Values and Competitive Prices', *Journal of Economic Literature* (1971).
J. A. Schumpeter, *Ten Great Economists* (1951).

[24] By the late 1960s, the orthodox histories of economic thought and textbook introductions to economics generally included a respectful discussion of the Marxian model. More important still, it was by then common for the pillars of the neo-classical orthodoxy to engage in serious and live debate on theoretical issues raised by Marx.

10

NEO-CLASSICAL ORTHODOXY IN THE INTER-WAR PERIOD

It is the function of an economic theory to bring some aspects of reality sharply into focus at the expense of making simplifying assumptions that are patently untrue of the real world. Classical and neo-classical theory, for example, assumed an unchanging political and social environment and by so doing made it easier to isolate the inter-connections between the distinctively economic factors in the economic process. Walrasian general equilibrium theory exploited mathematical tools of analysis to illuminate the overall interdependence of commodity and factor markets, but could be applied to the study of the real world only on the assumption that most of the inter-relationships were constant. The Marshallian partial equilibrium analysis made the stability assumptions less crucial by focusing on the behaviour of the micro-units in the economic system (the individual consumer or firm) and through the additional assumption of the 'representative firm' sought to extend its scope to cover the market situations of whole industries.

The neo-classical framework of analysis defined in Marshall's *Principles of Economics* (1890) established the main foundation of orthodox economic thought for roughly half a century after its publication. The scientific community of economists reared in this tradition found themselves endowed with an integrated set of theories and tools of analysis which were useful and flexible over a wide range of currently interesting problems. There was a lot for them to do both in applying the techniques to current problems and in tying up loose ends in the theory. For unlike J. S. Mill, Marshall had encouraged his pupils to see theoretical economics as a developing, rather than as a developed, subject and had himself footnoted many of the salient deficiencies in his theory.

The methodological views characteristic of the neo-classical orthodoxy at what was probably the fullest extent of its power over the minds of mainstream economists were defined for the profession by Lionel Robbins' *The Nature and Significance of Economic Science* first published in 1932. Its essential message was the same as that given by Neville Keynes roughly four decades before. It was that the claim of economics to be a scientific discipline rested exclusively on its *positive* aspects, that the main achievement of the economists was a system of abstract analysis based on logical inference from simple postulates and capable of universal applicability. Economics, insisted Robbins 'is entirely neutral as between ends'.[1]

There are many such echoes of Neville Keynes' earlier statement in Robbins' book. Robbins rejected for example the hedonistic doctrines with which Jevons supported his subjective theory of value without rejecting the theory itself: 'the hedonistic trimmings of the works of Jevons and his followers were incidental to the main structure of a theory which . . . is capable of being set out and defended in absolutely non-hedonistic terms'.[2] He acknowledged the close links between economic history and economic theory and the value of empirical research generally in very much the same terms as Neville Keynes had done: e.g. 'Economic Theory describes the forms, Economic History the substance':[3] and again 'Realistic studies may suggest the problem to be solved. They may test the range of applicability of the answer when it is forthcoming. They may suggest assumptions for further theoretical elaboration. But it is theory and theory alone which is capable of supplying the solution.'[4]

However, Robbins made the case in a more confident and more extreme form, which tended to emphasise its distinctive methodology and the restrictions which it placed on the scope of the subject. He brushed aside the methodological controversies which Neville Keynes had tried to expound in a balanced 'non-partisan' spirit. For example, the aim of the essay is des-

---

[1] Cf. Neville Keynes' description of political economy as 'standing neutral between competing social sciences' (J. N. Keynes, *Scope and Method of Political Economy*, p. 13).

[2] L. Robbins, *The Nature and Significance of Economic Science*, p. 85. Cf. J. N. Keynes, *op. cit.*, pp. 91–2, n.: 'The outcome of Jevons's conception of a calculus of pleasure and pain is a theory of utility, whose economic importance it would be difficult to exaggerate. Still, this theory does not itself constitute the central theory of economics. It should be regarded as an essential datum or basis of economic reasonings rather than as itself an integral portion of the science at all.'

[3] L. Robbins, *The Nature and Significance of Economic Science*, p. 39.

[4] *Ibid*, p. 120.

cribed as 'not to discover how Economics should be pursued – that controversy, although we shall have occasion to refer to it *en passant*, may be regarded as settled as between reasonable people – but rather what significance is to be attached to the results which it has already achieved.'[5] The references '*en passant*' bundled the institutionalists and the historicists up with all other critics of neo-classical orthodoxy[6] as ideologically rather than scientifically motivated: for example, it is asserted that the main attacks on orthodox economic science 'have been *political* in nature. They have come from men with an axe to grind – from men who wished to pursue courses which the acknowledgment of law in the economic sphere would have suggested to be unwise...The only difference between Institutionalism and *Historismus* is that *Historismus* is much more interesting.'[7] Or, again 'We have had the Historical School. And now we have the Institutionalists ...sterile and incapable of helpful comment' in face of the great depression.[8]

Having asserted (as Neville Keynes had done) the primacy of *positive* economics and having dismissed the methodological critics, Robbins examined the question of the *scope* of economic science or 'pure' economics. In this he certainly achieved greater precision than any of his predecessors though by deliberately narrowing it. He rejected 'the traditional approach to Economics...by way of an inquiry into the causes determining the production and distribution of wealth',[9] because 'a change in the aggregate of production is not a definitive conception...Whenever the generalisations of economists have assumed the form of laws, they have related not to vague notions such as the total product, but to perfectly definite concepts such as price, supply, demand, and so on.'[10] Attempts to measure the social product in macroeconomic terms or to discuss either its development through time or its distribution as between individuals or groups

[5] *Ibid*, p. 72.

[6] Marxism is never explicitly confronted, though the 'materialist interpretation of history' is specifically disowned and there is a nice passage (p. 151) in which Lenin is visualised as the one dissentient voice in an imaginary Committee on State regulation of the rate of discount in which the other Members were Mr Hawtrey, Buddha and the Head of the US Steel Corporation.

[7] *Ibid*, pp. 82–3.   [8] *Ibid*, pp. 114–15.

[9] *Ibid*, p. 64. There is a footnote here quoting Cannan, *Wealth*, p. v: 'The fundamental questions of economics are why all of us taken together are as well off as we are and why some of us are much better off and others much worse off than average.'

[10] *Ibid*, pp. 66–7.

were dismissed as irrelevant except possibly to monetary theory: e.g. 'Both the concept of world money income and the national money income have strict significance only for monetary theory – the one in relation to the general theory of indirect exchange, the other to the Ricardian theory of the distribution of the precious metals.' For the rest national income estimates have 'conventional significance' only. 'They do not have an exact counterpart in fact and they do not follow from the main categories of pure theory.'[11]

So modern theorists, according to Robbins, had tended to abandon the traditional approach and to divide the

central body of analysis into...a theory of equilibrium, a theory of comparative statics and a theory of dynamic change. Instead of regarding the economic system as a gigantic machine for turning out an aggregate product and proceeding to enquire what causes make this product greater or less, and in what proportions this product is divided, we regard it as a series of interdependent but conceptually discrete relationships between men and economic goods; and we ask under what conditions these relationships are constant and what are the effects of changes in either the ends or the means between which they mediate and how such changes may be expected to take place through time.[12]

Even Adam Smith is said to have made his main contribution to economic science in this limited framework:

although Adam Smith's great work professed to deal with the causes of the wealth of nations, and did in fact make many remarks on the general question of the conditions of opulence which are of great importance in any history of applied Economics, yet from the point of view of the history of theoretical Economics, the central achievement of this book was his demonstration of the mode in which the division of labour tended to be kept in equilibrium by the mechanism of relative prices.[12]

Just as Ricardo's system 'which, in this respect, provides the archetype of all subsequent systems, is essentially a discussion of the tendencies to equilibrium of clear-cut quantities and relationships. It is no accident that wherever its discussions have related to separate types of economic goods and ratios of exchange between economic goods, there the generalisations of Economics have assumed the form of scientific laws.'[13] As a study of these market relationships Robbins claimed for economics great prognostic power because it was based on inferences from a few universally applicable postulates.[14]

[11] *Ibid*, p. 57.   [12] *Ibid*, p. 68.
[13] *Ibid*, p. 67.   [14] *Ibid*, pp. 78–9.

On the face of it Robbins' own definition of economics as 'the science which studies human behaviour as a relationship between ends and scarce means which have alternative uses'[15] was wider than earlier orthodox definitions in that it was not limited to goods and services actually exchanged on a market. In practice however it involved accepting a much narrower range of questions as being within the range of the economist *qua* economist to answer. Macroeconomic concepts were held to be relevant only to monetary theory. Welfare economics was excluded by the insistence that it is impossible to make inter-personal comparisons of satisfactions – still less to aggregate them. A theory of economic development was virtually excluded by Robbins (as it had been by Neville Keynes) because it must involve assumptions that are relative to time and place and/or must take account of changes in social and political organisation. 'How can we predict the substance of the political indifference systems?'[16]

Within this limited sphere, however, Robbins made confident claims about the superior (at times seemingly infallible) prognostic power of positive economics in relation to practical problems. Some of his illustrations of its universal applicability and virtual infallibility may appear less convincing today than they did in the early 1930s and some now seem curious in the context of a book written at the time of the great depression. For example, on the trade cycle, he wrote that 'it becomes more and more clear, for purely analytical reasons, that, once the signs of a major boom in trade have made their appearance, the coming of slump and depression is almost certain'.[17] And after a scathing reference to Wesley Mitchell's empirical researches on business cycles he concluded: 'Meanwhile, a few isolated thinkers, using the despised apparatus of deductive theory, have brought our knowledge of the theory of fluctuations to a point from which the fateful events of the last few years can be explained in general terms, and a complete solution of the riddle of depressions within the next few years does not seem outside the bounds of probability.'[18] But perhaps the most characteristic of the claims of neo-classical economists to infallibility at this period was in relation to wages policy. For example: 'It is a well-known generalisation of theoretical Economics that a wage which is held above the equilibrium level necessarily involves unemployment and a diminution of the value of capital. This is one of the most elementary deductions from the theory of economic equilibrium.

[15] *Ibid*, p. 16.
[17] *Ibid*, p. 126.
[16] *Ibid*, p. 134.
[18] *Ibid*, p. 115.

The history of this country since the War is one long vindication of its accuracy.'[19]

In the end, however, having eschewed all value judgments as being irrelevant to the thought process of the economist *qua* economist, Robbins admitted that his view of the 'nature and significance' of economic science rested on an ultimate valuation – the affirmation that rationality and ability to choose with knowledge is desirable.[20] It is arguable, moreover, that there were other, less explicit, value judgments determining his choice of the problems to which the economist was capable of finding a valid solution, the distinction he drew between 'basic postulates' and 'subsidiary assumptions' and the kind of complications that he was prepared to allow *ceteris paribus* to take care of. For an interest in the theory of economic development and in welfare economics tends to be associated with a readiness to approve government intervention in the economy; and a sharp focus on the analysis of price determination in a freely competitive economy tends to accompany a bias towards laissez-faire and economic individualism. Actually Robbins was quite frank about his ideological biases in these respects though he tended to relegate them to footnotes and deliberately to disassociate them from his economic analysis.[21]

The ideological premises which determined Robbins' choice of the questions that the scientific economist was competent to answer, his selection of methodology and of simplifying assumptions were the preconceptions of most 'reasonable people' (in Robbins' sense: orthodox economists) when the first edition of his book was in the writing, though by the time the second edition appeared, the depths of the great depression had extensively revised the political and social attitudes of those reared in the classical orthodoxy. The *General Theory* gave theoretical expression to some of these ideological shifts and the war and its aftermath completed the revolution. Robbins' objections of

---

[19] *Ibid*, p. 146.   [20] *Ibid*, p. 157.
[21] E.g. p. 125, n., on economic planning ends with 'Scratch a would-be planner and you usually find a would-be dictator'. See also p. 142n on inter-personal comparisons: 'It does not make me a more docile democrat to be told that *I* am equally capable of experiencing satisfaction as my neighbour; it fills me with indignation'; and on p. 147 on minimum wage policy: 'As private individuals we may think that such a system of preferences sacrifices tangible increments of the ingredients of real happiness for the false end of a mere diminution of inequality'.

principle to attempts to measure social income aggregates, to make inter-personal comparisons, to formulate a primarily economic theory of economic development were as valid after the Second World War as they had been before. The difference was that questions about 'how factors of production are distributed between the production of different goods by the mechanism of prices and costs, how given certain fundamental data, interest rates and price margins determine the distribution of factors between production for the present and production for the future',[22] had taken second place (even for academic economists) to questions of the relationships between macroeconomic aggregates, problems of welfare economics and the determinants of economic growth.

Meanwhile, however, some progress had been made within the neo-classical framework by economists engaged in modifying it along lines already suggested by Marshallian authority or in picking up some of the theoretical loose ends footnoted by Marshall himself. One such contribution was Piero Sraffa's *Economic Journal* article 'The Laws of Returns under Competitive Conditions' published in 1926.[23]

The Marshallian analysis represented a theory of optimal resource allocation based on the convenient assumption of perfect competition – implying that each individual firm could sell as much as it chose without affecting the market price and that its profits would always tend towards a normal level because as soon as they rose above that level they would attract competition from new firms. The beauty of this set of assumptions was that it made it possible to infer the output of a commodity from its price and that it illustrated a stable market in which price would always tend towards an equilibrium value: given *perfect* competition (and abstracting from the implications of the way income was distributed), economic welfare could be shown to be fully maximised. It was the assumption of perfect competition that justified the elegant demand and supply analysis of Book v of Marshall's *Principles*. It also gave neo-classical theory its strong normative bias in spite of the claims by its exponents to value-free analysis, for the equality of the rate of return in each resource in all uses which defines competition is also the condition for

[22] *Ibid*, p. 71.
[23] It had already been published in somewhat different form in Italian: 'Sulle relazione fra costo e quantita prodotta', *Annali di Economia* (1925).

maximum output from given resources.[24] The perfectly competitive economy, that is to say, could be shown to display a 'natural' efficiency, again provided that one accepted the income distribution as being outside one's frame of reference.

The difficulty was however that as soon as the analysis began to go beyond the static situation of a single time period, as soon as the possibility of abandoning the assumption of an upward sloping supply curve or horizontal demand curve was considered, the theory began to disintegrate. In particular it proved difficult to keep it consistent with either increasing or diminishing returns. Marshall himself saw the dilemma but as a problem in mathematics rather than in economics. He referred to it in a footnote:

Abstract reasonings as to the effect of the economies in production, which an individual firm gets from an increase of its output are apt to be misleading, not only in detail, but even in their general effect. This is nearly the same as saying that in such cases the conditions governing supply should be represented in their totality. They are often vitiated by difficulties which lie rather below the surface, and are especially troublesome in attempts to express the equilibrium conditions of trade by mathematical formulae. Some, among whom Cournot himself is to be counted, have before them what is in effect the supply schedule of an individual firm; representing that an increase in its output gives it command over so great internal economies as much to diminish its expenses of production; and they follow their mathematics boldly, but apparently without noticing that their premises lead inevitably to the conclusion that, whatever firm first gets a good start will obtain a monopoly of the whole business of its trade in its district. While others avoiding this horn of the dilemma, maintain that there is no equilibrium at all for commodities which obey the law of increasing return; and some again have called in question the validity of any supply schedule which represents prices diminishing as the amount produced increases.[25]

But the problem of course is not merely a problem in mathematics: it is a problem of economic logic. If a firm can be subject to increasing returns what is to stop it from expanding indefinitely and destroying perfect competition? If an industry (i.e. the group of firms producing a particular commodity) is subject to diminishing returns, so that increasing costs react on the prices of the products of other industries and thus reduce the demand for the product of the industry in question, how can one analyse its price and output behaviour in terms of partial

[24] See e.g. G. Stigler, *Essays in the Theory of Economics*, p. 265.
[25] Marshall, *Principles, op. cit.*, p. 380, n.

equilibrium analysis in which the factors affecting demand and supply operate independently? For it is only by ignoring such interactions between industries that we can isolate the demand and supply factors for a particular industry and discuss them independently of their interactions with other industries and with each other. If their interactions are significant then the only way of analysing them is by means of the complex system of simultaneous equations embodied in a general equilibrium analysis.

This in effect was what Sraffa brought out in his famous article. The problems of diminishing returns and increasing returns are asymmetrical but both are very damaging to the Marshallian partial equilibrium analysis based on competitive assumptions. If there *is* an input in absolutely scarce supply it is unlikely that a *single* competitive industry will absorb the whole of that input or that it will have no substitutes. Hence all industries requiring the scarce input or supplying substitutes for that industry's output will be interdependent as to costs and prices.[26] If there are increasing returns attributable to internal economies of scale, the notion of the representative firm is of no use to us and there is no reason to expect the factors on the side of supply and demand to lead to long-term competitive equilibrium.

In short, what Sraffa showed was that the laws of returns which Marshall had used as the basis of his theory of supply, cannot be reconciled with the Marshallian theory of value except under certain highly restrictive assumptions. For when unit cost is dependent on the size of output, the conditions which determine the demand curve are liable to affect the conditions which determine the supply curve (and *vice versa*) except on certain highly restrictive assumptions: viz (i) in cases where the production of an individual commodity uses the whole supply of a scarce

[26] See P. Sraffa, 'The Laws of Return under Competitive Conditions', *Economic Journal* (December 1926), p. 539: 'if in the production of a particular commodity a considerable part of a factor is employed, the total amount of which is fixed or can be increased only at a more than proportional cost, a small increase in the production of the commodity will necessitate a more intense utilisation of that factor, and this will affect in the same manner the cost of the commodity in question and the cost of the other commodities into the production of which that factor enters; and since commodities into the production of which a common special factor enters are frequently, to a certain extent, substitutes for one another (for example various kinds of agricultural produce), the modification in their price will not be without appreciable effects on demand in the industry concerned.'

factor (so that its cost cannot affect demand through its reactions on the output and cost of competing industries using this factor) and (ii) in cases where increasing returns are external to the individual firms in an industry so that they will all operate under the same cost conditions. Apart from these special cases, as Sraffa showed, if diminishing returns exist 'it becomes necessary to extent the field of investigation so as to examine the conditions of simultaneous equilibrium in numerous industries'. And if internal economies exist and generate increasing returns, then there is no such thing as 'normal' profit for an industry and no sense in the concept of a 'representative firm'. Either way the Marshallian theory of value under competitive conditions is shown to be inapplicable.

Finally, Sraffa indicated a way out of the Marshallian dilemma. He suggested that instead of trying to explain the market equilibrium of the *industry*, value theory should focus on the market equilibrium of the *firm*. Instead of starting from the level of a 'representative firm' faced with an infinitely elastic demand curve, theory should begin with an individual producer faced with a downward sloping demand curve.

The clue was already in Marshall who had pointed out that 'when we are considering an individual producer, we must couple his supply curve – not with the general demand curve for his commodity in a wide market – but with the particular demand curve of his own special market.'[27] Sraffa followed this tip to its logical conclusion by arguing that 'it is necessary, therefore, to abandon the path of free competition and turn in the opposite direction, namely towards monopoly.'[28] By focusing on the situation of the individual firm it was possible to escape from the problems raised by diminishing returns (which, at most, apply to an industry as a whole rather than to individual firms) and hence to use the familiar techniques of partial equilibrium analysis. By focusing on an individual firm faced by a downward sloping demand curve it was possible to reformulate the conditions of stable equilibrium in spite of increasing returns. The effective obstacle, that is to say, to the explosive growth of an individual firm under conditions of increasing returns is the fact that it cannot supply a larger quantity of goods to the market without lowering its prices.

The Sraffa article set off a hectic debate on problems of price,

[27] Marshall, *Principles, op. cit.*, p. 379n.
[28] P. Sraffa, *op. cit.*, p. 542.

cost and output which eventually shifted the whole emphasis of orthodox microeconomic analysis by opening the door to a theory of imperfect competition – a theory which was at once more relevant, on the face of it, to the real world of the inter-war period and more helpful in defining the conditions of long-period equilibrium in very general terms. In 1933 Joan Robinson published her classic *Economics of Imperfect Competition* which blended the Marshallian theories of monopolistic and perfect competition into a more general, more integrated, and more realistic theory of value: in this more general theory pure competition and pure monopoly figure as special limiting cases. The new theory formed the basis for the modern theory of the firm.[29]

Under the Marshallian theory of production with its focus on the conditions of supply for the industry of representative firms producing a single commodity there was actually very little scope for analysing the pricing behaviour of the individual firm. Under perfect competition all it had to do was to keep down its costs and produce the output which would be most profitable at given market prices. Adoption of the evidently more realistic assumption of imperfect competition showed a way out of this theoretical *impasse*. 'The notion that every firm is facing a falling demand curve for its own product and that profits are maximised at the output for which marginal revenue is equal to marginal cost provided an explanation for a situation in which firms could work their plants at less than full capacity and still earn a profit'.[30] The new theory provided explicit theoretical expression for the output-restricting and price-raising tendencies inherent in the monopolistic or imperfectly competitive market and led to another hectic theoretical controversy on the question of the best way of regulating monopoly prices. However it also blew a great hole in the normative implications of neo-classical analysis by showing that the natural tendencies of the market do not inevitably lead to an optimal distribution of scarce resources. The notions of consumer's sovereignty and maximum productivity which could be attached to analyses based on the assumption of perfect competition sat uneasily in an analysis based on the contrived variety of products in an imperfectly competitive market.

[29] Joan Robinson, has since abandoned the method of static equilibrium analysis on which her *Economics of Imperfect Competition* largely depended and now disowns much of the modern theory of the firm to which it led. See the preface to the 2nd (1969) edition.

[30] Joan Robinson, *Economics of Imperfect Competition*, 2nd edn (1969), p. vi.

However, Joan Robinson's theory of imperfect competition was rooted deep in the Marshallian tradition and followed a trail already indicated by Pigou, Marshall's successor in the Cambridge chair, in his *Economics of Welfare* (1920).[31] It used the techniques of partial equilibrium analysis to analyse the behaviour of one firm in isolation from the rest of industry. It sharpened the tools of marginal analysis, in particular by its use of the concept of marginal revenue, which became the keystone of a new theory of long-run imperfectly competitive equilibrium. In effect, the equilibrium conditions of the firm under imperfect or monopolistic competition, as outlined by John Robinson, differ from those under perfect competition in a number of significant ways: (i) in that marginal cost is less than price at the equilibrium output; (ii) in that the firm is always operating under conditions of falling average costs when the firm and the industry are in equilibrium; (iii) in that the producer has more than one set of average cost and revenue curves to choose from in deciding on his equilibrium output; and (iv) in that the way equilibrium is established when there are too few or too many firms in the industry is more complex, because a change in the number of firms alters the elasticity of demand for each firm as well as the average level of prices in the market. As a result of marginal costs being less than price at the equilibrium output it can be said that resources are not allocated as well as they might be. And because each firm confronts its own individual sales curve, different from that of other firms, because the commodity it produces is differentiated in some sense from the commodities produced by its competitors, it follows that the price charged by each firm in the industry does not have to be the same as that of every other firm.

The new theory could be integrated with the old, however, by regarding perfect competition on the one hand and monopoly on the other as being the two limiting cases of the one theory. The more firms there are in an industry the less effective are their attempts to attach to themselves a loyal clientele, until ultimately the number is so large that their attempts are entirely ineffective:

[31] In her own later judgment this analysis was based on 'a shameless fudge. I postulated that a firm could find out the conditions of demand for its product by trial and error – that is I treated the conditions of demand as being unchanged for an indefinitely long period and I assumed that experiments with prices would leave no traces in market conditions. The whole analysis, which in reality consists of comparisons of static equilibrium positions is dressed up to appear to represent a process going on through time' (*ibid*, p. vi).

that is, as the number of firms grows and differentiation becomes less emphatic the demand curve of each firm becomes flatter and flatter until when all are perfectly elastic we merge into perfect competition. Conversely, of course, if entry into the industry becomes less and less easy and the number of firms shrinks as a result of amalgamations and natural deaths, the demand curve of each producer becomes steeper and steeper until it merges into the case of pure monopoly. Clearly for anyone brought up in the Marshallian school a restatement of the theory of competition in a form which embraced the perfectly competitive case at one end of the spectrum and monopoly at the other end, and which permitted continued use of the techniques and concepts of partial equilibrium analysis, was an immensely attractive development. The fact that it seemed to reflect the practical problems of real firms in a real world made it even more attractive to those of Marshall's disciples who believed with the master that economic theory ought always to be founded on facts, to be relevant to current policy issues and to be intelligible to the practical man.

The interesting thing about this new development, this abandonment of perfect competition as the central assumption in analysing the formation of output and prices in favour of imperfect competition, is that it took place independently in two places at once – in Cambridge, England and in Cambridge, Massachusetts. As with the marginal analysis of the 1870s the reaction to orthodox economic thinking in the late 1920s, early 1930s, developed in two quite separate academic centres. While Piero Sraffa was writing his seminal article Edward Chamberlin was already working on a Harvard doctoral thesis which constituted the starting point for his *Theory of Monopolistic Competition* (1933), published in the same year as Joan Robinson's *Economics of Imperfect Competition*, and presenting essentially the same theory with differences of detail and presentation.[32]

[32] It was as Marshall would have put it 'the product of the age'. See the letter to L. L. Price dated August 1892 and printed in *Memorials*, ed. A. C. Pigou, pp. 378–9: 'In the early seventies when I was in my full fresh enthusiasm for the historical study of economics I set myself to trace the genesis of Adam Smith's doctrines... And then I grew to think that the substance of economic thought cannot well be to any great extent the work of any one man. It is the product of the age. Perhaps an exception should be made for Ricardo: but everything of importance that was said in the five generations 1740–65, 1765–90, 1815–40, 1840–65, 1865–90 seems to be to have been thought out concurrently more or less by many people.'

The printed controversy which took place when the authors became aware of the coincidence of their views has tended to over-emphasise the differences between their approaches. Seen in long-term perspective what is interesting about these two books is not their differences but their similarities. While both held to Marshallian partial equilibrium techniques of analysis, both dropped the perfect competition assumption and both did so by shifting the focus of their price theory from an industry to an enterprise context. Marshall had begun with the commodity and had called the list of firms producing it an industry. His object was to show the way outputs and prices came into equilibrium for each commodity. The notion of a representative firm was merely a device by which the behaviour of a whole industry could be seen in terms of the producing units of which it was composed. Chamberlin and Robinson, however, focused attention not so much on the commodity (and hence the industry) as on the firm. They analysed the behaviour of the individual firm – each firm producing a commodity more or less differentiated from that produced by other firms. Joan Robinson still used the concept of the industry to cover the case of a group of firms producing broadly similar commodities which are close substitutes for each other: however, what she was really concerned with was not the conditions governing the production and distribution of parti-cular commodities but the decisions of the firm considered as a profit-maximising unit. Similarly, Chamberlin referred to the 'group of firms' composing a given 'industry' but in practice he proceeded on the assumption that 'both demand and cost curves for all products are uniform throughout the group'. So that his idea of an industry was just a group of identical firms. In short, both Chamberlin and Robinson substituted a theory of the firm for the Marshallian theory of the market.

The concept of perfect competition with all its normative implications had not disappeared from active service, however. Wherever problems of the optimum allocation of resources are paramount economists have tended to revert to the assumption that the market is competitive in the sense that there is no over-riding monopoly power on the market. It remains the standard, basic, model of microeconomic analysis.[33] Moreover,

[33] See e.g. G. Stigler, in an article originally published in the February 1957 *Journal of Political Economy*: 'Today the concept of perfect competition is being used more widely by the profession in its theoretical work than at any time in the past.' Reprinted in Stigler, *Essays on the History of Economics*, p. 267.

although, on the face of it, the assumption of imperfect competition was a more realistic approximation to the conditions of the capitalistic economy of the twentieth century it would be a mistake to imagine that its adoption necessarily involved a more realistic type of economic theory. In some ways the methodology of Joan Robinson's kind of analysis represents a purer kind of theorising than anything in Marshall. Marshall had always tried to keep as close as possible to the facts of the real world and although he had by his later editions shifted a good deal of the rambling complexities of the real world into extensive appendices, the argument of the *Principles* never attains the remorseless streamlined logic of Joan Robinson's *Economics of Imperfect Competition*. For this was among the earliest exercises in systematic economic model building, a method which set the fashion for a good deal of subsequent theorising. A major reason why Joan Robinson's book had such a dramatic and powerful impact on English economic thinking was almost certainly the distinctive methodology of the Robinsonian approach, i.e. in the careful preliminary spelling out of definitions and assumptions, the systematic recourse to diagrammatic reasoning techniques and the deliberate abstention from attempts to confuse abstract logic with real sequences of events. What her book provided was a handy 'box of tools' for the analysis of microeconomic questions in the Marshallian tradition.

Marshall had indeed introduced his undergraduate audiences to the use of diagrammatic techniques of exposition in his earliest lectures, though in his *Principles*, which was deliberately angled at a wider readership than professional economists or students, he had carefully relegated even his simple demand and supply curves to a modest footnote. However, in his *Pure Theory of Foreign Trade* (1879) which *was* designed for an academic audience (and was privately published at the instigation of Henry Sidgwick, his Professor at Cambridge) he made his position clear:

The pure theory of economic science requires the aid of an apparatus which can grasp and handle the general quantitative relations on the assumption of which the theory is based. The most powerful engines for such a purpose are supplied by the various branches of mathematical calculus. But diagrams are of great service, wherever they are applicable, in interpreting to the eye, the processes by which the methods of mathematical analysis obtain their results. It happens that with a few unimportant exceptions all the results which have been obtained by the application of mathematical methods to pure economic theory can be obtained independently by the method of diagrams.[34]

The other area in which the existence of a Marshallian loose end stimulated his disciples to make a significant dent in the current orthodoxy during the inter-war period was in the theory of consumer's behaviour. Again the solution depended heavily on mathematical techniques of analysis. Marshall's theory of consumers' demand was founded on his famous law of demand, i.e. that 'the greater the amount to be sold the smaller the price at which it is offered in order that it may find purchasers; or in other words, the amount demanded increases with a fall in price and diminishes with a rise in price'. From this he went on to derive the characteristically downward sloping demand curve and went on at a later stage to develop the notion of consumers' surplus.

Now there are several fundamental and disputable assumptions implicit in this theory. The first is a law which Marshall describes as due to a 'familiar and fundamental tendency of human nature', viz that 'the additional benefit which a person derives from a given increase in his stock of a thing diminishes with every increase in the stock he already has'. In other words it is based on Marshall's 'law of satiable wants or diminishing utility'. The second is that an increment in utility (i.e. marginal utility) can be measured independently and absolutely of the individual concerned. The third is that it can be measured in money terms (and it is the second and third assumptions that provide the rationale for the consumers' demand price). The fourth assumption (implicit in the third) is that the marginal utility of money is constant, or in other words that the unit of measurement is stable. The Marshallian theory of consumers' behaviour thus depended on the assumption that utility was measurable in cardinal terms. A consumer with given tastes and a given money income, confronted by a system of market prices, over which he has no influence, will maximise his total utility by ensuring that a marginal unit of expenditure in each direction brings in the same increment of utility. Which means that in equilibrium marginal utilities will be proportional to prices.

The assumption that the marginal utility of money was constant however meant in effect ignoring the consequences of

[34] A. Marshall, *The Pure Theory of Foreign Trade* (1879), LSE Reprints, 1930, p. 4.

changes in the consumer's income level on the price he was prepared to pay. It meant making the consumer's demand for a good independent of his income. Generations of economists, Marshall included, regretted this unrealistic assumption. But it was not until 1934 when an article by J. R. Hicks and R. G. D. Allen appeared in *Economica* that a way out of the dilemma was suggested.[35] The solution was to abandon the idea of measuring utility and to analyse consumers' behaviour in terms of their preference for different goods as expressed graphically in the notion of an indifference curve. Hicks and Allen did not invent the indifference curve. That appeared first in the literature in 1881 when it was introduced by Edgeworth to illustrate a contract curve between Crusoe and Man Friday and was revived by Pareto around the turn of the century in his *Manual of Political Economy* as a device for illustrating the individual's scale of preference for combinations of certain goods. However, the advantage of the indifference curve approach over the Marshallian theory of demand was that it did not involve measuring the consumer's utilities in any absolute sense, only ordering them in the light of his preferences, preferences that were assumed to have been revealed by the choices he actually made.

The new way of analysing consumers' demand and the new theory of value to which it gave rise was elaborated and formalised by Hicks in his classic *Value and Capital* (1939). The new theory was at once more general and more precise. Henceforth it was possible to start from the assumption that the consumer preferred one collection of goods to another without measuring the extent to which he preferred it. Allen and Hicks demonstrated by means of the indifference curve technique that it was sufficient to assume that consumers were capable of choosing between products and hence of ranking them, i.e. of measuring the strength of their desires for different commodities in an ordinal (relative) sense, in order to explain the downward slope of the demand curve. They thus succeeded in emptying the Marshallian demand curve of some of its classical heritage of armchair psychology by making it unnecessary to assume that

[35] Actually the Hicks–Allen solution had been anticipated by an article by Slutsky that had been published in Italian in the July 1915 issue of the *Giornale degli Economisti*, which seems to have been overlooked by English-speaking economists. R. G. D. Allen and J. R. Hicks, 'A reconsideration of the theory of value', *Economica* (1934). See also R. G. D. Allen, 'Professor Slutsky's Theory of Consumers' Choice', *Review of Economic Studies* (February 1936).

consumers were capable of measuring utility in a cardinal (additive) sense; and offered an alternative criterion to the principle that a consumer maximises his satisfaction from a given income by laying it out in such a way that the marginal utility of his expenditure on each good is proportionate to its price. Given an indifference curve describing consumers' preferences for different combinations of any pair of goods, and a price line which reflects the price ratio of the goods in question, it can be shown that a consumer maximises his satisfaction at their point of tangency, i.e. where the marginal rate of substitution between the two products is exactly equal to their price ratio. It was also possible with the new technique to distinguish clearly between the income effects and substitution effects of a consumer's reaction to a change in the price of a particular commodity.

However, the new theory stuck close to the Marshallian traditional methodology. Indeed from some points of view the changes seem almost entirely terminological and expository. Instead of diminishing marginal utility we have diminishing marginal rate of substitution. Instead of proportionality of marginal utilities to prices we have as equilibrium condition the tangency of the price line to the indifference curve. According to the new theory the marginal rate of substitution between two classes of goods (as expressed by the slope of the indifference curve) is equal in equilibrium to the ratio of prices. In essence, that is to say, the indifference curve approach as worked out by Allen and Hicks represented a development and an extension of Marshallian concepts and methods. Its path-breaking quality was due largely to the fact that it introduced a new analytical concept which seemed to free Marshallian value theory from some of its more awkward assumptions and the innovation was rapidly incorporated into the textbooks.

So both of the two major theoretical development in microeconomics that emerged in the inter-war period – the theory of imperfect competition and the theory of consumers' demand based on indifference curves – represented revisions of the orthodox Marshallian theory rather than frontal attacks on it. Some of the faithful had begun to see before the end of the period that these piecemeal revisions were undermining the whole structure of the microeconomic analysis of the *Principles*. Hicks for example in 1939 described the new work on imperfect competition as involving 'the wreckage of the great part of economic theory'. Some – even more faithful – went on adhering to the old techniques. The cardinalist school (who adhered to the assumption that utilities were measurable in money terms) fought a determined rearguard action against the ordinalists (with their less restrictive assumption that utilities could be ordered in revealed preference rankings but not measured) who played happily with their indifference curves. As late as 1956/57, Sir Dennis Robertson, the most distinguished of the cardinalist school, was insisting in his lectures to Cambridge undergraduates that the concept of measurable utility made good economic sense and was refusing to clutter up his lectures on demand with any treatment of the indifference curve analysis which by then was standard fare in the textbooks.[36]

The real onslaught on the traditional orthodoxy of the early twentieth century however came from another side, by way of the theory of money to which Marshall had never made a major published contribution, though he had given a great deal of thought to monetary questions in preparing his Cambridge lectures or in response to various parliamentary committees and Royal Commissions.[37] But as in other directions, it was Marshall's own teaching that gave his ablest pupils the first scent of a new trail which was to lead them to displace and reconstruct those parts of the conventional analysis which had outgrown their usefulness. The pupil who has most claim to the title of having effectively overthrown the neo-classical orthodoxy was John Maynard Keynes, who had sat appreciatively through Marshall's 1906 lectures on money and who bore witness in 1924 to the importance, originality and insight of Marshall's contributions to the theory of money.[38]

[36] D. Robertson, *Lectures on Economic Principles*, Vol. I, Lecture VI.

[37] Marshall's *Money, Credit and Commerce* (1923), was published in his old age and (to quote Keynes) 'its jejune treatment, carefully avoiding difficulties and complications, yields the mere shadow of what he had had it in him to bring forth twenty or (better) thirty years earlier'. *Essays in Biography, J.M.K. Collected Writings* Vol. X, p. 190.

[38] *Ibid*, pp. 189–95. See also below p. 168 for Keynes' warm obituary tribute to the importance, originality and insight of Marshall's contributions to monetary theory.

FURTHER READING

Primary literature

R. G. D. Allen and J. R. Hicks, 'A Reconsideration of the Theory of Value', *Economica* (1934).

J. R. Hicks, *Value and Capital*, 2nd edn (1946).

Lionel Robbins, *The Nature and Significance of Economic Science*, 2nd edn (1936).

Joan Robinson, *The Economics of Imperfect Competition*, 2nd edn (1969).

Piero Sraffa, 'The Laws of Returns under Competitive Conditions', *Economic Journal* (1926).

Secondary literature

G. L. S. Shackle, *The Years of High Theory* (1967).

11

MONETARY THEORY IN THE NEO-CLASSICAL ERA

Although the later classical theorists, such as J. S. Mill, had been aware that theories formulated in real/physical terms could not be applied to the complex system of credit prevailing in the leading commercialised countries, they settled rather readily for the relatively simple monetarist doctrines they had inherited from Ricardo. Nor were their immediate successors among the neo-classical theorists much inclined to explore the links between the supply of money and the level of output to which Thornton had drawn attention at the beginning of the nineteenth century. The main reason for this blind spot was no doubt the fact that economic policy problems originating in the financial sector did not present themselves in such an urgent and acute form as they had in the early years of the nineteenth century or as they were to do in the twentieth century inter-war period. Whatever the reason, the Ricardian example of separating the problems of price determination into two separate compartments of analysis was carried over into the neo-classical paradigm. The structure of relative prices was explained in real, micro, terms – as dependent on marginal cost and/or utility – essentially in terms applicable to a competitive barter economy in long-term equilibrium. The absolute price of each commodity or the general level of prices, was given a monetary, macro, explanation dependent on a short-term fixed relationship between the stock of money and the stock of commodities. As a result real and monetary theory developed independently of each other and the former took precedence over the latter in the textbooks.[1]

[1] Cf. J. M. Keynes' obituary memoir of Marshall, listing among his main contributions to monetary economics an analysis of the link between the supply of money, the rate of interest and prices: 'It was an odd state of affairs that one of the most fundamental parts of Monetary Theory should, for about a quarter of a century, have been available to students nowhere except embedded in the form of question-and-answer before a Government Commission interested in a transitory practical problem' (J. M. Keynes, *Collected Writings*, Vol. x, *Essays in Biography*, p. 192).

Nowhere did this dichotomy between real and monetary theory show up more clearly than in the classical theories of the rate of interest. True to their Ricardian origins the classical theorists put their main efforts into developing theories of value and distribution in long-term competitive equilibrium: the neo-classicals focused even more narrowly on the theory of markets – a micro theory of prices – also in long-period competitive equilibrium. The rate of interest for long-term loans was explained as the price of capital, its level governed on the one hand by the demand of entrepreneurs for capital to invest (hence dependent on the marginal productivity of capital); and on the other by the supply of uncommitted real capital resources (hence dependent on the supply of gross savings). In short, the real rate of interest was a function of the twin exogenous forces of productivity and thrift. The possible influence of monetary policy on these variables did not come into the picture at all, for in the long run money was irrelevant and could realistically be ignored as having no lasting effect on the fundamental tendencies of real factors.

Side by side with this theory of the way real economic resources were produced and distributed or allocated in the long run, the classical economists had accepted a short-term theory of a market for credit where the rate of interest was a function of the demand and supply of loanable funds. In the original version of this theory, as developed by Thornton, overall monetary equilibrium was held to depend on the real rate of return to physical capital being equivalent to the market rate of return on loanable funds and there was thus an explicit (if unexplained) connection between the money market and the commodity markets. However, the real gap in nineteenth-century thinking on this point (at least until Wicksell) lay in the lack of any systematic attempt to explore the relationship between the market rate of interest (which would be directly influenced by the monetary authorities) and the 'real' or 'natural' rate of interest which Ricardo had called the rate of profits on stock. Conventional classical doctrine treated the former as a sort of shadow of the latter, in effect denying the possibility that the actions of the monetary authorities operating under the gold standard rules would be able to create a divergence between the market rate and the real rate for any appreciable period. Thus the classical school steadfastly refused to allow that changes in the money supply might have any effect on the rate of interest persistent enough to affect the accumu-

lation of real capital. The orthodox quantity theorist argument
was that an increase in the money supply would raise the prices
of *all* commodities without affecting the rate of profit (hence of
interest) in any but the very short run. In evidence before the
Lords Committee on the Resumption of Cash Payments (1819),
for example, Ricardo had insisted that: 'Reduction or Increase
of the Quantity of Money always ultimately raises or lowers the
Price of Commodities, when this is effected the Rate of Interest
will be precisely the same as before; it is only during the Interval,
that is before the Prices are settled at the new Rate, that the Rate
of Interest is either raised or lowered.'[2]

However, even when applied to the short term, the classical
quantity-theory level of analysis left loose ends which could be
held to have implications for the long-run assumption that money
could be treated as neutral, merely a veil behind which the real
factors and tendencies worked towards their long-run equilibrium position. The implication of the orthodox quantity-theory
doctrine, for example, was that an increase in the quantity of
money would in the first instance lower interest rates as well as
raise prices and a decrease would have the opposite effect. Yet
empirical evidence, as Tooke demonstrated in his *History of Prices*,
suggested that in fact interest rates had generally been low when
prices were falling and high in times of rising prices. If it were
really true that a restrictive credit policy (a high discount rate)
could lead to rising prices, and an expansive policy to falling
prices, then not only was the conventional role of monetary policy
as prescribed by the quantity theorists suspect, but doubt was also
cast on the self-equilibrating characteristics of the classical
monetary system.

It was this loose end and its implications for both monetary
policy and orthodox monetary theory that bothered Wicksell in
the 1890s. The preface to his *Interest and Prices* first published in
German in 1898 illustrates his bewilderment. 'If the Quantity
Theory is false – or to the extent that it is false – there is so far
available only one false theory of money and no true theory...It
is no exaggeration to say that even today many of the most
distinguished economists lack any real logically worked out
theory of money.'[3]

The result of Wicksell's inquiry into the relation between

[2] Sraffa edn, *Works etc. of David Ricardo*, Vol. v, p. 445.
[3] Knut Wicksell, *Interest and Prices*, translated by R. F. Kahn (1936), p. xxiii.

interest and prices was to suggest a new theory of interest and price determination which gave more causal substance to the quantity-theory framework of analysis and integrated the orthodox monetary theory of interest with the orthodox real theory of interest. The basic question for Wicksell was 'why do prices rise or fall?' The key to its solution he found in the relationship between the market or money rate of interest (manipulable by monetary policy) and the 'natural' or 'real' rate of interest (dependent on the marginal productivity of physical capital). For if the monetary authorities should set the market rate below the natural rate this would put an artificial premium on capital expenditure financed by credit, so pushing up prices, which will go on rising cumulatively until the shortage of loanable funds has pulled up the market rate to match the natural rate. Conversely, of course, if the monetary authorities set a market rate which is above the natural rate, investment expenditures will be postponed and prices will tend to fall until the slack demand for funds brings down the money rate.

Wicksell therefore concluded that his inquiry fully vindicated the quantity theory and at the same time explained 'the observed fact that rising prices have seldom been associated with low or falling rates of interest, that far more often they are associated with high or rising rates of interest and that falling prices accompany falling interest rates'.[4] In effect he argued that the rate of interest was the crucial link in the quantity theory argument which made prices depend on the money supply, for

an increase or relative diminution in the stock of money must always tend to raise or lower prices – by its opposite effect in the first place on rates of interest. But monetary conditions are only one factor in the situation... The other factor, which is often of more weight, takes the form of the independent movements of the natural capital rate itself, which must necessarily, but in general only gradually, be accompanied by corresponding movements of the money rate.[5]

On the other hand, as was ultimately recognised by the twentieth-century theorists who pursued the same trail – his theory destroyed the rationale for the assumption that money can be conveniently treated as neutral in analysing changes in real output and investment for it showed that manipulations of short-term interest rates could be expected to have considerable effects on actual economic activity. It also, as Wicksell himself noted, had

⁴ *Ibid*, Preface.   ⁵ *Ibid*, p. xxviii.

practical implications for the active role of monetary policy which were at variance with the current orthodoxy: 'Banks and credit institutions have hitherto exerted only an *involuntary* influence on prices, and consequently it has sometimes been in a favourable direction and sometimes in an unfavourable direction. Now, however, they will be able in full consciousness to pursue their objective, to the indisputable benefit of the world economy.'[6]

Significantly, however, Wicksell's *Interest and Prices* seems to have been largely ignored by mainstream theorists in English speaking countries and was not translated into English until the 1930s – by which time the problems of monetary policy had assumed a dominant importance and the world was ripe for a revolution in monetary theory. Indeed before he died in 1926 Wicksell had himself begun to doubt whether his own theory was adequate to explain the wartime inflation and the 'puzzling price fluctuations' of the 1920s. In the words of his compatriot B. Ohlin he had come 'more and more to doubt the solidity of what had been regarded as the cornerstone of his monetary theory: the idea that if the money rate coincided with a normal rate, which brought about equality between savings and investment, the commodity price level would remain constant'.[7]

Wicksell was not the only theorist to find traditional monetary theory inadequate as a basis for explaining or prescribing for the chaotic monetary problems of the 1920s. The 1914–18 war had shattered the international gold standard, though the complexity of the national and international problems confronting the post-war world was such that it took time for the fact that it was impossible to put the clock back to penetrate to the majority of informed observers. The disruption of world trade and payments patterns – the need for massive unrequited transfers of capital in the form of reparations and loan repayments, the persistent weakness of sterling whose unique strength had made it the keystone of the pre-1914 gold standard, the sudden swings in the direction taken by 'hot money' movements, the national hyper-inflations and balance of payments disequilibria – all combined to present a thoroughly confusing context of empirical evidence about the way the national and international monetary systems were operating. On the other hand, this was precisely the envi-

[6] *Ibid*, p. 176.
[7] *Ibid*, p. xix. The evidence is in Wicksell's last paper, originally published in *Ekonomisk Tidskrift* 1925 and reprinted as an appendix to the Kahn translation, *op. cit.*

ronment to challenge theoretical economists to a systematic reconsideration of the concepts and theories which had constituted the traditional orthodoxy on monetary issues for over a century, and to get heretical ideas a hearing among respectable academics.

Meanwhile, however, even before the outbreak of the First World War, there was developing in Cambridge a lively intellectual interest in monetary economics, nurtured by Marshall's direct, if unsystematic, teaching. It was out of this fertile, open-minded, monetary theorising begun by Marshall and continued after his retirement by his successors, Pigou and then Robertson, and by such active disciples as Hawtrey, Lavington and Keynes, that the most influential of the twentieth-century heresies grew. John Maynard Keynes – whose first major publication was a monograph on *Indian Currency and Finance* (1913) – testified to the quality and stimulus of the Cambridge oral tradition in monetary theory in his 1924 obituary Memoir of Alfred Marshall.[8] Regretting the master's postponement of publication of his theory of money 'until extreme old age', Keynes insisted that: 'There is no part of Economics where Marshall's originality and priority of thought are more marked than here, or where his superiority of insight and knowledge over his contemporaries was greater.'[9] He then went on to list his contributions to this area, and it is interesting to note, in view of what has been said above about the conventional neo-classical dichotomy between real and monetary theory, that Keynes gave primary importance to Marshall's

exposition of the Quantity Theory of Money as a part of the General Theory of Value. He always taught that the value of money is a function of its supply on one hand, and the demand for it, on the other, as measured by 'the average stock of command over commodities which each person cares to keep in a ready form'. He went on to explain how each individual decides how much to keep in a ready form as the result of a *balance* of advantage between this and alternative forms of wealth.[10]

Keynes' own *Tract on Monetary Reform* (1923) appeared before Marshall died, in the same year as the latter's *Money, Credit and Commerce*, and did not depart from the basic Marshallian quantity-theory framework of analysis. However, it reacted – significantly

---

[8] Reprinted in *Essays in Biography*, Vol. x of *Collected Writings*.
[9] *Ibid*, p. 189.
[10] *Ibid*, p. 191 (italics in the original). See also the quotation from Marshall on p. 170 below.

in the light of the later Keynesian theorising – against some of
the values traditionally associated with the quantity theory, for
example against the belief that it was always better to run the risk
of deflation than of inflation;[11] and also against the equally
solidly-entrenched notion (given a legal backing in the 1844 Bank
Charter Act) that the prosperity of the economy depended on
the strength of the foreign exchanges and hence that domestic
policies ought to be subordinated to the over-riding objective of
maintaining a stable exchange rate. Here too, Keynes reacted
against the classical and neo-classical schools' obsessive concentration on the economics of long-term equilibrium with his
famous quip: 'In the long-run we are all dead. Economists set
themselves too easy a task if in tempestuous seasons they can only
tell us that when the storm is long past the ocean is flat again.'[12]
Finally, as Moggridge and Howson have noted, the policy inferences drawn in the *Tract* are more interventionist in sympathy than was consistent with the traditional Marshallian
quantity-theory approach.[13]

The *Tract* was, of course, a polemic. However, in the universities the theorists had already begun to subject the variables of
the quantity theory to a closer scrutiny than had been fashionable
in the halcyon pre-1914 era, in an effort to elucidate their causal-
significance. The Cambridge School, under the direct influence
of Marshall, began by shifting the emphasis of the so-called
'equation of exchange' so as to convert the tautologous formulation associated with Irving Fisher i.e. $MV = PT$, into a beha-
vioural formulation, e.g. $M = kY$, where k is the proportion of
the public's income which it chooses to hold in the form of cash
balances. In a purely formal sense the Marshallian k is merely
the reciprocal of V, and of course $Y = PT$ but the new formulation reflected a view of the causal relationships involved, in
particular the strategic importance of changes in the behaviour
of income velocity; or, to put it another way, on the demand for
cash balances.

Cambridge theorising, however, was never sufficiently abstract

[11] See J. M. Keynes, *Collected Writings*, Vol. IV, p. 36: 'Thus inflation is unjust
and deflation is inexpedient. Of the two perhaps deflation is, if we rule out
exaggerated inflations such as that of Germany, the worse: because it is worse,
in an impoverished world to provoke unemployment than to disappoint the
rentier.'

[12] *Ibid*, p. 80.

[13] D. E. Moggridge and Susan Howson, 'Keynes on Monetary Policy, 1910–46',
Oxford Economic Papers (July 1974), pp. 232–3.

or precise to be captured in a simple algebraic formula and one needs to go back to the verbal exposition to pick up the threads leading to its later development – in particular to note its focus on the psychological motives for holding or parting with cash balances and its explicit awareness of the fact that there were stocks of wealth considerations as well as flow of income considerations entering into the decisions made at any point of time.

Both clues are present in Marshall's statement that

currency held in the hand yields no income: therefore everyone balances (more or less automatically and instinctively) the benefits which he would get by investing some of it either in a commodity – say a coat or piano – from which he would derive direct benefit: or in some business plant or stock exchange security, which would yield him a money income.[14]

Also in Marshall (already expressed in evidence to the Indian Currency Committee of 1899) is a scepticism about the stability of the velocity of circulation of money, the assumption which underlies the naive quantity theory, e.g.: 'This "quantity doctrine" is helpful as far as it goes; but it does not indicate what are the "other things" which must be assumed to be equal in order to justify the proposition: and it does not explain the causes which govern "rapidity of circulation".'[15]

   The Cambridge approach to the quantity theory had the effect of stressing a quality of money which had been ignored in earlier versions, viz its role as a store of value. The original neo-classical formulation of the equation of exchange was a way of describing (without explaining) a simple relationship between the level of money in circulation and the level of prices, given a situation where the velocity of circulation was institutionally determined and money was needed merely as a medium of exchange. Once it was recognised that the demand for money might be affected not only by its need for immediate transaction purposes but also by its usefulness as a store of value for later purchases, then it was no longer possible to treat velocity as an essentially exogenous variable, for the demand for cash balances would then depend not only on the level of activity and on institutional factors, but also on trends in the supply of money and prices, and on entrepreneurial expectations *vis-à-vis* all these variables. The use of the equation of exchange for predictive or explanatory purposes must then depend crucially on the assumptions made

[14] A. Marshall, *Money Credit and Commerce* (1923), pp. 38–9.
[15] *Ibid*, p. 48.

about the links between V and M or P, i.e. on a theory of money which had not as yet been satisfactorily worked out.

The other direction in which monetary theory developed in the 1920s was along the path already indicated by Wicksell at the end of the 1892 – i.e. an attempt to analyse the connections between prices, interest, savings and investment in such a way as to bridge the classical dichotomy between the orthodox monetary theory of the factors affecting the general price level and the orthodox real theory of factors affecting investment, output and relative (as opposed to general) prices. The fact is that the problems of the inter-war period took a different shape from the pre-war problems. Apart altogether from the new importance of monetary issues, narrowly defined, it was increasingly obvious that the major real problems (above all the problems associated with chronic unemployment) were affecting and being affected by monetary factors in ways that the existing corpus of economic theory did little to illuminate. In effect, the questions that concerned most economists (at any rate in Britain and Sweden) had changed radically in form and it was no longer convenient to attack them with analytical concepts and theories drawn from two separate, and at times mutually inconsistent, intellectual compartments. Nor was it merely that the theory of markets was relevant only to long-run problems, whereas the questions that currently mattered were all cast in a short-run context; in the event, the received theory of money was as unsatisfactory as a tool for analysing short-term problems as the received theory of markets.

The other feature of the inter-war period which encouraged a radical reconstruction of orthodox monetary theory was that the institutional context was plainly different from that presumed in nineteenth-century quantity-theory doctrine. The skills in monetary management which the Bank of England had been developing, almost clandestinely, in the quarter century before 1914 and the greatly increased scope for open market operations implicit in the enormous weight of the National Debt were two examples of the changed situation in the United Kingdom: in the United States the most important new fact was the Federal Reserve System. Clearly it was time for economists to think in terms not only of a more sophisticated and active monetary policy but also in terms of a more complex gamut of monetary influences on output and employment.

The Swedish School made important strides along the Wick-

sellian path in the 1920s and 1930s while in England the lead
was taken by D. H. Robertson and J. M. Keynes working as colleagues and in such close consultation that, as Robertson wrote
of his *Banking Policy and the Price Level* (1926): 'neither of us now
know how much of the ideas is his...and how much is mine'.
Keynes' principal contribution to the revision of orthodox monetary theory came four years later in the form of his two volume
Treatise on Money (1930) a work which seems in some ways to have
been 'overtaken by events'. It was the most academic and least
polemical of all Keynes' books, a richer and more developed
version than Robertson's *Banking Policy* had been of the innovative ideas that they and others had been working on in the
1920s.[16] But it did not seem to contemporaries to fill the gap
lamented by the Macmillan Committee (of which Keynes was
himself a member) and which noted that 'there are no general
principles universally accepted as to the mode in which monetary
institutions and activities affect the economic situation, still less
as to the precise degree of their importance as compared with
other causes'. Indeed Keynes' Preface to the *Treatise* suggested
that his own ideas had already overtaken it by the time it came
into print. Then when the *General Theory* appeared, beginning
with a dramatic rejection of the classical frame of thought in
which the *Treatise* was unquestionably set, it seemed to those who
had embraced the Keynesian revolution that the latter was no
longer relevant and it slipped quietly off the core-course academic reading lists.

Recent research into the nature of the Keynesian revolution,
however, has tended to reinstate the *Treatise* not merely as being
the more complete and systematic exposition of Maynard Keynes'
contribution to monetary theory, but also as being an integral
part of the revolution in ideas that was characteristically Keynesian. Sir John Hicks, for example, has pointed out that the
General Theory relates to a closed economy and that it is the
Treatise which contains Keynes' contribution to the theory of
international money.[17] Leijonhufvud has argued that the essential Keynesian break with tradition shows up between the *Tract*

[16] There are many echoes of D. H. Robertson in the *Treatise* but it is here that
the differences between Keynes and Robertson began to be most clearly defined.
After publication of the *Treatise* Robertsonian and Keynesian monetary theories
explicitly and increasingly diverged.
[17] John Hicks, 'Note on the *Treatise*', *Critical Essays in Monetary Theory* (1967),
p. 189.

– which respected the traditional boundary between monetary
theory (dealing with the value of money and the demand for
output at the macro-level) and value theory (with its focus on
relative prices) – and the *Treatise* which effectively abandoned
this 'traditional compartmentalization'.[18] Others, however, have
stressed the rejection of the Quantity Theory which distinguishes
the *General Theory* from the *Treatise* as the crucial break with
monetary tradition:[19] and there is evidence that Keynes himself
saw his escape from the 'confusions of the Quantity Theory,
which once entangled me' as the breakthrough which enabled
him finally to integrate the theory of money with the 'fundamental theory of value', and thus to construct a completely
new theory of the monetary economy.[20]

By the time he came to write the *General Theory*, however,
Maynard Keynes had adapted his analytical techniques to the
fact that he was endeavouring to answer a different set of questions and to prescribe for a different range of policy issues, within
a different institutional context, to those confronting the neo-
classical economists who had taught him his trade. The policy
problem which had come to occupy the centre of Keynes' attention by the 1930s was not the problem of fluctuations in the value
of money, but the problem of mass unemployment, which led
him to focus in the *General Theory* on what determined the level
of output. In a real world subject to continuous change and often
deep uncertainty, the importance of money lay in its being a
refuge for those who wanted to postpone a definitive commitment of their real resources either to consumption or to investment; and the crucial variables that needed identification were
not the quantity of money in circulation or the factors through
which it affected the price level, but the market and real rates
of return from investment and their impact on the level of
economic activity. With those considerations in mind Keynes
fashioned new analytical tools and methodological techniques in
the field of money. Some of the new tools and techniques passed
into the commonly accepted heritage of all economists, whether

[18] Axel Leijonhufvud, *On Keynesian Economics and the Economics of Keynes*
(1968), p. 22.
[19] E.g. Donald Winch, *Economics and Policy* (1969); Don Patinkin, 'The Collected
Writings of John Maynard Keynes: From the Tract to the General Theory',
Economic Journal (June 1975), p. 260; Lord Kahn, *On Rereading Keynes* (1975), 4th
British Academy Lecture on Keynes.
[20] See the preface to the French Edition of the *General Theory*, reprinted in
J. M. Keynes, *Collected Writings*, Vol. VII, p. xxxiv.

or not they were persuaded to follow his overall change of methodological emphasis and to focus on a historical short term rather than on a long-term equilibrium economics. In the monetary sphere, for example, Keynes' liquidity-preference analysis (itself a development of the Cambridge cash-balance version of the quantity theory) has become a conventional part of the orthodox textbooks and has generated a whole new branch of monetary theory concerned with the choice of an optimum portfolio of assets. In the event, these Keynesian developments in monetary theory were merely a part of the more radical reconstruction of economic theory which arose out of his attempt to arrive at a general system of analysis appropriate to a twentieth-century monetary economy.

FURTHER READING

Primary literature

J. M. Keynes, *A Tract on Monetary Reform*, Vol. IV of *The Collected Writings of John Maynard Keynes*, ed. E. Johnson and D. E. Moggridge for the Royal Economic Society (1971).
J. M. Keynes, *A Treatise on Money*, Vols. V and VI of *Collected Writings*, ed. E. Johnson and D. E. Moggridge (1971).
D. H. Robertson, *Banking Policy and the Price Level* (1926).
Knut Wicksell, *Interest and Prices*, translated by R. F. Kahn (1936).

Secondary literature

E. Eshag, *From Marshall to Keynes. An Essay on the Monetary Theory of the Cambridge School* (1963).
D. E. Moggridge and Susan Howson, 'Keynes on Monetary Policy, 1910–46', *Oxford Economic Papers* (1974).
D. Patinkin, *Money, Interest and Prices* (1969).
D. Winch, *Economics and Policy* (1969).

12

THE KEYNESIAN REVOLUTION

The academic community of economists had by the early 1930s reached a sufficient disciplinary solidarity in their commitment to marginal analysis, and the associated analytical techniques, to provide the learned journals with a steady flow of articles that were often incomprehensible to the laymen, and sometimes too abstract either for the increasing body of empirical researchers, or for the broad fringe of economics graduates who continued to provide professional advice and explanation in their capacities as journalists, politicians, bankers, government officials, etc. Nevertheless, the common objective of the purest of theorists was still to provide a framework for the explanations or predictions that could assist policy makers to formulate rational economic policies. The fact is that the problems which professional economists have accepted as important have never been defined exclusively by an academic community. When economic science fails effectively to focus on the problems which society at large regards as important, all practising economists are vulnerable to the sense of intellectual insecurity that spreads through the rank and file of the profession.

In the 1930s the problem that dominated the mature capitalist economies was the problem of intense, persistent, trade depression, associated with widespread, unprecedentedly heavy unemployment. The unemployment problem was already chronic in Britain and some other Western European countries in the 1920s. By the 1930s it was universal in capitalist economies; and it was aggravated rather than relieved by laissez-faire economic policies. Even Britain, the last stronghold of free trade, adopted a protectionist strategy in the 1930s. Even in the United States, the proverbial home of economic individualism, the New Deal licensed an unprecedented level of government intervention. The ideological bias associated with the neo-classical paradigm was becoming an anachro-

nism,[1] and Robbins' view that the cause of Britain's difficulties since
the War was due to wages being 'held above the equilibrium
level',[2] though still shared by many politicians and officials provided little practical guidance to policy makers. This then was the
context in which Keynes produced his new theory. In what sense
did it constitute a new paradigm?

John Maynard Keynes himself certainly viewed his theory as
a complete break with current orthodoxy. The first chapter of
the *General Theory* consists of a single dramatic paragraph saying
just that. Like Marshall before him he set out deliberately to make
the economic theory in which he had been brought up more
general, i.e. more useful over a wider frame of reference in its
explanatory power. Unlike Marshall, however, he saw himself as
an innovator rather than an adaptor: though this was perhaps
more a difference in temperament or of starting-point[3] than a
difference of substance. Marshall, that is to say, changed more
than he was prepared to admit of the basic classical model and
Keynes retained more than might appear of the neo-classical
tradition.

Keynes took issue with what he chose to call 'classical' theory
but which embraced neo-classical theory,[4] i.e. with the current
economic orthodoxy. A major objection to orthodox economic

[1] Keynes had consigned the laissez-faire ideology to the lumber-room of
'vulgar economics' as early as November 1924 in a lecture on 'The End of
Laissez-faire'. See J. M. Keynes, *Collected Writings*, Vol. IX, e.g. p. 277: 'I have said
that it was the economists who furnished the scientific pretext by which the
practical man could solve the contradiction between egoism and socialism which
emerged out of the philosophising of the eighteenth century and the decay of
revealed religion. But having said this for shortness' sake, I hasten to qualify it.
This is what the economists are *supposed* to have said. No such doctrine is really
to be found in the writings of the greatest authorities. It is what the popularisers
and the vulgarisers said.'

[2] Quoted above, pp. 147–8.

[3] Keynes was conscious of a real struggle to free himself from classical theoretical ruts. See e.g. a letter to Harrod dated 30 August 1936: 'What some people
treat as unnecessarily controversial is really due to the importance in my own
mind of what I *used* to believe, and of the moments of transition which were for
me personally moments of illumination' (J. M. Keynes, *Collected Writings*, Vol.
XIV, pp. 84–5).

[4] '"The classical economists" was a name invented by Marx to cover Ricardo
and James Mill and their *predecessors*, that is to say for the founders of the theory
which culminated in the Ricardian economics. I have become accustomed,
perhaps perpetrating a solecism, to include in "the classical school" the *followers*
of Ricardo, those, that is to say, who adopted and perfected the theory of the
Ricardian economics, including (for example) J. S. Mill, Marshall, Edgeworth and
Prof. Pigou' (footnote to Chapter 1 of the *General Theory*, p. 3).

theory in the context of the 1930s was that it assumed an economy which was tending towards full employment – *not* of course that the economy was necessarily in a position of full employment, but that its eventual equilibrium was a full employment position. But for Britain in the prolonged depression of the inter-war period, with unemployment averaging 10 per cent of the insured labour force even in the prosperous years, the assumption seemed blatantly to disregard the crucial problem of economic policy.

It was thus the classical theory of employment with which Keynes took issue *first* in his second chapter, which is a critique of what he chose to specify as 'the postulates of classical economics'. These on his account were fourfold:

(1) That the real wage is equal to the marginal product of labour;
(2) That the real wage is equal to the marginal disutility of the existing employment;
(3) – which is a logical corollary of (2) – that there is no such thing as involuntary unemployment in the strict sense; i.e. that all the unemployed could get employment merely by accepting a fall in wages, and
(4) that supply creates its own demand in the sense that the aggregate demand price is equal to the aggregate supply price for all levels of output and employment.

With the first of the postulates he did not quarrel. With the second and its logical corollary the third, he came into head-on clash. The implication of the second classical assumption, that the real wage equals the marginal disutility of labour, is that an individual could increase his employment by revising his notion of the disutility of labour and accepting a lower wage. At a macroeconomic level it implies that 'if labour as a whole would agree to a reduction of money-wages more employment would be forthcoming'. Keynes' objections to these assumptions were based partly on an appeal to facts: 'It is not very plausible to assert that unemployment in the United States was due either to labour obstinately refusing to accept a reduction of money wages or to its obstinately demanding a real wage beyond what the productivity of the economic machine was capable of furnishing.'[5] Of course the facts were not necessarily in conflict with the classical assumption for this was not that there could never be any involuntary unemployment or depression but that there would not

[5] *General Theory, op. cit.*, p. 9.

be any involuntary unemployment when the economy was in long-run equilibrium. Pigou, for example, whose *Theory of Unemployment* Keynes chose as his target in his attack on classical theory recognised that in times of depression (i.e. in a position of disequilibrium) real wages could be falling while unemployment was rising.

More significantly, however, Keynes objected that classical theory failed to take account of the role of money in the situation, and in particular of the fact that money wages did not necessarily move in the same way as real wages. Wage bargains he pointed out are made in money terms and money wage rates do not determine real wage rates, and

the struggle about money wages primarily affects the *distribution* of the aggregate real wage between different labour-groups, and not its average amount per unit of employment... The effect of combination on the part of a group of workers is to protect their *relative* real wage. The *general* level of real wages depends on other forces of the economic system.[6]

Only on very special assumptions concerning the flexibility of wages, prices and interest rates could it be argued that a wage cut would necessarily lead to an increase in employment.

The other postulate of the classical economists with which Keynes took issue at the outset of his *General Theory* was Say's Law – the proposition that for the economy as a whole supply necessarily creates a demand of equivalent magnitude. In its plainest form it states that 'the whole of the costs of production must necessarily be spent in the aggregate, directly or indirectly, on purchasing the product'.[7] Here, as elsewhere in his assault on the current orthodoxy, Keynes was setting up what Dennis Robertson was to describe as 'a composite Aunt Sally of uncertain age'[8] for he did not really believe that many of his contemporaries actually accepted Say's Law. It was crucial to his own position, however, because it was tantamount to the proposition that there was no real obstacle to full employment and as such, he believed, was one of the tacit assumptions which prevented the classical theorists from thinking clearly about the economic situation in which they found themselves in the 1930s. If Say's Law (read as an economic law rather than as a logical consequence of certain

---

[6] *Ibid*, p. 14. [7] *Ibid*, p. 18.
[8] In the course of a debate on the *General Theory* in the 1937 *Economic Journal*. Keynes admitted the justice of the quip. J. M. Keynes, *Collected Writings*, Vol. XIV, p. 215.

restrictive assumptions) had fallen into disuse among contemporary theorists before Keynes proceeded to demolish it so devastatingly, it was because classical and neo-classical theory had largely turned away from the macroeconomic questions to which it was relevant, i.e. from questions of the demand and supply for output as a whole. This, however, did not prevent the implicit assumptions from exerting a stranglehold on conventional economic analysis when the macro-economic policy issues of the inter-war period forced their way into the centre of economic discussion. For example, the official 'Treasury view' that a public works programme would increase rather than relieve the unemployment problem by diverting funds from private productive investments to unproductive public investment, was largely justified by an appeal to Say's Law.[9]

There is no real doubt, both that Maynard Keynes intended to revise radically the analytical framework of the discipline, and that the publication of the *General Theory* marked the beginning of a revolution in economic ideas. However, whether the revolution was what Keynes had intended and exactly how destructive it was of the neo-classical paradigm are matters of considerable current controversy.

Beginning then with his own view of what he was doing in the *General Theory*, he claimed to show that the classical theory was based on postulates that were applicable to a special case – the case of an economy in which the *natural* forces were such that aggregate demand would always adjust to aggregate supply so as to produce a persistent tendency towards full employment. 'The classical theorists resemble Euclidean geometers in a non-Euclidean world who, discovering that in experience straight lines apparently parallel often meet, rebuke the lines for not keeping straight – as the only remedy for the unfortunate collisions which are occurring.'[10] What was needed was a new model of economic reality which started from the facts of experience, i.e. a system with a persistent tendency towards something less than full employment. He then developed a theory in which the level of employment depended on (i) the propensity to consume, (ii) the marginal efficiency of capital, (iii) the quantity of money and (iv) the level of wages. The key factors in the system were (a) the 'principle of effective demand' which acted through the propensity to consume and the rate of new investment to set a

---

[9] See L. L. Pasinetti, *Growth and Income Distribution* (1974), p. 35.
[10] *General Theory*, p. 16.

ceiling to the level of economic activity, and (b) the role played
by money as 'the link between the present and the future' in
reflecting past and present uncertainties about the future on the
part of lenders and borrowers, and reflecting them on the rate
of interest and hence of investment. The system was enriched
by the introduction of a set of concepts which were novel not in
origin but in the dynamic use to which they were put, viz the
marginal propensity to save and its inverse the multiplier,
liquidity preference which made the demand for money hinge
on choices between stocks of assets as well as flows of income
and expenditure, and the marginal efficiency of capital which
depended on the relation between the supply price of assets and
the variable expectations of investors.

It is a testament both to the tenacity of the ruling paradigm
and to the capacity of some of the most enthusiastic converts to
a new set of ideas to reinterpret the ideas of the master in the
light of the conventional wisdom in which they were trained that
the Keynesian theory has come to be interpreted by the textbooks
in exactly the opposite sense to which Keynes saw it himself, i.e.
it is treated as a special case of neo-classical theory, the case of
unemployment equilibrium.[11] The argument runs that, with a
given money wage rate, the equilibrium levels of aggregate income
and the rate of investment are determined by (1) the propensity
to consume, (2) the investment demand schedule (defined on
conventional neo-classical lines with investment a decreasing
function of interest), (3) liquidity preference and (4) the quantity
of money: with (1) and (2) being stable functions in the short
run and (3) being stable (and highly elastic) at low interest rates.
From this standpoint the special assumptions which justify the
Keynesian theory within a neo-classical framework are rigid
money wages, a 'liquidity trap' (in which the demand for money
becomes infinitely elastic at low interest rates and so prevents
rates from falling when the supply of money increases), plus,
possibly, a low interest elasticity of investment.

The novelty of the *General Theory*, then, boils down to Keynes'
use of the 'psychological' concepts of the consumption function
and liquidity preference, his treatment of the role of effective
demand in generating output changes (rather than price changes
as in the general classical case where prices and wages are flex-

---

[11] For a detailed analysis of the way Keynesian economics differs from the
economics of Keynes see A. Leijonhufvud, *On Keynesian Economics and the Economics of Keynes* (1968).

ible), in making the demand for money hinge on choices between assets rather than between flows of income and expenditure, and in shifting the stress from savings to investment as the primary cause of capital accumulation.[12] It is a corollary of this reinterpretation of the *General Theory* that more than one Keynesian has doubted that Keynes understood the significance of his own analysis.[13]

It is debatable, however, whether Keynes would have accepted modern Keynesian economics as the textbooks expound it. For one thing he did not regard the tentative assumptions necessary to absorb his general theory into the neo-classical framework as valid in themselves. He was quite explicit for example in regarding the stable wage assumption as merely a preliminary expository convenience with no relevance for the logic of his argument.[14] Nor did he believe in the actuality of the liquidity trap and referred to it as hypothetical possibility only in order to show how easy it would be for a farsighted public authority to fill the gap in investment by borrowing from the banking system at nominal rates.[15]

But more important than the restrictive assumptions that have been attached to Keynesian economics, is the fact that his departures from the neo-classical paradigm were more radical in spirit than the modern interpretation allows. In particular, for example, he was in revolt against the tendency, implicit in the mechanistic analytical techniques of marginal economics, towards visualising economic science as capable of providing a vehicle for scientific prediction by analogy with the natural sciences. 'Economics' he maintained, in a letter to Harrod in 1938, 'is essentially a moral science and not a natural science.'

I mentioned before that it deals with introspection and with values. I might have added that it deals with motives, expectations, psychological uncertainties. One has to be constantly on guard against treating the material as constant and homogeneous. It is as though the fall of the apple to the ground depended on the apple's motives on whether

[12] See e.g. James Meade, 'The Keynesian Revolution', *op. cit.*, ed. Milo Keynes (1975), p. 82: 'Keynes's intellectual revolution was to shift economists from thinking normally in terms of a model of reality in which a dog called *savings* wagged his tail labelled *investment* to thinking in terms of a model in which a dog called *investment* wagged his tail labelled *savings*.'

[13] E.g. P. Samuelson in R. Lekachman (ed.), *Keynes' General Theory: Reports of Three Decades*, p. 321; and L. Klein, *The Keynesian Revolution* (1960), p. 83.

[14] *General Theory*, p. 27: 'The essential character of the argument is precisely the same whether or not money-wages, etc. are liable to change.'

[15] *General Theory*, p. 207.

it is worthwhile falling to the ground, and whether the ground
wanted the apple to fall, and on mistaken calculations on the part of the
apple as to how far it was from the centre of the earth.[16]
Hence his emphasis on psychological propensities and on expectations under uncertainty. Investment he argued, for example,
'depends on two sets of judgments about the future, neither of
which rests on an adequate or secure foundation – on the
propensity to hoard and on opinions of the future yield of
capital assets'.[17] His own view of the object of an economic model
was that it was a vehicle for analysis rather than for prediction.
'The object of a model is to segregate the semi-permanent or
relatively constant factors from those which are transitory or
fluctuating so as to develop a logical way of thinking about the
latter, and of understanding the time sequences to which they
give rise in particular cases'.[18] His primary concern was with states
of disequilibrium rather than of equilibrium and although – true
to his classical upbringing, he made frequent use of the concept
of equilibrium in his *General Theory* – it was a short-period
equilibrium rather than a long-period equilibrium that he had in
mind.

It can be said that there were three respects in which the
General Theory broke away from the classical mould and generated a new economics. The first was in the questions it asked,
the second was in its conclusions and the third was in the route
to these conclusions. The central question on which Keynes
focused, as has already been stressed, was a question which
neo-classical theory had so far failed effectively to confront, viz
what were the determinants of the supply and demand for
aggregate output.

The iconoclastic conclusion of his analysis was that there was
no invisible hand translating private self-interest into social
benefit. This was the nub of the Keynesian heresy. It had already
been formulated in 1924 in the lecture which provided the basis
for the essay on *The End of Laissez-faire* – though the leading
classical and neo-classical economists from John Stuart Mill onwards were there exonerated by Keynes from having subscribed
to the ideological doctrine of laissez-faire.[19] In 1934 while he was

[16] J. M. Keynes, *Collected Writings*, Vol. xiv, pp. 297–300.
[17] J. M. Keynes, 'The General Theory of Employment', *Quarterly Journal of
Economics* (1937), Reprinted in *Collected Writings*, Vol. xiv, p. 218.
[18] J. M. Keynes, *Collected Writings*, Vol. xiv, pp. 296–7.
[19] J. M. Keynes, *Collected Writings*, Vol. ix, p. 281: 'Economists no longer have
any link with the theological or political philosophies out of which the dogma

primarily engaged in drafting the *General Theory* Keynes put the point more aggressively in a BBC talk on the theme 'Is the Economic System Self-Adjusting?' in which he argued that those who believed the system embodied significant tendencies towards self-adjustment had behind them 'almost the whole body of organised economic thinking and doctrine of the last hundred years' and went on to range himself unequivocally on the side of the heretics with this statement: 'There is, I am convinced, a fatal flaw in that part of the orthodox reasoning which deals with the theory of what determines the level of effective demand and the volume of aggregate employment: the flaw being largely due to the failure of the classical doctrine to develop a satisfactory theory of the rate of interest.'[20] The really shattering conclusion to emerge from the *General Theory* in the context of the 1930s was that a cut in wages, far from relieving unemployment as the classical theory implied, could actually increase it by reducing the level of effective demand.

The method was to set up an aggregative model of the economy as a whole – so simple in basic construction that it was readily intelligible to the average student or interested politician, deliberately relevant to contemporary economic problems and convincing in the range of its vision. According to Pigou: 'Nobody before him... had brought all the relevant factors, real and monetary at once, together in a single scheme, through which their interplay could be coherently investigated.'[21] Keynes concentrated attention on national expenditure–income and income–expenditure relationships which were superficially easier to understand and to manipulate than the classical quantity-theory relationships. He demonstrated in a way that had never been so dramatically and clearly brought out before, the dependence of aggregate expenditure on itself in its income-generating capacity. In so doing he filled a large gap in classical theory and added a new dimension to economic analysis. Macro-economics as we know it today starts from Keynes' *General Theory*.

When one examines in detail the innovations introduced by the *General Theory* into current economic thought one can trace many of them back to earlier writers as Keynes did himself. Malthus had recognised a link between effective demand, con-

of social harmony was born, and their scientific analysis leads them to no such conclusions.'
[20] J. M. Keynes, *Collected Writings*, Vol. XIII, p. 489.
[21] Quoted by Haberler in Lekachman (ed.), *op. cit.*, pp. 290–1.

sumption and total output as long ago as 1820 when in his *Principles of Political Economy* he had formally denied Say's Law. Hobson pursued the same line of thought by pointing to the tendency for production to outrun consumption as a consequence of over-saving. The Swedish school of economists, focusing in the early 1930s on the problem of the gap between savings and investment, developed a theory of monetary equilibrium which was essentially the same as that which emerged from the *General Theory*. In some ways indeed the Swedish school, with their explicit distinction between *ex-ante* and *ex-post* concepts of savings and investment brought out more clearly than Keynes himself was to do the dynamic significance of the savings–investment disequilibrium – viz that it is the divergence beteween planned lending and planned investment which accounts for the gap whereas *ex-post* savings and *ex-post* investment are always equal.[22] The concept of the multiplier had been formally expounded by R. F. Kahn in an article published in the 1931 *Economic Journal*.[23]

However, it was in its broad outlines – (a) in the way it formulated the fundamental theoretical problem as one of accounting for the level of economic activity rather than of prices, (b) in its method – the national-income–expenditure framework of analysis and (c) in its policy implications for deliberate demand-management on the part of the political and monetary authority – that the *General Theory* produced a revolution in economic ideas. Whether or not the revolution took the shape which Keynes would have approved is of course another matter.

No doubt the principal reason why the *General Theory* had such a powerful impact on the community of professional economists inside and outside the universities, internationally as well as in Britain, was that the time was ripe. Its abstractions seemed more relevant to the conditions of the 1930s than the competing theories. Its analysis gave a theoretical basis for policy-

[22] According to G. L. S. Shackle, *The Years of High Theory*, p. 144, Myrdal's *Monetary Equilibrium*, written 5 years or more before the appearance of Keynes' *General Theory* 'anticipated the *General Theory* in almost every respect except that of its huge impact on economics and the world'.

[23] As Dr Moggridge has noted in his account of the Cambridge debates which preceded and helped to shape the *General Theory*, Kahn's article was stimulated by a line of thought already suggested by Keynes and H. D. Henderson in the 1929 essay *Can Lloyd George do it?* and was in Keynes' hands as early as 1930 – before publication of the *Treatise* but too late to affect its exposition. See *The Collected Writings of John Maynard Keynes*, ed. D. E. Moggridge, Vol. XIII, p. 340.

prescriptions that were more in tune with existing political trends in a world that was already in massive retreat from a laissez-faire ideology. It thus attracted the interest of economists over a very wide spectrum of political affinity. Marxian economists who had been unable to come to terms with socially complacent starting assumptions which took for granted the legendary virtues of laissez-faire competitive capitalism, welcomed this breath of fresh air. Sweezy, for example, in a warm obituary written in 1946 suggested that Keynes' greatest achievement was that of liberating Anglo-American economics from the 'tyrannical dogma' of Say's Law, and of exploding 'once and for all the myth of a harmony between private and public interests which was the corner-stone of nineteenth century liberalism'.[24] Liberal economists on the other hand were attracted by the profoundly capitalistic nature of Keynesian philosophy, offering as it did both an antidote to social revolution and an analytical framework which could 'swallow the classical system as a special case'.[25] Many more academic economists uncommitted to either ideological extreme, found it intellectually stimulating to identify with Keynes' attempt to modernise economic theory without jettisoning the familiar Marshallian methodological techniques and concepts.

For applied economists, particularly the growing number of empirical research workers, a prime attraction of the Keynesian system was that it was a coherent system of thought which lent itself readily to quantification and statistical testing. It opened a whole new programme of research with particularly exciting possibilities for those whose interest in economics was policy oriented. It is doubtful whether the new system could have seduced so many theorists and empirical research workers away from the neo-classical orthodoxy in which they had been trained, or could have inspired so many practical policy makers with confidence that economics, had, after all, something useful to contribute to their decisions, if it had not been focused on a more urgent set of questions than the Marshallian ones. The classical economists had asked what determined prices and output in particular commodity markets and at the level of the individual producer or industry: they examined the behaviour of the individual consumer. As by-products of this analysis they drew macroeconomic inferences and they suggested general welfare

[24] P. Sweezy in Lekachman (ed.), *op. cit.*, p. 301.
[25] P. Samuelson in Lekachman (ed.), *op. cit.*, p. 318.

criteria for policy makers to take into account. But most of the time they were looking at the economy in terms of the behaviour of its atomistic particles and the way these reacted on each other. Except in relation to monetary theory – which was never fully integrated with the basic theories of demand, production and distribution – their techniques of analysis were micro-economic rather than macro-economic. By starting from the national, aggregative level of analysis Keynes focused on problems that academics and politicians alike regarded as important and he tackled them by making assumptions drawn from a close and acute observation of the way the economic system was working in his own time.

In view of the developments that have taken place in Keynesian economics in the 1950s and 1960s and in the immense volume of statistical and econometric research that stemmed from these developments it may be worth emphasising that Keynes' commitment to realism did not imply an anti-theoretical bias. On the contrary he accused Marshall, for example, of confusing his models with superfluous realism and of 'being unnecessarily ashamed of lean and abstract outlines'. Most of all, however, he objected to the attempts of the econometricians such as Schultz and Tinbergen, to quantify their models in order to use them as a basis for prediction.[26]

In chemistry and physics and other natural sciences the object of the experiment is to fill the actual values of the various quantities and factors appearing in an equation or a formula; and the work when done is once and for all. In economics this is not the case and to convert a model into a quantitative formula is to destroy its usefulness as an instrument of thought.[27]

For Keynes the role of the statistician was not to turn economic models into forecasting instruments but to test their relevance and validity.

On the other hand, although the Keynesian theory was not intended to displace the neo-classical theories at the micro-

[26] In his Presidential Address to the Econometric Society Don Patinkin noted that 'the statistical revolution as represented by Clark's and Kuznets' national income estimates precedes the "Keynesian Revolution" as represented by the *General Theory*' and criticised Keynes for not having been more active in pressing the UK authorities to follow the US example in setting up an official national income unit as early as 1932. See 'Keynes and Econometrics: on the interaction between the macroeconomic Revolutions of the Interwar Period' (*Econometrica*, November 1976, p. 1104).

[27] J. M. Keynes, *Collected Writings*, Vol. XIV, p. 299.

economic level of analysis, and although Keynesian economics has retained more of the neo-classical framework than Keynes had intended, the elements of a distinctively Keynesian model have been indelibly written into modern economic thought and have to a large extent determined the way it has developed. The revolution in ideas about the role of government in the economic system – in particular the deliberate attempt to influence the level of effective demand, which was a feature of all advanced capitalist economies in the post Second World War era – was facilitated by, and guaranteed a central importance in economic thought for, the Keynesian macroeconomic variables and relationships. The Keynesian model turned out to be an operational model which constituted the basic prototype for all later macroeconomic general equilibrium and dynamic models. The systematic rethinking of the assumptions underlying classical economic theory, which was an inevitable consequence of its confrontation by a vigorous competing system, effectively broke the stabilising effect of orthodoxy, so that neo-classical theory itself gained a new lease of life and began to take off in new, non-Keynesian directions. Finally the sheer range of the Keynesian model made it a convenient frame of reference against which to consider almost any problem in pure or applied economics.

Nevertheless, as Professor Leijonhufvud has now shown,[28] in the event Keynesian economics turned into something wholly different from the economics which Keynes expounded in the *General Theory* and which was a development of theories which he had worked out in his *Treatise on Money* (1930). He has argued that the familiar income–expenditure theory which is a basic component of the orthodox macroeconomic texts published in the 1950s and 1960s is substantially different in structure and emphasis from the original Keynesian model. In particular, for example, the emphasis on the superior effectiveness of fiscal policy as opposed to monetary policy is a subsequent development and is not reflected in the arguments of the *General Theory*. The assumptions that wages are rigid and that savings (and indeed investment too) are interest-inelastic – assumptions which have been used to justify the modern neo-classical contention that Keynes' so-called 'general' theory is merely a special case of the traditional neo-classical theory of markets – are not, it turns out, necessary assumptions in Keynes' own theory.

[28] A. Leijonhufvud, *On Keynesian Economics and the Economics of Keynes* (1968).

Leijonhufvud's interpretation of 'what Keynes really meant' is of course debatable and has indeed already been revised: but it brought sharply into question the pedigree of much of contemporary macroeconomic theory which currently passes for Keynesian economics. More recently, since the publication of the *Collected Works of John Maynard Keynes*, edited for the Royal Economic Society by Elizabeth Johnson and Donald Moggridge, it has been possible to draw extensively on Keynes' less accessible, or hitherto unpublished, letters and papers to assess his views: and the debate stimulated by Leijonhufvud accordingly continues. Of particular interest, for example, is Moggridge's note on Keynes' response (in a letter dated 31 March 1937) to Hicks' well-known formulation of the Keynesian model of the relationships between savings, investment, income and the rate of interest.[29] For as Moggridge points out, one of the points at which Keynes took issue with Hicks' formulation (which in the event became basic to the textbook version of orthodox Keynesian economics) was its treatment of expectations as given by the current level of income. This suggested for the model an unrealistic degree of predictive potential by in effect ignoring the influence of uncertainty on investment decisions – a device which has frequently characterised Keynesian economics, but was missing a vital point as far as Keynes was concerned.

In the event then, the macroeconomic concepts and theories associated with the Keynesian revolution inspired a variety of theoretical and empirical research programmes[30] and there are wide divergencies between the basic assumptions and analytical techniques adopted by economists who would regard themselves as working within a Keynesian tradition. Partly because of the intervention of the war which raised totally different policy

[29] Hicks' article 'Mr. Keynes and the Classics' appeared originally in *Econometrica* (1937), but has since been reprinted in J. R. Hicks, *Critical Essays in Monetary Theory* (1973), which also reprints Keynes' letter. Moggridge's note on this matter is contained in an appendix to D. E. Moggridge, *Keynes* (1976).

[30] That is to say the Keynesian revolution did not lead the economics profession into the kind of narrowly constrained research tradition that is implied in Kuhn's concept of Normal Science and which in the Kuhnian model of scientific revolutions marks the success of a new paradigm. Cf. I. Lakatos, 'Falsification and the Methodology of Scientific Research Programmes', in I. Lakatos and A. Musgrave (eds.), *Criticism and the Growth of Knowledge* (1970), p. 155: '*The history of science has been and should be a history of competing research programmes (or, if you wish, "paradigms"), but it has not been and must not become a succession of periods of normal science.* "Theoretical pluralism" is better than "theoretical monism": on this point Popper and Feyerabend are right and Kuhn is wrong.'

problems from those which the *General Theory* was designed to analyse, and partly because Keynes died before the peacetime problems assumed their distinctive shape – and indeed before the academic economists had effectively digested the revolutionary quality of his message – the *General Theory* never became the bible of the 'new economics' in the way that Marshall's *Principles* had done. It graduated rapidly to the status of a 'classic' which the average undergraduate of the 1950s and 1960s absorbed through secondary sources (guides to Keynes or macroeconomic texts) rather than in the original.[31]

FURTHER READING

Primary literature

J. M. Keynes, *The General Theory of Employment, Interest and Money*, Vol. VIII, in *Collected Writings of John Maynard Keynes* (1971).

J. M. Keynes, 'The General Theory of Employment', *Quarterly Journal of Economics* (1937).

Secondary literature

Milo Keynes (ed.), *Essays on John Maynard Keynes* (1975).

L. Klein, *The Keynesian Revolution* (1960).

Axel Leijonhufvud, *On Keynesian Economics and the Economics of Keynes* (1968).

R. Lekachman, *Keynes' General Theory after Three Decades* (1964).

D. E. Moggridge, *Keynes* (1976).

Don Patinkin, 'The Collected Writings of John Maynard Keynes: From the *Tract* to the *General Theory*', *Economic Journal* (1975).

[31] It became conventional to describe the *General Theory* as being 'too difficult' or 'badly written' – a convention which owed more to the inability of the teachers to reconcile its contents with orthodox Keynesian economics than to the expository deficiencies of a book which in its first edition was read with excitement and enthusiasm by the rank and file of the economics profession.

13

TWENTIETH CENTURY GROWTH THEORY

The theory of economic growth was not a promising area in which to apply marginal techniques of analysis. It therefore fell largely outside the scope of what the neo-classical orthodoxy which triumphed as a result of the marginal revolution chose to define as 'pure economic science'. At the beginning of the twentieth century, however, one man, far ahead of his time in theoretical interests and insight, was working in Europe on a theory of economic development which was essentially a theory of cyclical growth. Joseph Schumpeter's *Theory of Economic Development* was first published in Germany in 1911 but was not translated into English until 1934. By then English and American economists were deeply concerned by problems of trade cycles and secular stagnation in the mature capitalist countries from which developed a new interest in analysing the economic development of industrial society. But it was not until after the Second World War when the condition of the under-developed countries became a primary policy issue that economists began to study growth again in the form in which it had interested Adam Smith, Karl Marx and the classical economists generally, i.e. as an inquiry into the nature and causes of the wealth of nations.

Unlike most of his contemporaries among English speaking economists, Schumpeter was well-acquainted with the works of both Marx and Walras as well as Marshall, and, of course, of the members of the Austrian school in which he was trained.[1] His ideas on economics thus developed in an unusually open framework of theories, concepts and methodological techniques. While recognising, with Marx, that 'the social process is really one indivisible whole', he shared Marshall's view that an econo-

[1] The Austrian school developed out of Carl Menger's contribution to the marginal revolution and among its most influential ideas was Böhm-Bawerk's theory of capital.

mist should develop explanations for economic variables. To quote:

When we succeed in finding a definite causal relation between two phenomena, our problem is solved if the one which plays the 'causal' rôle is non-economic. We have then accomplished what we, as economists, are capable of in the case in question and we must give place to other disciplines. If, on the other hand, the causal factor is itself economic in nature, we must continue our explanatory efforts until we ground upon a non-economic bottom.[2]

However, like Marx he looked to 'business cycles for material with which to build the fundamental theory of capitalist reality'[3] and to history, sociology, and political science for the basis of his assumptions concerning the nature and structural characteristics of economic development. His *Theory of Economic Development* (1911) was an outline of the theoretical model which was basic to all his analysis of economic growth; and his later books *Business Cycles* (1939) and *Capitalism Socialism and Democracy* (1943) put empirical flesh on to these bare bones and set them within the broader context of the social process as a whole.

Classical theory had produced models which set up a mechanism, rather than a reason, for economic expansion and growth – though it was a mechanism which was destined eventually to run down: neo-classical theory took total output for the economy as a whole as given and focused on the problem of ensuring the optimum allocation of resources in a stationary state. What Schumpeter set out to do was to identify an endogenous source of productivity growth and a mechanism which would generate long-term continuity, but persistent fluctuations, in the growth of total output. He found an answer in the character of the profit-maximising entrepreneur and in the act of innovation – the latter being widely defined to include any change in the method of production which was expected to add to profits, e.g. new machines, new processes, new products, new markets or sources of inputs, industrial reorganisation and so on. Unlike the neo-classical theorists he was more interested in conditions of disequilibrium than of equilibrium and he brought the credit mechanism purposefully within his explanations for real sequences of events.

The novel characteristic of the Schumpeterian theory then was the emphasis it put on technical progress in the growth process.

[2] J. Schumpeter, *Theory of Economic Development* (1934), pp. 4–5.
[3] Schumpeter, *History of Economic Analysis*, p. 1135.

In effect the result of trying to explain economic development as a phenomenon that takes place in spurts and slumps, instead of in terms of a long-term trend, was to focus his interest on the cyclical impact of technical progress, on the psychology of crises and on the role of the entrepreneur in initiating or imitating innovation. It is through the decisions of the entrepreneur that technical progress gives direction and momentum to capital and it is his psychology (his readiness to take the lead in pursuit of profits associated with 'those tragi-comic aberrations of the frightened business world' which break the boom) that causes the growth process to fluctuate. Labour is a passive element in Schumpeter's system and 'Capital is nothing but the lever by which the entrepreneur subjects to his control the concrete goods which he needs, nothing but a means of diverting the factors of production to new uses or of dictating a new direction to production.'[4]

Schumpeter begins with the concept of a stationary state, i.e. he 'describes economic life from the standpoint of a "circular flow" running on in channels essentially the same year after year, similar to the circulation of the blood in an animal organism.'[5] This quasi-equilibrium starting point is characterised by the fact that labour, capital and output are all growing at the same rate and just enough capital is being annually accumulated to equip additions to the labour force at a constant capital–labour ratio. The circular flow is periodically broken, either by a new discovery, or by the emergence of a few gifted entrepreneurs capable of recognising already existing opportunities for profitable new investment. These entrepreneurs persuade the banking system to advance them credit, so inflating the supply of money, raising prices and creating the forced savings necessary to finance the additional capital formation.[6] Their example attracts imitators and their investment may create new opportunities for innovation in other sectors of the economy or stimulate new research or invention so that innovations tend to cluster in time. The sheeplike trail of less gifted imitators and the working out of the cost-reducing possibilities of a given cluster of innovations tends to overproduction and recession (sometimes precipitated by panic) but not before the system has been lifted to new levels of productivity and to a higher capital–labour ratio. It was crucial

---

[4] *Theory of Economic Development*, p. 116.   [5] *Ibid*, p. 61.
[6] The mechanism suggested here resembles Keynes' analysis, but lacks the multiplier link between savings and investment.

to Schumpeter's theory (and added to its realism) that there should be enough imperfection in the competitive system to permit an innovating entrepreneur to reap super-normal (monopoly) profits from his risk-taking: for if competition (and foresight) were quite perfect, imitation would be instantaneous and profits at once forced back to normal levels, leaving no incentive for technological change. However, given a degree of hindrance to instant imitation (often supported by institutional constraints, e.g. patent laws), growth takes place in bursts of creative activity where entrepreneurs, attracted by the monopoly profits of innovation, get credit from the banking system to expand investment, and earn supernormal profits until they are forced by competition into overproduction and contraction.

None of the classical theories had visualised growth going on forever. Most saw output per head reaching an upper asymptote in the form of a stationary state, brought about by diminishing returns to new investment and a falling rate of profit, as the stock of capital expanded faster than the supply of labour and natural resources. In the end Schumpeter also visualised a slowing down in the growth process but he attributed it to changes in the institutional context of economic activity. He saw the growth in the scale of production leading to a bureaucratisation of corporate enterprise and a change in the character of the entrepreneur. He thus came in his *Capitalism, Socialism and Democracy* (1943) to an explanation for secular stagnation which hinges with the rest of his theory on the psychology of the innovating entrepreneur.

Not surprisingly, economists in the inter-war period were more interested in theories of stagnation than theories of growth and theories of secular stagnation began to proliferate. Some were no more than a reversion to classical growth theories of the gradual drift towards the stationary state as the race between diminishing returns and increasing returns was steadily tipped in favour of the former. Others developed within a more specifically Keynesian framework. In its simplest form the stagnation thesis that became popular in the 1930s states that in a mature capitalistic economy (mature in the sense that it is exploiting the full level of technological know-how and enjoys average incomes well above subsistence level) the opportunities for investment are unlikely to keep pace with the growing supply of savings and of labour. With incomes (and hence savings) rising continuously the economy faces problems not only of recurring cyclical unemployment but also of growing *chronic* unemployment.

There are various versions of this theory, but the best known is Alvin Hansen's, which he illustrated by reference to the world's most technologically progressive and high-income economy – the United States. Basically Hansen's argument was that a mature economy tends to confront increasingly diminishing returns to investment and that in the American case this tendency, which first became obvious in the 1930s, was due to a combination of four characteristically twentieth-century causes – one of which made the supply of new savings relatively abundant and three of which weakened the demand for loanable funds. They were: (1) the rise in both personal and corporate savings ratios; (2) the declining rate of population growth; (3) the end to the expansion of the geographical frontier; and (4) the tendency for inventions to become capital-saving rather than capital-absorbing. It was the historical coincidence of these four factors that gave the Hansen argument its cogency. The rate of profit is likely to fall faster if *both* labour supply and natural resources fail to grow in step with capital formation: and the contraction of new investment opportunities will be more serious when the propensity to consume is falling.

The contrast between the inter-war stagnation thesis and the classical theory of the stationary state is that the former saw a decline in the rate of population growth as a reason for the falling rate of return on capital in mature societies, and the latter saw a rising population (associated with diminishing returns from land and a constant real wage) as the cause of a fall in the share of profits. The classical economists (with the exception of Malthus) were prepared to assume full employment as normal. The heirs of the Keynesian Revolution were not. To them it was the gap between potential and effective productivity that determined actual productivity in the long run. 'The problem of our generation' said Hansen in his presidential address to the American Economic Association 'is above all the problem of inadequate private investment outlets.'[7] According to this view, a rapidly growing population demands more capital resources (construction, residential building, public utilities) than a stationary population and hence stimulates a high rate of investment. A high-income community with a slowly growing population and

[7] A. Hansen, 'Economic progress and declining population', *American Economic Review* (1939).

a substantial heritage of fixed capital has a relatively high propensity to save and to consume personal services (with little capital content), plus a relatively large scope for capital-saving innovation or for financing new investment by liquidating old capital in competing uses. Moreover, the other side of the high propensity to save, i.e. a low propensity to consume, tends to depress entrepreneurial expectations and inhibit the flow of innovation. In addition to these deficiencies on the side of demand, the development of capitalism has raised a series of barriers to the exploitation of potential productivity in the form of restrictive practices by businesses or trade unions, and of government intervention through taxation, regulation or direct participation.

It is easy to see why this theory gained popularity amongst economists in a period of chronic unemployment and depressed entrepreneurial expectations though it depended on a series of untested and possibly untestable propositions of doubtful generality. How does one test empirically, for example, the proposition that mature economies are characterised by a rising *ex-ante* propensity to save? *Ex-post* savings showed a historical decline, reflecting the decline in *ex-post* investment. Moreover, by formulating the relation between average incomes and the marginal propensity to save in these aggregative terms, the stagnation theory obscured the fact that the national propensity to save depends on the distribution of incomes between groups with a high propensity to consume and groups with a high propensity to save. A redistribution of incomes in favour of the former might be expected to check the inexorable slide to stagnation. The declining rate of population growth was clear for all to see (though as it turned out it was not irreversible), but its effect on the capital-intensity of the production process was a presumption for which there was no empirical evidence. Similarly there was no *a priori* reason or empirical evidence to justify the assumption that a new trend for innovations to be capital-saving had suddenly appeared in the inter-war period. Finally, the concept of the frontier as used in the context of Hansen's theory is a relative one, and neither migration of industry nor the discovery of new resources is necessarily associated with or dependent on the opening up of new geographical territory.[8]

[8] E.g. the discovery (or exhaustion) of minerals may be as significant as the extension (or closing) of the land frontier in determining the scope for new investment.

By the time the Second World War was over, growth theory was in vogue again on a level of relative importance that recalled Adam Smith and was stimulated by contemporary problems that were as far removed as they could be from the problems of the 1930s. They were the problems of low-income countries struggling to get on to a path of sustained growth for the first time or of high-income countries trying to expand investment in conditions of near full employment. Neither the stagnation theories nor the cyclical growth theories seemed to have much relevance to these problems and a spate of new growth theories developed on neo-classical or Keynesian foundations.

Meanwhile, however, there had been two developments in analytical technique which ensured that the growth theories of the 1950s and 1960s would be methodologically different to all previous thinking in this field. The first was the Keynesian revolution, i.e. the development of macroeconomic analysis. The second was the development of econometrics – a combination of theoretical and statistical analysis.[9] The first development stimulated a type of growth theory that was formulated in broad aggregative terms i.e. in the familiar Keynesian national income aggregates. The second created a demand for theoretical concepts that were selected and defined in empirically measurable forms.

As it happened, modern growth theory itself split into two separate lines of development which have taken divergent routes and constitute different branches of economic theory. The first route has been directed mainly to the problems of developing countries and has been concerned to formulate theories which can be applied to particular cases to yield conclusions of relevance to practical policy formulation. This route, close in spirit to Adam Smith's trail, was taken by W. Arthur Lewis, for example, in his *Theory of Economic Growth*, and a long line of development economists.[10] The second route was almost exclusively theoretical, in aim as well as in scope, and has been empirically tested,

[9] This development led in the early 1930s to the formation of the Econometric Society, an international society committed to the promotion of an essentially new area of economic research characterised by 'unification of the theoretical–quantitative and the empirical–quantitative approach to economic problems'. See R. Frisch's editorial in the first issue of *Econometrica* (1933).

[10] Some of these theories are reviewed in H. Chenery, 'Comparative Advantage and Development Policy', *American Economic Review* (1963), reprinted (1965) in Royal Economic Society/American Economic Association, *Surveys of Economic Theory*.

if at all, in terms of the data relating to mature capitalist countries.

Both routes have embraced a wide variety of issues and models in the field of economic development, but while the former has drawn heavily on theories of international trade and optimum resource allocation the second route has been almost exclusively macroeconomic in orientation. It is the second route that is generally accepted, as being the mainstream of the theory of economic growth. It dates effectively from an article by Harrod published in the 1939 *Economic Journal* (and subsequently developed as a set of lectures published in 1948 as *Towards a Dynamic Economics*) which was essentially an attempt to extract the long-run dynamic implications of Keynes' primarily static and short-run analysis. It consists, in Harrod's own words 'in a marriage of the "acceleration principle" and the "multiplier" theory'. Evsey Domar was independently developing a similar framework of analysis in the United States in the early 1940s and the 'Keynesian dynamics' that is the simple basis of most modern growth models has therefore generally been called the Harrod–Domar model.

The broad purpose of the growth theory that stemmed from this source was to explain the fluctuating behaviour of per capita income through time, to introduce into the Keynesian static system the hypotheses that would generate an equilibrium path of growth and to illustrate the effects of instability in the system on the actual path of growth. In the Harrod–Domar formulation this was achieved by adopting the Keynesian assumption that saving is a function of income, introducing the concept of the capital stock, i.e. the notion that investment is capacity-creating as well as income-generating, and linking to the latter the effects of the quality of entrepreneurial expectations on investment decisions. Steady growth then depends on effective demand growing at the rate warranted by the growth of the capital stock. It is the failure of entrepreneurs to predict the growth of demand accurately enough to make the right investment decisions that throws the economy off the equilibrium path of growth. Thus the actual rate of growth for a given economy can be explained as a function of entrepreneurial expectations on the one hand and the factors determining the natural long-term growth of demand (i.e. the growth of population and technical progress) on the other.

At the heart of the Harrod–Domar model was what Joan

Robinson has succinctly described as the 'simple piece of arithmetic' which stems from the twin assumptions fixing savings as a proportion of income and output as a proportion of the capital stock.[11]

When a constant proportion of income is added to capital every year and capital bears a constant ratio to income then income expands continuously at a constant proportional rate. Thus when 10% of net income is invested every year and the stock of capital is five years purchase of net income then the stock of capital, the rate of investment per annum and net income per annum all expand cumulatively at 2 per cent per annum.

This truism gave Harrod his basic dynamic equation, $G = s/v$ where G is the actual growth rate, s is the propensity to save and v is the capital–output ratio. The distinctive feature of his model however was the introduction of entrepreneurial expectations; and given perfect foresight on the part of entrepreneurs, an economy could find its equilibrium growth path. Thus his second dynamic equation defined a 'warranted' growth rate which equates planned savings and required investment and so justifies entrepreneurial expectations. How fast the rate of growth would be over the long run, however, would depend on the basic underlying factors governing the growth in labour supply and productivity, viz the growth of population and technical progress. Harrod then completed his model by postulating a 'natural' rate of growth representing the feasible long-term growth rate in total output.

The significant characteristic of Harrod's (as of Domar's) theory of growth was that it rested on the capacity-creating as well as the income-generating properties of new investment. Its demonstration of the logical possibility of steady economic growth in a model based on the twin assumptions of a fixed capital–output ratio and a fixed savings–income ratio was of particular interest to planners trying to identify feasible growth targets and to draw relevant policy conclusions for developing countries. For, to the extent that the state can determine the savings–output ratio, and that the capital–output ratio reflects the current state of technology, it may be possible to manipulate the rate of investment to match a desired growth target. In practice it turned out to be less of a magic formula than it at first seemed, for the assumption of a rigid capital–output ratio was a singularly inappropriate starting-point for a developing country.

[11] J. Robinson, 'The model of an expanding economy', *Economic Journal* (March 1952), p. 42.

For the industrialised capitalist market economies to which the Harrod model was designed to apply, however, the most striking implication that emerged from it was that growth was likely to be steady only on very special assumptions. Not only was it possible - as Keynes had shown – for planned investment to diverge from the level warranted by the actual level of effective demand, when this did occur in the context of Harrod's model the divergence was likely to widen violently before being brought back on line. In a typically uncertain world, changes in the rate of growth of demand or of technical improvements would normally take entrepreneurs by surprise, raising (or lowering) the actual rate of growth of incomes by comparison with the expected rate of growth. If entrepreneurs find that the actual rate of growth G falls short of the rate of growth for which they were planning they will see themselves as having ordered too much capital equipment – and by cutting back their investment plans will tend to reduce the actual rate of growth still further. Conversely if the actual rate of growth exceeds the expected rate, producers will find themselves running short of stocks, or of equipment, and will adjust their orders upwards, thus inflating the actual rate the more.

Thus an initial, even modest, divergence between expectations and events will falsify the expectations of entrepreneurs and push them into cumulative slump or cumulative boom. Unless the rate of growth on which investors base their decisions corresponds exactly with the rate of growth in output actually achieved, the disappointment of entrepreneurial expectations will set in motion centrifugal forces driving the economy towards boom or slump. What Harrod had done in effect was to introduce into the simple model of an expanding economy given by a constant relationship between the savings/income and capital/output ratios, a cyclical element which stemmed from the Keynesian analysis.

The explosive instability of the Harrod model was of course a result of the simplicity and rigidity of its assumptions. In the real world neither the multiplier nor the accelerator could be expected to operate with undiluted ferocity. There are leakages in the multiplier when part of expenditure goes out of the domestic income stream to imports or when it is diverted into taxation. Only a proportion of each year's new expenditure on investment goods is directly induced by the rise in incomes: some of it is autonomous in the sense that it is independent of the rate of growth of output (e.g. government expenditure) and may actually be a stabilising influence on changes in investment demand. However many of the post Second World War developments in growth theory, most of which owed their stimulus to Harrod's basic model, have been focused on attempts to develop a model of steady growth which did not have to creep along the knife-edge growth path implied by the assumption that both the savings ratio and the capital output ratio are fixed.

From the Harrod–Domar beginnings in dynamic theory there sprang an enormous and varied progeny of growth models. Many of them dropped the assumption of fixed factor proportions in search of more realistic assumptions concerning the rates of growth of capital and labour. For as soon as attempts were made to use the model to analyse the process of long-term economic growth it became necessary to explore the causes and consequences of changes in the ratio and in technology. This led on to models illustrating the resulting structural changes and their influence on the income-generating power of the economy: and thence to models (of increasing mathematical complexity) which take account of monetary factors, or of different varieties of technical progress, or that define alternative criteria for steady-state growth or maximal growth paths.

There has, however, been a deep rift between the directions taken by the two main varieties of growth theory since the Second World War. On the one hand there has been the neo-classical direction taken by the production function theorists who have applied marginalist techniques of analysis to Keynesian-type aggregates and who have been prepared to make non-Keynesian assumptions about the way savings decisions govern the rate of capital formation. On the other is the direction generally associated with the modern Cambridge school which stands closer to the Harrodian version and has a predilection for assumptions which are either Keynesian or Ricardian in their inspiration.

The neo-classical school sought to escape from the rigidities and the instability problems associated with the Harrod–Domar model by postulating an aggregative production function with two flexible inputs – capital and labour – which are smoothly substitutable over the whole range defined by current technology, and where movements in factor input prices would automatically ensure that the available capital and labour would be fully employed. Obviously this is unrealistic but they would argue that price adjustments and factor substitutions clearly *do* take place in the real world in response to technological change and relative factor scarcities, and that when changes in underlying conditions create imbalances between demand and supply it is reasonable to suppose that the system will generate the appropriate price signals and responses to shift the input-mix back in the direction of the optimum.[12] In effect, the assumptions of perfect substitutability between factors, perfect foresight and a total absence of constraints on the real wage or interest rate, makes it possible to define a stable equilibrium growth rate in which the warranted growth rate is tied to the natural growth rate by factor price shifts which induce appropriate variations in the input-mix.

The attractions of this type of model for the ordinary research economist are its great simplicity, its use of Keynesian macroeconomic aggregates on the one hand and microeconomic techniques of analysis on the other (both familiar ingredients in any comprehensive economics principles course) and the fact that it seems to lend itself readily to empirical tests and predictions. Its disadvantages are that it is designed for full-employment situations, that it says nothing about the mutual interactions between growth and factor income distribution or about the role of entrepreneurial expectations and that its analytical results are ambiguous because it provides no practical means of distinguishing between changes in the input-mix that are a consequence of changes in relative factor scarcities (i.e. a movement along the production function) and those which are a consequence of technological progress (i.e. a shift in the production function). Of course the objections of those who reject the neoclassical model, because it does not provide a suitable framework for the questions they require a theory of growth to answer, tend to revolve around its choice of assumptions. Those who share the Ricardian (and Marxian) interest in the changing pattern of income distribution associated with capitalist economic development, for example, have been particularly critical of the measure of capital implicit in the production function approach and of the assumption that capital goods are 'malleable' – which is needed to postulate continuous substitutability between factors.

[12] Cf. Samuelson's statement of faith: 'Until the laws of thermo-dynamics are repealed, I shall continue to relate outputs to inputs, i.e. to believe in production functions. Until factors cease to have their rewards determined by bidding in quasi-competitive markets, I shall adhere to (generalized) neo-classical approximations in which relative factor prices are important in explaining their market remunerations.'

The Cambridge school made their escape from the Harrodian rigidities and instability problems by altering instead the assumptions concerning the savings coefficient. Their approach is classical (or Marxian) in that they insist on analysing growth in relation to changes in factor income distribution, and Keynesian in that it makes investment depend on entrepreneurial expectations rather than on saving. So they disaggregate the national savings ratio by assuming that profit recipients and wage earners are likely to save different proportions of their income (the simplest version of this is that capitalists save all their profits and wage earners spend all their wages). Thus Kaldor's model for example, postulates a savings–income ratio which is dependent on the distribution of incomes.[13] They ridicule the neo-classical assumptions necessary to treat labour and capital as smoothly and continuously substitutable, e.g. the assumption that real capital, i.e. fixed capital, is like putty, homogeneous and malleable, as easily transferred from one use to another as putty. Above all, they reject as untenable the neo-classical assumption that the prices of labour and capital are proportional to their marginal productivity, on the grounds that there is a profound ambiguity in the concept of capital, physical or financial capital, i.e. capital as a real input into the productive process, or capital as a property owned by certain individuals; for this carries with it a corresponding ambiguity in the concept of a price for capital – interest as the expected rate of discount on financial assets or actual profit on the current stock of assets.

It is indeed there that the basic difference of viewpoint between the neo-classical and post Keynesian schools comes to a crunch and the protagonists are clearly seen to be fighting on different battle grounds. For in the extreme neo-classical world where competition and foresight are perfect, and the past and the future melt into one, the rate of discount and the rate of profit are indistinguishable. In this kind of context we can focus on the supply side of the growth process and analyse the contribution that capital accumulation, labour and technical progress make to the rate of growth of aggregate output within the empirical framework of the national accounts, and develop explanatory or predictive models whose success or failure, when applied to real-world data, may tell us something about the way actual

[13] Nicholas Kaldor, 'Alternative Theories of Distribution', *Review of Economic Studies* (1956).

economies have behaved in these respects. If one is concerned, however, to assess the role of demand and entrepreneurial expectations in the growth process, and if one believes that changes in the distribution of incomes between factors of production (representing social classes) are also a crucial part of the explanation for variations in national rates of economic growth, then one needs an entirely different set of abstractions to those embodied in the timeless neo-classical framework.

Probably the most distinctive general characteristics of the Cambridge school's approach to growth theory are that its models tend to be explanatory rather than predictive, involving behaviouristic rather than mechanistic assumptions, and strongly concerned with directions of causation through time rather than with mutually determining sets of variables. They focus (as Keynes did) on the causes and mechanism of change rather than the conditions of equilibrium and they stress the need to develop theories which are designed to apply to specific types of economy and to particular periods of historical time i.e. to construct 'historical' or causal models. Joan Robinson, one of the leading exponents of this approach, describes it in the following terms:

To build up a causal model, we must start not from equilibrium relations but from the rules and motives governing human behaviour. We therefore have to specify to what kind of economy the model applies, for various kinds of economies have different rules... The independent elements in the model must correspond with the features of reality which are given independently of each other, either by the brute facts of nature or by the freedom of individuals to decide how they will behave.[14]

She then goes on to list the 'determinants of equilibrium' for a modern capitalist society under seven main headings – (1) technical conditions, (2) investment policy, (3) thriftiness conditions, (4) competitive conditions, (5) the wage bargain, (6) financial conditions and (7) the initial stock of capital and the state of expectations formed by past experience.

A post-Keynesian growth model is thus less general, takes into account a much wider range of variables, links them together much less rigidly, and since it is designed for analytical rather than for predictive purposes, the process of verification is more often logical than experimental. One result is that it is not easy to describe the main features of a generalised post-Keynesian growth model and individual members of the school tend to

[14] J. Robinson, *Essays in the Theory of Economic Growth*, p. 34.

develop highly distinctive models of their own and sometimes indeed a succession of own-models. The particular assumption that distinguishes the post-Keynesian approach most strongly is its use of a Keynesian-type investment function which implies that investment determines savings rather than savings investment. However, it is not possible to define a specific list of assumptions or axioms which distinguish a typically post-Keynesian approach. What is noticeable however is that the typical model in this genre is less easy to quantify, and hence less easy to test, or to apply empirically using a standard analytical technique such as that generated by a neo-classical production function model.

Again the choice between the different varieties of model depends partly on the questions to which an answer is sought, partly on the analytical concepts and techniques followed by the theorists and partly on their preconceptions as to which set of simplifying assumptions is most palatable. In each of these respects there is often a strong ideological bias to the choices made and the debates between opposing schools of thought accordingly tend to generate more heat than light. It is doubtful, however, whether either of these two major strains of pure theory have yet succeeded in influencing current economic policy nor do they show much interest in reconsidering their basic premises on more realistic lines.

FURTHER READING

Primary literature

E. V. Domar, *Essays in the Theory of Economic Growth* (1957).
Alvin Hansen, 'Economic Progress and Declining Population', *American Economic Review* (1939).
R. F. Harrod, *Towards a Dynamic Economics* (1948).
J. V. Robinson, *The Accumulation of Capital* (1956).
J. Schumpeter, *The Theory of Economic Development* (1951).
A. K. Sen (ed.), *Growth Economics* (1970).
M. Kalecki, *Theory of Economic Dynamics* (1954).

Secondary literature

F. H. Hahn and R. C. O. Matthews, 'The Theory of Economic Growth', *Economic Journal* (1954).
J. A. Kregel, *The Theory of Economic Growth* (1972).

14

METHODOLOGICAL DIVISIONS IN ECONOMICS SINCE KEYNES

Use of the term Keynesian Revolution to characterise the impact of Keynes' *General Theory* on the evolution of economic ideas follows a convention approved by Keynes and his contemporaries and rendered commonplace by subsequent usage. There is a similar textbook tradition justifying the use of the term Marginal Revolution to denote the change-over as between the two systems of economic analysis – classical and neo-classical – which were sufficiently different in their leading questions, assumptions and techniques of analysis to imply an intellectual shift of revolutionary proportions. It may be unhelpful to stretch the Kuhnian analogy of a scientific revolution too far: but there is no doubt that the neo-classical system of thought which stemmed from the adoption of marginal techniques of analysis brought with it a radical and far-reaching change in the disciplinary framework and research priorities of the professional economist. The hallmark of the neo-classical economist is his formulation of the fundamental economic problem as primarily a question of optimal allocation of scarce resources, his mastery of marginal techniques of analysis designed to solve the problem of maximising output or utility, and a conceptual apparatus in which the assumption of long-term competitive equilibrium plays a crucial role. These are the professional attributes of any contemporary economist faced with a problem soluble at the microeconomic level as many of the current public policy problems certainly are.

Whatever the Keynesian Revolution did then it did not displace the neo-classical paradigm in the standard textbooks for that remains the foundation of a wide area of orthodox economic theory today. So what effect *did* it have on the views of the scientific community of economists concerning the scope and methodology of their discipline? The obvious, though not the complete, answer to this question is that it added an extra dimension to orthodox economic doctrine by providing it with a new integrated set of theories, concepts and tools for analysing macro-economic problems. Basically this involved two things: (1) the conceptualisation of the notions of aggregate demand and aggregate supply, which enabled Maynard Keynes to make the principle of effective demand the key concept in his theory of economic activity;[1] and (2) integrating monetary theory into the core of a general theory of macroeconomic activity instead of treating money as an artificial veil which could conveniently be ignored, or neutralised, by those seeking to analyse the real forces driving the capitalist economy.

At the same time, Keynes' general theory used many of the traditional techniques of classical economics; e.g. the typical *a priori* assumption based on nothing more solid than introspection and/or casual observation, such as the 'fundamental psychological law' underlying the consumption function; or the maximising propensities that are assumed to underlie the behaviour of his consumers, businessmen or speculators; e.g. also the comparative-static techniques and the framework of equilibrium analysis in which the whole argument is formally couched. Like all other classical and neo-classical economists he accepted as given (and therefore as outside the range of problems susceptible to economic analysis) the whole social and economic power-structure and distribution of wealth, though it is fair to say that this assumption was more realistic in a short-period framework of analysis than in the neo-classical long period.

> We take as given the existing skill and quantity of available labour, the existing quality and quantity of available equipment, the existing technique, the degree of competition, the tastes and habits of the consumer, the disutility of different intensities of labour and of the activities of supervision and organisation, as well as the social structure including the forces, other than our variables set forth below, which determine the distribution of the national income.[2]

Keynes' general theory was thus an outcrop of (if also a reaction against) the Marshallian neo-classical orthodoxy. This is hardly surprising. For he was nearly 53 when the first edition of the *General Theory* was published. He had been a Cambridge don for more than a quarter of a century and an Editor of the *Economic Journal* for almost as long. He had acquired a formidable repu-

[1] See e.g. *General Theory*, p. 32: 'The idea that we can safely neglect the aggregate demand function is fundamental to the Ricardian economics, which underlie what we have been taught for more than a century.'

[2] Keynes, *General Theory*, p. 245.

tation as a Treasury official (heading the Treasury delegation to the Peace conference in 1919). While publishing a stream of economic heresies in the late 1920s and early 1930s he was appointed a member first of the Macmillan Committee on Finance and Industry and later of the Economic Advisory Council. Although Keynes seems to have felt an increasing sense of detachment from the community of academic economists who had been his teachers or in his own age-set there seems little doubt that his intellectual prestige was almost as 'staggering' as Ricardo's had seemed to Malthus – even among those who disagreed with him.[3] The impact of the Keynesian revolution was thus largely confined to the (younger) heirs of the neo-classical orthodoxy and left virtually unscathed the adherents of the Marxian alternative. True, contemporary Marxists welcomed the Keynesian shift of emphasis from the theory of prices to the theory of income determination – for they had no interest in the theory of prices and no competition to offer to the neo-classical theory of resource allocation. But at least in the initial stages they seem to have got little direct stimulus from Keynes' macroeconomic framework.[4]

From one point of view then, the Keynesian revolution can be assessed as simply a major extension to the neo-classical paradigm, adding a macroeconomic dimension to the myopically microeconomic vision of mainstream economic doctrine. This is the way it could reasonably be interpreted by the majority of North American and British economists who have absorbed Keynesian concepts and aggregative techniques of analysis into a neo-classical or a general equilibrium framework. The fact that Keynesian economics as it is expounded in the textbooks on which most of today's undergraduates are reared, or as it is embodied in the income–expenditure model which is the ac-

[3] See Keynes' account, in a letter to Harrod dated 30 August 1936, of his own sense of detachment from orthodox economists: 'experience seems to show that people are divided between the old ones whom nothing will shift and are merely amazed by my attempts to underline the points of transition so vital in my own progress, and the young ones who have not been properly brought up and believe nothing in particular...I have no companions it seems, in my own generation, either of earliest teachers or of earliest pupils' (J. M. Keynes, *Collected Writings*, Vol. XIV, p. 85). Nevertheless, as Dr Moggridge attests, by 1939, Keynes – on the evidence of his mother's scrapbook 'was by far the most distinguished economist of his generation, both within "the profession" and amongst the larger public' (Milo Keynes (ed.), *Essays on John Maynard Keynes*, p. 177).
[4] See e.g. P. M. Sweezy, 'The First Quarter Century', pp. 312–13, in R. Lekachman, *Keynes' General Theory. Reports on Three Decades*.

cepted framework of economic analysis for most business and government economists, does not much resemble the economics of Keynes, is beside the point for those who would favour this interpretation.

Looked at however in the context of recent methodological debate, it might seem that the most characteristically Keynesian break with the classical heritage – a difference which is currently the distinctive badge of the modern post-Keynesians, was a change in the formulation of the central economic question. Keynes was interested in the problems of an economy in a state of disequilibrium and in the process of its change through time, rather than in the forces which were tending to bring the economy into a hypothetical equilibrium.[5] For, as he saw it, in time – i.e. real historical time, subject to all the shocks and aberrations of a continuously changing world – there was no reason to suppose either that an economy would ever approach an equilibrium in the classical sense, or that there was any concept of an equilibrium towards which it might be tending, that might help to explain the actual pace and directions of economic change in the short period within which all the economic policy problems inevitably arise. Even the best informed entrepreneur is incapable of making rational economic decisions when 'there is no scientific basis on which to form any calculable probability whatever' and where the expectations themselves are subject to sudden and violent change. 'I accuse the classical economic theory' wrote Keynes, in an article written shortly after the *General Theory* was published, 'of being one of those pretty polite techniques which tries to deal with the present by abstracting from the fact that we know very little about the future.'[6]

Nevertheless orthodox economics in the post Second World War era, in spite of its Keynesian legacy, has abandoned neither its general equilibrium nor its quantity-theory traditions. Equilibrium theory has taken on a new lease of life, largely under the inspiration of Sir John Hicks, building on Walrasian and Keynesian foundations; and general equilibrium economics now attracts distinguished theoretical talents. In spite of having been 'thoroughly discredited' by Keynes the quantity theory has staged a theoretical come-back (a monetarist counter-revolution), largely at the hands of Milton Friedman (also building on

[5] *Quarterly Journal of Economics* (February 1937). Reprinted in J. M. Keynes, *Collected Writings*, Vol. XIV, pp. 109–23.
[6] *Ibid.*, p. 115.

Keynesian foundations), in a post-war world where the economic questions have changed and the problem of the price level is again a dominating policy issue, comparable in importance to, if not actually over-riding the unemployment problem. At the same time the self-professed Keynesians, the theorists who are the direct products of the 'new economics' of the Keynesian Revolution, have followed the path of macroeconomic income–expenditure analysis in a direction which, as Leijonhufvud has convincingly demonstrated 'is antithetical to monetary approaches and unrelated to value theory'[7] and indeed is now a long way off the course set by Keynes in the *Treatise* and the *General Theory*. In particular the integration of monetary and value theory which Keynes hoped to achieve is as far off as ever it was, while some of his keenest disciples have tended to denigrate the significance of monetary policy and to neglect monetary theory.

However, we are too near the doctrinal debates triggered off by the *General Theory* to assess its *ultimate* impact at all reliably. All we can usefully do at this stage is to try to identify some of the ways in which opinions on the scope and methodology of economics have developed since Keynes and look at the leading strands in the current methodological controversies. If there really is a new paradigm waiting its cue already in the wings, waiting its opportunity to turn methodological confusion into a clearly defined research programme for the economics profession, these controversies contain the materials of which it will be woven as well as the material destined for the scrap heap. But before considering doctrinal differences, it is worth noting that the intellectual environment in which economic ideas and theories are now developing differs in important respects from that of the 1930s.

For one thing, economists are currently challenged by a different set of questions from those which were interesting Keynes at the time he wrote the *General Theory*, because the most urgent economic problems dominating the post Second World War period differ from those of the inter-war period. Perhaps the most radical and far-reaching of the underlying shifts have been those associated with the changing role of government in the economy. There remain of course profound ideological differences between economists as to the extent to which, and the ways in which, they believe government should use its power to

---

[7] Leijonhufvud, *op. cit.*, p. 31.

intervene in the economic system: and naturally these differences tend to be associated with the school of theory with which they identify. Nevertheless, the sheer weight of government expenditures and assets in a modern industrial society is such that it has transformed the context within which economic policy decisions are made and economic theories formulated. Thus there is debate, for example, as to whether monetary policy or fiscal policy is the most effective channel of government influence, or as to whether government should attempt to direct or stabilise economic change. But that it must play a conscious managing role in the allocation of the nation's economic resources is scarcely in dispute.

There were also certain other consequences of the new environment which influenced the shape of the economic questions to which post-war economists were reacting. One of these was a loss of interest at the empirical and theoretical level in the traditional capitalist problem of economic crises. For when the weight of exogenous government expenditures reached its post-war levels, business cycles, trade cycles and building cycles were so flattened as to be virtually invisible in the time series. In these circumstances, the emphasis which Keynes' theory of money had attached to the effects on the level of economic activity of relative price changes as between investment goods and consumption goods (an essential key to the explanation for industrial fluctuations) fell into the background, and the main stream of Keynesian economics went on to develop within a neo-neo-classical framework of analysis the prototype of which was the aggregative production function model.

Secondly, the problem of unemployment ceased to be a leading problem in the same sense as it had been in the inter-war period, for experience in the 1950s suggested that any government that was prepared to adopt the appropriate fiscal policy could so manage demand as to generate any level of employment that it chose. However, by the same token, since fiscal policy was apparently sufficient to eliminate unemployment, the role of monetary policy and the range of monetary theory was correspondingly attenuated. Keynes' passionate concern with the level of interest rates and with the need to hit the appropriate rate to maintain full employment was not shared by his post-war successors. The bridge he built between monetary theory and value theory has fallen into disuse and the classical dichotomy has opened up again – mirrored by the dichotomy between macro-economics and micro-economics. The dichotomy is still a challenge to modern theorists but it is the general equilibrium school, not the mainstream Keynesian succession, that is taking it up.

Thirdly, the problem of inflation has reappeared in more acute guise in the 1960s and 1970s than ever before. The orthodox Keynesians saw it as a trade-off against unemployment, and the Phillips-curve analysis formalised this viewpoint. More important, however, from the point of view of monetary theory has been the revival and development of quantity-theory analysis stimulated by the chronic post-war inflation. Just as neo-classical economics had, in effect, swept the unemployment problem out of court by assuming full employment, so Keynesian economics ignored the dangers of inflation by assuming stable prices.[8] To those who are concerned by the problem of chronic inflation and its implications for economic behaviour, therefore, orthodox Keynesian economics is irrelevant and Milton Friedman's re-statement of the quantity theory holds considerable attractions.

The other change in intellectual environment that requires notice is the professionalisation of the discipline of economics which gathered momentum in the mid-decades of the twentieth century. To begin with, there has been a remarkable expansion in the number of practising professional economists. The water-shed for the United Kingdom can be dated within the Second World War. During the war the majority of academic economists moved into government service to take an active part *qua* econo-mists in organising the national war effort. It was a task which economists reared in the neo-classical tradition were peculiarly well-equipped to perform for it was essentially a problem of optimal resource allocation.[9] In peacetime the economist's role in economic policy making is necessarily subordinate to that of the politician because the multiplicity of (often conflicting) policy objectives makes it impossible to take the value judgments as given. In wartime the victory objective over-rides all else and the optimising techniques of the economist were allowed maximum

---

[8] Keynes himself had been particularly intrigued by 'the apparent asymmetry between Inflation and Deflation' and Book v of the *General Theory* developed a theory of prices as a corollary of his theory of employment. As Leijonhufvud and others have now demonstrated, however, orthodox Keynesian economics often bears little resemblance to the economics of Keynes.

[9] In conditions of total war even the most doctrinaire adherents to the laissez-faire tradition were freed from their ideological objections to government inter-vention in the economic process.

scope. The result of this active involvement of economists in the war effort was to increase both their prestige and their practical experience of applying their training to the solution of real-world problems.[10]

The most prestigious of all the British economists both in official and in academic circles was John Maynard Keynes, and the War enabled him and his devotees (a small band at the outset) to introduce the innovations of the *General Theory* to the wider circle of practising economists *outside* the universities as rapidly as (more rapidly than indeed) they converted most teaching academics still struggling to absorb the complex theoretical implications of the *General Theory*. Keynes' *How to Pay for the War*, first published in 1939 as a series of articles in the *Times* was a direct application of the *General Theory*. Since that date economists in government service have been continuously engaged in applying and adapting to their policy-oriented analysis the Keynesian body of macroeconomic ideas.

The accident of war thus gave Keynes and his closest disciples a unique opportunity to demonstrate the operational usefulness of his macroeconomic conceptual framework, not only to the informed public and to the official civil servants, but also to the majority of academic economists who came under his direct personal influence in the government service. During the war years senior members of the profession (such as Dennis Robertson and Lionel Robbins) who had initially resisted the *General Theory* found themselves working in harness with younger Keynesian converts (such as E. A. G. Robinson, J. E. Meade, J. R. N. Stone, A. K. Cairncross) in a methodological harmony which economists have rarely displayed in peacetime when they conduct their arguments remotely through the pages of the learned journals and select their own research agenda. In wartime the order of priority of the problems requiring solution was firmly imposed from outside: and they were envisaged primarily (though never exclusively) as macroeconomic problems.

In the immediate post-war period the context of economic policy formation was similar in many ways to the wartime context. The problems of reconstruction and of conversion to a peacetime economy demanded a continuing high level of government inter-

---

[10] Though the prestige was considerably shaken by the unsuccessful experiments of the 1960s (see e.g. M. M. Postan, 'A Plague of Economists?', *Encounter*, 1968) its persistence is attested by the increasing extent to which economists have been employed in the policy-making departments of government or business.

vention. The policy objectives were different from those of war but their order of priority was again generally accepted. There were few objectors to the view that the main danger to the post-war economy was that of runaway inflation, and the objective of stabilisation assumed the kind of over-riding quality that had attached to the victory objective. It called for tight economic controls, controls which the post-war Labour government, with its built-in ideological bias towards government intervention, was politically attuned to maintain. Significantly, the post-war governments published (1947–51) an annual *Economic Survey* making explicit quantitative macroeconomic forecasts for the subsequent year.

The high tide of prestige and influence in economic policy making which the academic economists enjoyed in wartime, began to turn, however, as the nation's economic problems reverted to their more complex peacetime shape. For one thing most of the leaders of the profession moved rapidly out of Whitehall to resume their university careers. For another, the falsification of many of the quantitative forecasts that had been boldly published in the *Economic Survey* strained the credibility of those who were trying to apply to the more open peacetime economy, predictive techniques that had worked rather well in the tightly controlled conditions of total war. And for another, the steady dismantling of war-time controls in response to public demand tended to reduce the number of issues on which the technical skills of the economist were the major ingredient in successful policy making. The Conservative governments of the 1950s followed their political bias by putting into reverse the economic dirigisme of the war and post-war period.

However, the return to peacetime conditions did not reduce the number of practising economists – as first it merely shifted the main field of their operations back to the universities and research institutes. When government in the 1950s stopped publishing the quantitative economic forecasts that were still being set up at the Treasury, an independent body – the National Institute of Economic and Social Research – took up the task in its *Economic Review*. The wartime trickle of newly trained economists expanded into a flood as soon as the universities returned to normal. Economics was a popular option for the ex-servicemen who returned as mature students on government grant, or to take up an opportunity that they had never even considered in the more straitened circumstances of the pre-war period. In the great post-war expansion of the universities and the colleges of advanced technology the social sciences in general, and economics in particular, attracted a disproportionate number of students.

The other consequence of the war and the heavily controlled post-war era was that it generated an unprecedented and irreversible flow of statistical data, data designed to measure the levels, structure and growth in the nation's economic activity in relation to a Keynesian macroeconomic framework. A Central Statistical Office, set up in 1941 within the War Cabinet Office, embarked at once on the task of producing an integrated set of national income and expenditure accounts to fit the Keynesian model. A small elite constituting the Prime Minister's Statistical Section answered directly to the keystone of the wartime power-structure. Henceforth it would have been virtually impossible to test macroeconomic theories or to carry out substantive empirical research *outside* a Keynesian analytical framework, for the aggregative data, were available in that form and no other. This, if nothing else, ensured that the formal Keynesian model became the prevailing orthodoxy to which normal scientific work in macro-economics had to conform.[11]

The textbooks were already being rewritten in the 1940s so as to incorporate the conceptual apparatus of the *General Theory* and to give macro-economics at least an equal prominence to micro-economics as part of the economist's basic training, though without trying to integrate the two forms of theory. The first introductory textbook in the new tradition was Hicks' *The Social Framework* first published in 1942.[12] Because of its immediate and obvious relevance to urgent contemporary national policy problems, macro-economics rapidly took a popular position in undergraduate teaching and in Workers' Educational Association and other adult education courses. The fact that many of the spate of new statistical series, currently being published in official sources, were conceptually linked to the Keynesian system made macro-economics a favourite area of research for applied economists inside or outside the universities. A whole vast programme of applied research projects unfolded out of theorems

[11] The above narrative relates to development in the UK but a similar story could be told for other western countries. A national income unit had been set up in the US before the war and American official statistics took the same Keynesian form as did, eventually, those of all other capitalist economies. Cf. D. Patinkin, 'Keynes and Econometrics', *Econometrica* (November 1976).

[12] It went into a 4th edn in 1971.

and hypothesis based on the Keynesian income–expenditure model and overshadowed the microeconomic puzzles which had been occupying economists in the inter-war period.

With the Master dead, however, long before the implications of his theoretical innovations had been fully explored, and with the problems assuming totally new shapes, it is not surprising that the implementation of the Keynesian Revolution took off in directions which were not altogether consistent with the original message of the *General Theory*.

The mainstream economic doctrines of the post Second World War era are thus a mixture of the neo-classical micro-economics which developed out of the marginal revolution, and the macro-economics which developed out of the Keynesian revolution. Within a broadly accepted disciplinary framework, however, there is considerable doctrinal controversy and a wide variety of theorists, concepts and assumptions in continuous dispute. The liveliness of the debate is an encouraging sign for it is this kind of critical attitude to current theory that distinguishes the scientific from the pre-scientific tradition.[13] It is thus neither surprising, nor necessarily regrettable, if Keynesian economics turned out to be different from the economics of Keynes, and Marxian economics to diverge from the gospel of *Das Kapital*. Marx however ever lived long enough to deny that he was a Marxist, whereas Keynes died in 1946, in what was still a war-dominated economic situation, before he or his followers had begun to formulate the typical economic problems of the post Second World War era in the analytical framework of the *General Theory*.

The variety of methodological approaches to economics currently being articulated in the learned journals and even expounded to students through introductory texts, has encouraged attempts to map the doctrinal battleground and to set contemporary controversies in systematic perspective. Probably the most popular criterion of classification is an ideological yardstick, its use justified in the eyes of its users by the tendency of left-wing sympathisers to focus on questions relating to the distribution of income as between social classes, and to favour policy implications involving a relatively high degree of government economic

[13] Cf. K. Popper, *Conjectures and Refutations* (1957), p. 50: 'The scientific tradition is distinguished from the pre-scientific tradition in having two layers. Like the latter it passes on its theories: but it also passes on a critical attitude towards them. The theories are passed on, not as dogmas, but rather with the challenge to discuss them and improve upon them.'

intervention.[14] One interesting example of its use is Paul Davidson's attempt to define 'five relatively homogeneous schools of
thought' on post-Keynesian macroeconomic monetary and
growth theory, along a spectrum from socialist extreme left to
laissez-faire extreme right.[15] The disadvantage of most attempts
at an ideological classification of economic theories, however, is
that they tend to reveal more about the political and intellectual
bias of the compiler and his mentors, than about the methodological qualities of the economic doctrines thus labelled. Indeed,
as an aid to an objective understanding of the nature and scope
of the methodological issues currently dividing the makers of
economic theory, the ideological yardstick may be positively
misleading. To stigmatise as extreme right in a political sense,
for example, all those who use 'well-behaved production functions' as tools of analysis is to drift into theological rather than
scientific ways of thought. The fact that the ideological implications that are commonly inferred from a particular economic
theory have undoubted bearing on its acceptance by economists
or politicians, and possibly even on its survival value in current
academic research programmes, does not justify the presumption that the leading economic theorists select their methods of
analysis, and their problem-focus, in accordance with ideological
rather than with logical or scientific criteria.

Nevertheless there is a crucial methodological split between a
positive and a normative approach to economic science underlying the current debate between the neo-classicals (sometimes
called the neo-neo-classicals) and the post-Keynesians (sometimes
called the 'Cambridge School'): and this division reflects a fundamental difference of viewpoint on whether economic theories
should express the personal value judgments of the theorists and
be relevant to a particular social and institutional context, or
whether theories should in principle be formulated in purely
objective terms and take account of ethical values and historical
contexts only at the point at which they are applied to empirical

[14] The natural inclination of some theorists to propagate their ideas through
polemical as well as logical arguments adds of course to the popularity of the
ideological criterion.
[15] Paul Davidson, *Money and the Real World* (1972), pp. 2–4. Davidson distinguishes five schools in the spectrum of modern macroeconomic monetary and
growth theory, viz: socialist radical, neo-Keynesian (approximating to what I have
called post-Keynesian), Keynes' school, neo-classical–bastard Keynesian and
monetarist–neoclassical.

analysis. Thus, the positive economist can be said to be more concerned with 'how' than with 'why', with the logic and internal consistency of his models than with their realism, with mechanical analogies than with biological analogies, with systems of inter-dependent functional relationships rather than with causal sequences. To quote Milton Friedman, a leading modern exponent of this methodology: 'Positive economics is in principle independent of any particular ethical position or normative judgements...Its task is to provide a system of generalisations than can be used to make correct predictions about the consequence of any change in circumstances. Its performance is to be judged by the precision, scope and conformity with experience of the predictions it yields.'[16] On the other hand, as Myrdal has pointed out, many of the basic concepts of economics are already loaded with normative implications, so that economic theories are never in practice value-free, however austerely objective the intentions of the theorists.[17]

Among the common characteristics of a positive neo-classical economist then, we can list the following:

(i) His emphasis on logical consistency – sometimes reflected in a tendency to move in the direction of abstract mathematical models and, in particular, models of general equilibrium.

(ii) His disregard for the realism of his basic assumptions on the grounds that the acid test of his theory is whether it works, i.e. whether its implications (descriptive, explanatory or pre-dictive) are confirmed by experience. This is sometimes re-flected in a tendency to develop sophisticated techniques of quantification and statistical analysis. In the end, of course, however powerful the techniques, it is still the empirical validity of the assumptions which determines the significance of the statistical conclusions. For example, among the assumptions that underlie Denison's quantitative analysis of inter-country differences in growth rates is the assumption that factor pro-ductivities are measured by factor returns i.e. that wages, for example, are normally equal to the value of the marginal product of labour.[18] If this is not true (and it is only in perfectly competitive micro equilibrium that it is a logically defensible

---

[16] M. Friedman, 'The Methodology of Positive Economics', in *Essays in Positive Economics* (1953), p. 4.

[17] G. Myrdal, *The Political Element in the Development of Economic Theory* (1953), See the quotation cited in n34, p. 111 above.

[18] E. Denison, *Why Growth Rates Differ* (1967).

assumption[19]) then what Denison explained is not *why* growth rates differ but *how* the calculated growth rates differ on certain assumptions. It is indeed of the essence of formal equilibrium analysis that it is more concerned with relationships between variables than with directions of causation. According to Frank Hahn for example 'equilibrium theory in general and the neo-classical theory in particular has nothing causal to say'.[20]

(iii) Finally, a third hallmark of a positive theorist is a disinclination to take account of changes in motivations, institutions, information systems, cultural attitudes and indeed of the whole complex of factors affecting economic ends and associated behaviour. Samuelson's theory of revealed preference, for example, was a typical neo-classical solution to the problem of explaining consumer behaviour: the trick is to assume that preferences are revealed by actual choices made in the market – though to do so leaves one without any explanation for, e.g., lag effects, inconsistencies in preferences or collective desires.[21]

Among the characteristics which distinguish the post-Keynesian methodology from its neo-classical counterpart are first that the post-Keynesians have closer affinities to Marxian and Ricardian methodology than do the neo-classicals. Like Marx's theory of the evolution of the capitalist system the post-Keynesian type of model owes little to the mechanical analogies of the neo-classical system and recognises the possibility of organic change. Again like Marx, the post-Keynesians favour sociological categories of analysis (e.g. workers and capitalists) whereas the neo-classical school restricts itself to producers and consumers and asks sociologically-oriented questions about the distribution of aggregate income between social classes. They hark back to Ricardo, and to ideas prevailing before the marginal revolution, in emphasising the interdependence of production rather than the interdependence of markets. They are more interested in technological and institutional relations, that is to say, than in

---

[19] As Marshall recognised. See e.g. his *Principles of Economics*, pp. 429–30: 'The doctrine that the earnings of a worker tend to be equal to the net product of his work, has by itself no real meaning; since in order to estimate net product, we have to take for granted all the expenses of production of the commodity on which he works, other than his own wages.'

[20] F. H. Hahn, *The Share of Wages in the National Income*, p. 3.

[21] Cf. K. Boulding, *Economics as a Science*, pp. 118–9: 'One of the most peculiar illusions of economists is the doctrine of what might be called the "Immaculate Conception" of the indifference curve, that is the doctrine that tastes are simply given and we cannot inquire into the process by which they are formed.'

commodity and factor relations. They adopt the Keynesian assumptions that investment decisions are independent of savings decisions, that equilibrium depends on savings being equal to investment, and they explain investment (as Keynes did) in terms of animal spirits, or expectations, or technical dynamism. They reject the notion that consumers' sovereignty can ever be effective so long as the initiative lies with the producer.[22] Above all they reject the timeless aggregative production function approach, with its assumptions of perfect substitution between factors, wholly impersonal market relations, perfect knowledge and foresight, and exclusive dependence on prices in information flows. In place of a production function approach they prefer an accounting approach in which 'capitalists get what they spend and workers spend what they get' and where the structural characteristics of the economy under study can be specified in principle in considerable detail. Their object is not primarily to predict but to analyse and explain, and they do not therefore attempt to force their variables into a readily quantifiable form.[23]

In the event it has been the neo-classical approach that has so far offered most scope for the ambitious researcher looking for specific puzzles to solve with sophisticated mathematical and statistical tools. Partly because the post-Keynesians have set their faces against quantifying the unquantifiable, and against manipulating questionable data with powerful mathematical or econometric tools, their growth models remain essentially theoretical constructs from which their authors may or may not draw a selection of speculative policy conclusions. Their disciples have been mainly, like the creators of the models, theoreticians; and the post-Keynesians have failed to spawn a numerous following of applied researchers. Paradoxically enough it is the neo-classical school with its consciously unrealistic assumptions that has provided most of the exemplars, and the standardised rules, and the stock of ready-made puzzles for an endless empirical research programme; while the 'historical' growth models, whose assumptions the post-Keynesians have deliberately sought to make directly relevant to the real world[24] have only rarely been

[22] J. Robinson, Preface to the 2nd edn of *Economics of Imperfect Competition*, p. xii.

[23] Joan Robinson's determinants of equilibrium listed on p. 203, for example, would be hard to quantify in principle – still harder in practice.

[24] Not always convincingly. Cf. Worswick's comments on modern growth theory: 'Facts hardly ever occur in this literature: the nearest we get is what Professor Kaldor has called stylised facts, which sometimes means no more than

confronted with real-world data and systematically tested. At the moment, for example, a research student setting out to investigate empirically a problem in the field of economic growth finds himself provided with an articulated set of neo-classical theories, concepts and research tools *and* a stock of data collected with these concepts and tools in mind. However convinced he may be of the superior insight of the heretics, he needs an immense self-confidence in his own ability to create the tools and the data to match these untested theories and concepts, and to abandon the well-stocked neo-classical tool box. Not surprisingly therefore, the so-called 'new' economic history, for example, is almost exclusively neo-classical in technique, though the theoretical concern with a historical approach to the analysis of economic growth is peculiarly post-Keynesian.

The other major branch of theory in which the route taken by the heirs to the Keynesian revolution does not seem to lie in the direction indicated by Maynard Keynes, is in the sphere of monetary theory. Here the main arena of conflict is between the Keynesians (widely interpreted), on the one hand, and the monetarists rather than the general equilibrium theorists on the other: although both the two latter groups tend to assume that the price system has a self-equilibrating tendency in the long run and both tend to stress price-theoretical rather than institutional factors in explaining the process of inflation. On the other hand, all three groups are a product of the Keynesian revolution, in that they pose questions concerned with the process of income determination, and with levels of aggregate demand and output, which are not at all the questions that were posed by the traditional quantity theorists.

New developments in monetary theory are thus currently proceeding along three main lines.

(1) There is the general equilibrium school, which aims at producing an integrated theory of money and prices in which the theory of money is one branch of the theory of prices.[25] They stress the real as opposed to the nominal stock of money and see

convenient assumptions without which determinate solutions of theoretical problems cannot be obtained' (G. D. N. Worswick, 'Is Progress in Economic Science Possible?', *Economic Journal*, March 1972, p. 78).

[25] See R. W. Clower (ed.), *Monetary Theory*, p. 20: 'In all such neo-Walrasian models money appears as just one among many analytically indistinguishable commodities in a world where trading activities are costlessly co-ordinated by a central market authority in such a way that all feasible trades ultimately can be carried out directly without the use of exchange intermediaries.'

its main effects in inducing a corresponding change in the real level of domestic expenditure. These ideas hark back to the late nineteenth-century neo-classicists, and particularly to Walras, and have a strong abstract mathematical bias.

(2) There is the Keynesian school, which sees financial short-term assets as being such close substitutes for money that they are virtually indistinguishable from it. They envisage the effects of a change in the money supply on expenditure decisions as taking place through interest rates rather than prices – in the form of a weakening ripple across the whole range of financial assets from short to long. In so far as they accept the quantity-theory formulation of the relation between money supply and prices, they see the direction of causation running as readily from an increase in prices to an increase in money supply, as in the opposite direction.[26] The implication of their analysis is that the effect of monetary policy, taken by itself, on investment or consumption decisions (and hence on the levels of either economic activity or prices) is rather weak and unpredictable,[27] especially since liquidity preference is highly sensitive to the state of expectations and hence unstable. Their views have clear links with those of the early nineteenth-century Banking School and with the relatively realistic analysis of J. S. Mill.

(3) Finally, there are the monetarists, for whom money is a unique kind of asset, substitutable as readily for real as for financial assets, the demand function for which is in real terms (i.e. after allowing for the rate of inflation) rather stable. In this model a change in the money supply will have pervasive direct effects on all planned expenditures whether on consumer goods, or investment goods, or financial assets. The implication of this analysis, which is a modern version of the Currency School quantity theory, is that monetary policy has a powerful effect (for good or ill) on the level of economic activity and of prices.

In sum, it is not surprising that the monetarists and the Keynesians, for example, fail to agree on monetary theory, because they are essentially arguing about different concepts within a different methodological framework. They agree neither about

[26] See e.g. Kaldor's view given in evidence before the Radcliffe Committee: 'It cannot be emphasized too strongly that there is no direct relationship in a modern community between the amount of money in circulation...and the amount of money spent on goods and services per unit of time' (Committee on the Working of the Monetary System, *Principal Memoranda of Evidence*, Vol. 3, p. 146).

[27] Hence their tendency to advocate incomes policies and/or fiscal policies as part of the solution for the modern stagflation problem.

'what is money?', for example, nor about what is the mechanism of the economic system. They take diametrically opposed views on most methodological issues (equilibrium v. disequilibrium analysis, for example, or the relevance of institutional factors). They differ most fundamentally on ideological issues i.e. on the extent to which the market economy is inherently stable or on the degree of State intervention which is in principle desirable. True, some of their assertions and counter-assertions about what actually happened in the past to key economic variables are empirically testable and some have actually been tested.[28] So some of the more extreme versions of both theories have been knocked out of the academic debate: and on some practical policy issues (e.g. that the lags and complexities in the monetary mechanism are such as to make monetary policy unsuitable for 'fine tuning' purposes) there is broad agreement by a majority on both sides. On the other hand, theoretical disagreements of this fundamental kind are not really susceptible to empirical test. For even where the protagonists can agree on which are the crucial variables to be tested and how to match the theoretical concepts with empirical constructs, the economic system does not stand still. So if, say, the income velocity of money can be shown to have been relatively stable in the recent past, this does not establish that an appropriate change in monetary policy, or in institutional factors, or in expectations, would not cause it to become highly unstable in the future.

For the applied economist, a viable system of economic theory is one which structures questions about economic behaviour in ways that make it possible to generate reliable predictions and hence successful prescriptions in the problem areas that policy makers consider important. It is in this respect that orthodox economics is currently disappointing the professionals. Evidence for a generalised professional unease can be found in the recent spate of 'laments for economics' uttered not only by the usual complainants at orthodox theory (e.g. economic historians and empirical analysts who lose patience when the theory gets too abstract or radical economists with their ideological objections)

[28] See, e.g. C. A. E. Goodhart, 'The Importance of Money', *Bank of England Quarterly Bulletin* (June 1970), e.g. p. 169: 'It is no longer possible to aver, without flying in the face of much collected evidence, that the interest-elasticity of demand for money is, on the one hand so large as to make monetary policy impotent, or on the other hand, so small that it is sufficient to concentrate entirely on the direct relationship between movements in the money stock and in money incomes while ignoring inter-relationships in the financial system.'

but also by some of the leaders in the economic establishment, viz the President of the American Economic Association, the President of the Royal Economic Society, the President of the Economic Section of the British Association, the President of the Econometric Society and various 'elder statesmen'.[29]

Three persistent and interdependent themes have been stressed in these critiques. They are that substantial further progress in economic science depends on:

(1) A much broader base of systematically collected data. Morgenstern, for example, draws an analogy with the Newtonian breakthrough which would have been impossible without the substantial foundation of careful observation and measurement laid down by preceding astronomers: 'Describing the economy may be more difficult since we know that our economies are subject to tremendous and rapid changes, while up to Newton and for Newton's purposes the sky could be considered static.'[30]

(2) Opening up the discipline to receive the theories, concepts and new ideas generated in allied disciplines (e.g. sociology and psychology). Phelps Brown for example, argues for

the removal of the traditional boundary between the subject matter of economic and other social sciences. Specialisation there must be, and there are clearly some activities that are primarily for the economist to study; but in trying to get to the heart of them he cannot separate certain propensities as properly economic from those studied by the social psychologist or social anthropologist.[31]

(3) Taking account of the fact that economics, like other social sciences is confronted by a different kind of system from that under investigation in the physical sciences. Not only is it in a state of constant flux, its development is subject to a high degree of uncertainty and auto-correlation. Of all the innovations that Keynes tried to introduce into economic thought it was the notion of taking uncertainty into account that proved most difficult to absorb into the neo-classical paradigm. For a world of uncertainty is a world in perpetual disequilibrium, and the neo-classical concept of a self-regulating system becomes irrelevant. As a result

[29] See e.g. F. H. Hahn, *Econometrica* (1970); W. Leontief, 'Theoretical Assumptions and Non-Observed Facts', *American Economic Review* (March 1971); E. H. Phelps Brown, 'The Underdevelopment of Economics', *Economic Journal* (March 1972); G. D. N. Worswick, 'Is Progress in Economic Science Possible?', *Economic Journal* (March 1972); O. Morgenstern, 'Descriptive, Predictive and Normative Theory', *Kyklos* (1972); Hahn, *op. cit.* (1970).

[30] Morgenstern (1972), *op. cit.*, p. 701.

[31] Phelps Brown (1972), *op. cit.*, p. 7.

the orthodox mainstream economics born out of a marriage of neo-classical and Keynesian ideas has tended to drop this awkward element overboard. Similarly, positive economics tends to lose sight of the fact that where the form of an accepted economic theory is one of the factors determining the economic behaviour it is supposed to explain, it is hard to rise to the objective standards possible in the natural sciences. Boulding puts this point more trenchantly thus: 'objectivity in the sense of investigating a world which is unchanged by the investigation of it is an absurdity'.[32]

Those who have studied Karl Marx's theories may be tempted to note at this point that his performance on at least two of these issues was manifestly more promising than mainstream economic theory has ever been. He was factually better informed than most modern theorists, less rigidly confined to narrowly economic concepts and categories, and more dynamic, if also more deterministic, in his approach to model-building. They may therefore feel justified in concluding that the new paradigm for economic science is most likely to emerge out of a development of the Marxian alternative. Certainly there has recently been a notable revival of interest in Marx on the part of leading mainstream theorists[33] as well as a resurgence of interest in Marxian economics among some of the younger economists who – being 'not properly brought up' as Keynes put it, may be more open to revolutionary new formulations of economic theory than their elders. On the other hand, the insights into economic and social behaviour yielded by intensive study of mid-nineteenth-century conditions in Western Europe, are no more likely to contribute to a well-founded system of theory appropriate to the later twentieth century mixed capitalist economy, than the existing basis of economic information, inadequate though it may be.

The theoretical controversies between the neo-classical and post-Keynesian schools of thought have also contributed to the renaissance of interest in Marxian economics, because the latter have developed a theory of growth and distribution which draws not only on Keynes but also on Ricardian and Marxian assump-

[32] K. Boulding, *Economics as a Science*, p. 121.
[33] See e.g. Paul Samuelson, *Journal of Economic Literature* (1971 and 1972). Cf. also M. Morishima's reinterpretation of Marx: *Marx's Economics: A Dual Theory of Value and Growth*, in which he argued that 'Marx's theory of reproduction and Walras' theory of capital accumulation should be honoured together with the parents of the modern dynamic theory of general equilibrium' (p. 1).

tions. The link with Ricardian economics has been formally demonstrated in a theoretical essay by Piero Sraffa, *Production of Commodities by Means of Commodities* (1960), representing an attempt to suggest a basis for a theory of value and distribution *outside* the framework of marginal analysis. The link with Marx goes through the Polish Marxian economist Kalecki, whose macroeconomic dynamic model, originally published in Polish in 1933, foreshadowed many of the ingredients of the Keynesian system. His visit to England in the late 1930s permitted a cross-fertilisation of ideas with the immediate Cambridge disciples of Keynes and as a result, according to Joan Robinson, his *Essays on the Theory of Economic Fluctuations* (1939) 'filled several gaps in Keynes' formulation of the theory of employment'.[34]

Which, if any, of the current efforts to formulate a more effective analytical framework for economics is likely to lay the foundations of a new paradigm for the discipline it is impossible to judge. In the end, however, what is necessary to achieve a revolution in economic ideas, is to convince the conventionally-trained economist that the new disciplinary matrix not only solves the newly-important problems, but also deals with the old more elegantly and effectively than the existing matrix. The new heresy has to build up an impressive stock of practical research achievements to its credit before it will dislodge the grip of the prevailing orthodoxy, and it is useless to reiterate that the latter fails to provide a meaningful answer to the really significant problems. While the hard core of the neo-classical research programme continues to supply the basic kit of techniques, concepts and theories applicable to a wide range of practical problems at both the micro and macro level, and while the basic empirical data continue to be compiled in the appropriate form, it is hard for graduate students to make the necessary leap to an alternative macroeconomic framework, however strongly they feel the need for a problem-shift. As far as the professional economist is concerned, his vested interests in preserving as much as possible of the hard-won technical skills in which he had been trained, makes it likely that the new paradigm will involve a marriage between schools rather than a total rejection of any one.

[34] Joan Robinson, 'Kalecki and Keynes', in *Problems of Economic Dynamics and Planning. Essays in honour of Michal Kalecki*, p. 338. See also L. R. Klein's essay on 'The Role of Econometrics in Socialist Economics' in the same volume for a discussion *inter alia* of the extent to which the Kalecki model based on Marxian premises anticipated much of the Keynesian model.

It is probably true also that economists will have to learn a great deal more about the behaviour of individuals in the economic aspects of their lives, and about the basic mechanism of the economic process, before they can begin to formulate better theories of a kind that are actually testable. It may be that they will have to abandon their search for axioms and formal theorems until they can base them on assumptions that are themselves empirically falsifiable.

FURTHER READING

M. Blaug, *The Cambridge Revolution. Success or Failure?* (1974).

K. Boulding, *Economics as a Science* (1970).

R. Clower (ed.), *Monetary Theory* (1969).

M. Friedman, 'The Methodology of Positive Economics', in *idem, Essays in Positive Economics* (1953).

F. H. Hahn, 'The Winter of our Discontent', *Economica* (1973).

G. C. Harcourt, *Some Cambridge Controversies in the Theory of Capital* (1972).

J. R. Hicks, *The Crisis in Keynesian Economics* (1974).

N. Kaldor, 'The Irrelevance of Equilibrium Economics', *Economic Journal* (1972).

Milo Keynes (ed.), *Essays on Keynes, op. cit.*

O. Morgenstern, 'Descriptive, Predictive and Normative Theory', *Kyklos* (1972).

M. Morishima, *Marx's Economics. A Dual Theory of Value and Growth* (1974).

L. L. Pasinetti, *Growth and Income Distribution: Essays in Economic Theory* (1974).

J. V. Robinson, 'The Second Crisis of Economic Theory', *American Economic Review* (1972). Also in her *Collected Economic Papers*, Vol. IV.

P. Sraffa, *Production of Commodities by Means of Commodities. Prelude to a Critique of Economic Theory* (1960).

INDEX OF NAMES

SUBJECT INDEX

abstinence, 69, 119, 131
accelerator, 197, 199
agriculture
  productivity of labour in, 135n
  role in economic development, 5, 13,
    30seq, 37, 39seq
  see also surplus, agricultural
allocation theory, 141, 164
  see also resource allocation and opti-
    mum resource allocation
anti-bullionist
  see bullionist controversy
American Economic Association, 223
armchair theory, 84, 122, 159
assets portfolio analysis, 174, 221
  assets, choice of, 180–1
astronomy, x, 223
Aunt Sally, 178
Australia, 127
Austrian school, 97n, 190

balance of payments, 45–6, 51, 54–5, 59,
  167
Bank Charter Act, 53–6, 58, 169
Bank of England, 45seq, 76, 171
  notes *see* money, paper
Bank of Ireland, 47
Banking School, 53, 59, 221
banks
  country, 46, 47, 51, 55
  Scottish chartered, 47
Berlin, University, 125n
biological analogies, 101, 110, 112n, 217
  sciences, x
bourgeois society, 127
  economists, 141, 142
Bristol, University of, 102
British Association for the Advance-
  ment of Science, 94, 100, 223
British Museum, 125, 127
Brussels, 125n

bullion, 46, 49, 55, 76
  mint price of, 47, 48, 49, 50
  see also gold, silver
Bullion Committee Report, 46n, 48n,
  50–3
bullionist controversy, 48–53

calculus
  differential, 95n, 107
  felicific, 95
  of pleasure and pain, 144n
California, 127
Cambridge, University of, xv, 91n, 95,
  102, 155, 161, 168, 184n, 206
  Wranglers, 99
Cambridge (Mass.), 155
Cambridge School, 169–70, 174, 200,
  202–3, 216, 225, 226
capital, 5, 12, 190n, 192
  accumulation of and growth, 30–1,
    32seq, 78, 84, 133seq, 192seq
  circulating, 66–7
  constant, 135–6
  durability of, 65–7, 115
  fixed, 40, 65–6, 134, 202
  marginal efficiency of, 123n, 179, 180
  malleable, 201–2
  organic composition of, 135–6
  overhead, 30
  return to, 119–20
  working, 30
  variable, 135–6
capital–output ratio, 197seq
Carron iron works, 11, 12
Census of population, 37, 82n
cash balance theory, 169–70, 174
Cash Payments
  Suspension of, 45seq
  Resumption of, 165
Central Bank, 47–8, 53–4
Central Statistical Office, 214